LENNON IN AMERICA

BASED IN PART ON THE LOST LENNON DIARIES
1971–1980

Geoffrey Giuliano

Cooper Square Press

Published by Cooper Square Press
An Imprint of the Rowman & Littlefield Publishing Group
150 Fifth Avenue, Suite 817
New York, New York 10011

Distributed by National Book Network

Library of Congress Cataloging-in-Publication Data

Giuliano, Geoffrey.
    Lennon in America : 1971–1980 : based in part on the lost
Lennon diaries / Geoffrey Giuliano.
      p. cm.
    Includes discography, bibliography, and index.
    ISBN 0-8154-1157-X (pbk. : alk. paper)
    1.   Lennon, John, 1940–1980. 2. Rock musicians—United
States—Biography. I. Title.

ML420.L38 G57 2001
782.42166'092—dc21
[B]
                                        2001028419

⊖™ The paper used in this publication meets the minimum requirements of
American National Standard for Information Sciences—Permanence of
Paper for Printed Library Materials, ANSI/NISO Z39.48–1992.
Manufactured in the United States of America.

Dedicated to

His Divine Grace
A. C. Bhaktivedanta Swami Prabhupada
My eternal master and mentor

and

Vrnda Devi
My everyday Goddess

CONTENTS

IMAGINE NATION

Introduction

Uncovering The Lennon Legacy

Now that John Lennon is twenty years dead, the law of the land will tell you that any appreciable remnant of his manifest time on this earth belongs chiefly to the corporate entity formed around his good name after his assassination. Still, if you think carefully about what Lennon stood for as an artist and a human being, it's difficult to go along with this suit-and-tie theory that anybody can ever actually *own* music. Let alone something as ethereal and delicate as the persona of a breakout artist like John. Certainly one's descendants should be allotted a share, perhaps even the lion's share, of any profits accruing from the remaining portfolio of their loved one's creative endeavors. Once an artist projects himself into the world, however, and is embraced by the public, how his works are regarded and what history has to say about him have little to do with anyone, not his business associates, his family, nor in the end, even himself.

Of course, there exists a profound interest in maintaining the status quo, thus protecting said commercial concerns, but some things are quite simply bigger than that. Bigger than money, bigger than ego, bigger often than even time itself. Things like the consciousness-expanding, life-altering, knee-trembling mind and music of John Winston Ono Lennon. There's a danger too (which is something we see now with the current Lennon estate) that in so tightly sitting on John's cultural legacy there is the urge to embrace revisionist history. That is, trying to sanitize (and therefore commercialize) the life and times of the artist toward a more satisfactory bottom line. That the several-hundred-million-dollar empire currently controlled by the acquisitive Yoko Ono is a significant impediment to the free flow of ideas regarding the truth about brother John seems to me obvious.

To see Yoko and her right-hand man Elliot Mintz rolling through life on the momentum of John's international love and goodwill is, frankly, frustrating. The fact is that John and Yoko endured a complicated, often explosive, ultimately painful relationship which, in my opinion, said much more about John's gnawing need, abject insecurity, and external emptiness than anything to do with universal love and peace. Mintz, too, has literally made a career from his relationship with John, but the truth is that Lennon, by his own admission, was generally contemptuous of the man, rarely wanting him around, and considered him exploitive, divisive, and even dangerous. With the publication of this book, when Mintz is out there blowing smoke about what great buddies he and John really were, it might be instructive to inquire as to what Lennon actually had to say about him in his journals. Elliot's profound silence, I'm sure, would very neatly fill the Albert Hall.

When you respect and admire someone as much as I do John Lennon, it's difficult to sit back and allow anyone to try to turn the man into some sort of psychedelized Disney character with their tatty line of happy Lennon greeting cards, barbecue aprons, eyewear, and so much else even less tasteful and more humiliating. I admit it may seem presumptuous for me, who only ever spent ten minutes in the man's company, to step forward with the kind of potentially myth-busting views presented in this book. I know too that the popular concept says one has to be personally intimate with one's subject to accurately portray them in print, but those familiar with the art of biography will realize this can actually be a serious impediment to the committed truth-seeker. Rather, in this case, I have spent some twenty-five years studying and writing about John Lennon and his milieu, not to mention the deep relationships I've developed along the way with John's Liverpool family and his inner circle of friends and associates.

Ultimately, I don't give a damn about what anyone says about me. All that seems to fade away rather rapidly after one reaches forty. But I do have a real interest in the facts about truth-teller John's life being told, and so far that hasn't happened. Not with May Pang's only occasionally insightful book; Albert Goldman's full frontal assault; tarot guru John Green's generally evenhanded memoir; or even Lennonturncoat Fred Seaman's pithy, self-serving tome. Further, John's English family doesn't really know anything about his later years, the Beatles certainly won't turn any heads with their own rumored multi-pound press release memoir, and Yoko has already said she's waiting for many of the principals in John's life to die before she even considers putting pen to paper or indeed publishing his lost diaries. As far as I'm concerned, that leaves me. An enthusiastic rebel ever since I was sent home from a junior high school dance for wearing a dickie instead of a tie in 1966, I have no problem going toe-to-toe with Yoko or anyone else. For all the deep internal trekking done by John on behalf of all of us, it seems a small price to pay.

Despite its early revolutionary overtones rock 'n' roll is perhaps the most deeply conservative business on earth. So patently incestuous and uptight are these old rock stars and the people around them that literally no one is ready to own up about anything. With so much money at the end of each dangling chord, these one-time precocious pop stars are now firmly fixed at the very pinnacle of the cautious institutions they once so abhorred. It seems only right therefore that someone, somewhere, call a halt to all this towering, temporal, self-interest and take up the challenge of John's great, still untold tale.

I have had possession of copies of John's never-published diaries (via my old chum Harry Nilsson) since early 1983 and was frankly very, very reticent to try and do anything with them. Can you imagine what it feels like to hold in your hand a document you know has the power to change the course of Beatles history completely and forever? What do you do with that?

Finally, after a great deal of concentrated soul searching I set off on my quest, amassing quite a lot of equally intoxicating source material, including much of Lennon's final private correspondence, rare audio tapes, and of course, many exclusive eyewitness accounts from insiders like May Pang, Fred Seaman, George Harrison, and Paul McCartney, to name only a few. What you will not find in this book, however, is the personal voice of John Lennon as quoted from his diaries. Lennon's journal entries were often incomplete thoughts and snippets—the exact meaning of which is difficult to discern, absent the knowledge I gleaned from my many other sources. Instead, the diaries served as firsthand source material for the provocative true story of Lennon's final years. I absorbed not only factual information from the diaries, but also a small mountain of other materials revealing more than twenty years of John's dangling thoughts and feelings as committed to both paper and magnetic tape by the great man himself. Perhaps the real challenge was "filtering" so much incredible source material through my poor Beatle-obsessed brain into the broader, rounder epic of Lennon's incredible life in America that is this book. Though Lennon was certainly my inspiration throughout, this is the story of John's final years from my viewpoint as told in my own words. On occasion you will find direct quotes of Lennon or others in his orbit. Those are not from his diaries, but rather, from the voluminous record I have gathered through the years by conducting numerous personal interviews, sleuthing amid piles of memorabilia, and combing through various biographies and memoirs.

Altogether some sixteen years of nearly full-time research and writing went into the book you now hold. I pray the narration herein ultimately proves enlightening as to the still largely misunderstood force and character of this troubled genius.

I'm sure some, perhaps many, will see this sometimes unusually frank memoir as yet more of the kind of self-interested Lennon bashing which has flared up from time to time since his murder in 1980. My heart, however, tells me something different. Lennon and the Beatles meant everything to me, a lonely kid in Tampa back in the sixties. I raced out and bought everything they ever did, concentrating my devotion primarily on John. To my small circle of friends this man's incredible music and searing lyrics were so much more than mere teen pop. This was important stuff: Lennon casting himself out over the edge of his own musical mortality, shuttling back his perceptions to a turned-on audience of pimply wannabe hipsters—many, like me, already flirting with psychedelic reality, mysticism, various eco-causes, and the like. Then, as now, John Lennon was a bona fide cultural hero. I admired him as much for his whimsy as his grit. It is out of my enduring affection for John that I now forever tie myself to the whipping post with the publication of this similarly in-your-face book about his unhappy last years. Providence, one might reason, bestowed upon me all this unseen info for a reason.

Frankly, the only audience whose often tender sensibilities give me some pause in relation to this work are the tens of thousands of dedicated Beatles People the world over whose enduring love for John Lennon and the Beatles compels them to attend just about every Fab-related anniversary, travel the world to stand where their heroes once stood, and scour Beatle conventions for the latest gunk from the ever-rolling memorabilia mill surrounding the group. I trust they will try and understand the sincerity of my mission to ferret out the facts on the dismal final days of the charismatic founder of the Beatles—a difficult task given one's personal hopes that Mr. Lennon's turbulent life had turned out less tragically than it ultimately did. Beyond that, I respect the solidarity of their affection for all of the Beatles and the almost transcendent aura which still surrounds their unbarreled persona some thirty years after they split up in April 1970.

Some may also question why, in this enlightened age of sexual choice, Lennon's various bedroom or bathroom habits are anyone's concern. The simple answer is that they wouldn't be if he were a plumber, or an accountant, but as a renowned poet who mirrored his innermost thoughts and feelings about life, all life, in his work, it is indeed most relevant.

Deeply ingrained in the public's neurotic need to pry into the private lives of famous people is the subtler quest for real insight into those whose life and work have so intimately impacted ours. To ignore something as fundamental as an artist's sensual proclivities, especially an artist of Lennon's mythic proportions, would be a profound disservice to his memory. Moreover, in John's case where his often bizarre sexual habits were key signposts to forming an accurate composite picture of the man, such a discussion is not only warranted but essential. Wasn't it Lennon who once sang "All I want is the truth. Just gimme some truth"? To settle for less would be a dreadful stain against the memory, the man, and his phenomenal work.

Here's to John: Flawed and human as he was, still the single greatest artist of the twentieth century.

Geoffrey Giuliano
Balaji Ashram
Vrndavana, Uttar Pradesh, India
December 9, 1999
http://www.geoffrey-giuliano.com
http://www.sri108@webtv.net
http://www.puripada.com
http://www.samba-records.com
http://www.oldgraygoose.com

Prologue
CRY BABY CRY
Early Neglect And Sex Thereafter

In many ways the true saga of John Lennon actually began on a blustery spring day in suburban Liverpool back in 1954. Sporadically estranged from his mother Julia, he made the brief bike ride from his Aunt Mimi's to the spacious corner home on Blomfield Road in hopes of spending some quality time with his mom before her lover Bobby Dykins returned from yet another drunken night in town and Lennon's kid sisters Julia and Jacqui came home from school.

Arriving around 11:00 John parked his bike by a bush outside the kitchen door and strode in. Calling Julia's name, he navigated his way under the clothesline hung with various items of her intimate apparel, strung from the icebox to an old sideboard at the opposite side of the room.

"John?" a cheery voice called back, "I'm in the bedroom." Standing now in the doorway, young Lennon exchanged pleasantries with his mother as she rose from her bed and, playfully grabbing him by the hand, led him to the edge of the mattress while she sank down on top of the covers. "Lay down with me, Luv," she whispered. "I haven't seen you in days. How's school?"

"Alright," he replied, sitting all at once on the side of the bed. "Mimi's driving me spare, though."

"As always," Julia chimed in, her still youthful voice cascading into a wave of laughter. Minutes later, after they exchanged family gossip and commented on the blooming of John's first peach-fuzz sideburns, they both fell suddenly silent, staying that way for a few minutes. Then, soundlessly, Julia reached over and placed John's hand on her breast. A jolt of native electricity went through the boy as he felt his mother slightly lift her body at his touch. It was a moment far too frightening and too real for the sensitive young man to ever forget.

While caught up in the steamy Greek tragedy on Blomfield Road, Lennon was acting out another drama with his mates on the street. As if trying to recreate himself, he assumed the role of a chain-smoking, pompadour-coiffed, foul-mouthed teddy boy. John also worked hard at earning a reputation as a lover. Before long, he couldn't even keep track of his conquests, later numbering them somewhere in the "hundreds."

Lennon's young Turk image—coarse, swaggering, deliberately intending to shock—served to compensate for a deep sense of abandonment and manipulation. John himself later admitted, "I was just a weird, psychotic kid covering up my insecurity with a macho facade."

His first wife Cynthia agreed: "He was never really a macho working-class man. John's talents were very much above and beyond that. He was a chrysalis. John had to *appear* macho to cope with some of the types he came across in Liverpool. He tended to try to look like the tough guys, so they wouldn't pick on him. What John later became was what he really was, underneath it all."

That facade also masked Lennon's burgeoning struggle against a force with which he could never fully come to terms. When, in late 1957, John Lennon met Stuart Sutcliffe, the gifted art student turned Beatle bassist, their deep mutual attraction seemed preordained. John instantly connected with his finely boned, waif-like fellow classmate. In turn, the refined, sensitive Sutcliffe was drawn to Lennon's fiery, take-no-prisoners persona. On the surface there were obvious parallels to Yoko Ono. John met both in the art world during times of great personal trial, and through both found renewed inspiration, direction, and purpose. But with Yoko there was always a degree of superficiality. She, the self-proclaimed "con artist" with her own agenda. In contrast, Sutcliffe was genuine: an introspective, talented purist suffering for his art. He was a dedicated loner who, before his introduction to Astrid Kirchherr, never really had time for girls. That Stu was willing to temporarily give up his art for John, and submit to the humiliation of playing in a scruffy rock band, proved his willingness to sacrifice his own dreams for John's. Author Sandra Shevy, who wrote a book on Lennon some years back, says: "Sutcliffe's expulsion from art school derives from his deep infatuation with Lennon and willingness to do anything for him. This dynamic was apparent on stage, where Stuart regularly crooned Elvis's 'Love Me Tender' directly to John."

Their connection was profound. Stu taught John about Kierkegaard and Nietzsche, philosophies far deeper than those Yoko later thrust upon him. John followed enthusiastically, not only in thought but in dress, first with purple tweed jackets, then in Germany with black leather, and finally with the trend-setting, French-style Beatle cuts and collarless suits that Brian Epstein subsequently selected as their stage persona. Both Sutcliffe and Epstein had key roles in softening the Beatles' rough-hewn image, a fact that must have at least had some subtle effect on Lennon's conflicted sexual identity.

While Stuart painted intimate portraits of John, Lennon wrote him long, thoughtful letters. Not the lusty bravado he penned to Cynthia, but reams of abstract, chapter-length poems, pouring out his deepest thoughts and feelings:

> I remember a time when everyone I loved hated me
> because I hated them, so what,
> So what so fucking what . . .
> I can't remember anything without a sadness
> So deep it hardly becomes known to me
> So deep that its tears leave me a spectator
> Of my own stupidity.

In 1983, this author was staying with "Legs" Larry Smith of the legendary Bonzo Dog Do Dah Band in Hamilden, Oxfordshire. George Harrison lives nearby. Over the months, I got to know many Beatles insiders, including their longtime public relations man Derek Taylor. He told me of an incident that John had related to him back in 1968. It occurred in Hamburg at the seedy Bambi Cinema, where the Beatles stayed during several early gigs. One day while Paul, George, and Pete Best were on a boat trip with some local fraüleins, Stu and John stayed behind, getting thoroughly drunk in one of the countless dives that lined the *Reeperbahn*. They commiserated with each other about their dismal lot: playing the cramped, noisy strip joints; enduring the filthy accommodations; being perpetually overworked and underpaid. Drunk and disconsolate, they returned to their dank one-room hole. Stu was sitting on the top bunk, while John rolled into the bottom. After a few minutes Lennon wordlessly climbed up to join Sutcliffe. What began as mutual consolation turned quietly sexual when Stu went down on him. Lennon disclosed the episode to Taylor during an intense acid trip at his home in suburban London.

Stu's death from a brain tumor on April 10, 1962 affected John on a profound level that didn't fully reveal itself until years later. The widely accepted story of Sutcliffe's early demise harkened back to a gang attack a year earlier. Apparently, Stu had been the victim of a beating, kicked in the head. One version of the tale suggests that Lennon, who charged into the scuffle, accidentally struck his mate with his boot.

Years later, however, Lennon confessed to Fred Seaman, among others, that he was to blame for Stu's death. According to John, while in Hamburg several months earlier, he and Sutcliffe had gotten into a heated argument when Lennon abruptly lost control. In a rage, he charged the slight artist, who stumbled and fell to the ground, blood running down the side of his head. A horrified John panicked and fled.

Lennon reacted to Stu's untimely death with hysterical laughter, which, according to former Beatle drummer Pete Best, dissolved into tears. "John wept like a child. I had never seen him break down in public before. . . . He was absolutely shattered." Family insiders claim that John's guilt over his friend's demise haunted him his entire life.

Lennon's conflicted feelings about other male friends included Paul McCartney. Theirs was a volatile relationship right up to the end, and was fraught with emotional summits and valleys. While the connection between them was strictly heterosexual, it was deep, passionate, and highly explosive. Jo Jo Laine, former wife of Moody Blues and Wings member Denny Laine, spoke to Lennon about his intense bond with McCartney during a chance encounter in a New York café early in 1979. Lennon spoke frankly about his feelings. As Laine relates the story: "I first met John during one of my many visits home to check on my dying father. I felt I had to get away, so I rang Wendy Rollins, a stewardess friend who offered me her Greenwich Village flat since she'd be away for two weeks jetting about the continent.

"One morning I stopped into La Fortuna, a ritzy coffee shop on Columbus Avenue. I spotted John instantly, seated alone in a corner table sipping a cappuccino over two monstrous eclairs. Pushing down my hesitation, I approached his table. 'I don't mean to disturb you,' I said, 'but I'm Jo Jo, Denny Laine's wife.'

"At that he bounced up and shook my hand, his eyes dancing with curiosity. 'Denny's wife? Don't tell me the sod finally found someone willing to take him on! How's he doing? Still winging round the world, is he?'

"After I caught him up on my wayward hubby, I looked down at his plate and ventured, 'Those seem like pretty hefty eclairs. Can I give you a hand?'

"'Sure,' he grinned. 'Sit down.' As we chatted, I kept waiting for the subject of our old nemesis Paul to come up. I was dying to compare notes, knowing full well there was no love lost between the two ex-Beatles.

"'How's Yoko?' I asked. 'Is she joining you?'

"'No, she's back at the office. I often come down here on my own. I can walk the streets fairly easily these days, thank God, especially here in New York. People don't really bother me anymore.'

"John was so charming and witty, so full of life, not at all the snobbish, caustic recluse I had come to expect from various media accounts. Unlike Paul, John was genuinely warm and responsive, not simply waiting for me to finish talking so he could rush forward with his own agenda.

"I didn't want to overstay my welcome, so after a few minutes I made my excuses and began edging away from the table. 'Wait a minute,' he stopped me. 'Listen, I have some time today. Mother [his pet name for Yoko] has things well in hand at the office and Sean is off with his friend Max for a few days. How about a drink tonight, say around 7:00? I'll give you a ring at 5:00 to confirm.'

"I practically flew out of the coffee shop, certain he wouldn't call. So sure was I that I even went ahead and made plans with my old pal, Rick Derringer, when precisely at 5:00 the phone rang. 'Who's this?' I asked.

"'It's John, you daft duck!'

"We spoke only briefly and I had the definite feeling Yoko might be nearby. He said he'd meet me at Lincoln Center. Even as I stood alone in the chilly Manhattan twilight, I was convinced he wouldn't show. After about twenty minutes I had given up, when there was a light tap on my shoulder. There he stood, somehow not quite real in his long gray tweed coat, a flamboyant African scarf flung carelessly about his neck. Only in New York could the greatest musical legend of the century go unnoticed as impervious pedestrians rushed by.

"One guy, however, did come up and politely requested an autograph. Not only did John oblige, but spent a good ten minutes chatting, even offering the kid some Belgium chocolates he'd just bought. John, I discovered, was an incurable chocoholic.

"'Who's she?' the young man asked, pointing to me.

"'My bodyguard,' John cracked, straight-faced, 'and she's a karate wiz, so watch out!'

"We stopped in a local Szechuan place, where John went virtually unrecognized, and we enjoyed a lovely dinner. Halfway through the meal he took my hand and the electricity flowed.

"John wrapped my arm in his as we strolled over to a buddy's who was off somewhere on the road. We took an elevator from the ground floor of an old warehouse and rode up three flights. John pulled out a key and opened the door to a large, lovely loft.

"We wasted no time on preliminaries. John proved amazingly gentle and patient as he undressed me. Unlike most men, who can't wait to put their hands all over you, John surprised me by wanting to be stroked. He purred as his hands directed my fingers up and down his legs and his hairless, freckled chest. Whether it was out of some quirky allegiance to Yoko or what, I quickly sensed it wasn't intercourse he wanted. I was happy to oblige and gave him a blowjob, and before the end of the night, a second.

"Afterwards, John pulled out a bit of coke and we got to talking. I noticed a guitar in a corner. John caught my glance and picked up the six-string, serenading me with an unfamiliar song he called 'Mucho Mungo.' I later discovered he wrote it with old friend Harry Nilsson.

"I waited for Paul to be mentioned. Was there still too much leftover hurt after all these years? Had passing time alienated the two

former mates even further? Or maybe he just didn't give a fuck anymore. As the final chords faded, I could see those compelling eyes
grow suddenly pensive and sober. John peered at me over the rim of
his glasses and whispered, 'You know, being in the Beatles was beautiful, and the work Paul and I did together pure magic. It's a fuckin'
shame it was spoiled by the incredible pressures around us. Many
times over the years we wanted to get back together. At one stage we
even planned it, but we were deathly afraid of the frenzy it would
cause, that it could be dangerous, never ending. Only now have we
been able to gain a modicum of peace in our lives, Paul on the farm,
George with the Hare Krishnas at Friar Park, Ringo with his new
lady, and me with Yoko and Sean.'

"'Actually,' he continued, 'there's a film we've been working on with
Neil Aspinall ever since the last days of Apple. It's a documentary
called *The Long and Winding Road*. We always took tons of footage
wherever we went. The idea is that we'll all get together somewhere
in the world for a session and film it. Now that I've got my immigration, which was one of the many things that kept us from getting back
together anyway, we'll do at least two or three new songs for the
soundtrack. I've already got a few kicking around.'

"I almost didn't dare breathe, overcome by the magnitude of what
John was so freely telling me. After nearly ten years of speculation the
Beatles were actually going to reunite for a new project!

"Around 1:30, John walked me out into the drizzly night and
flagged down a taxi. He gave me a warm hug and put me in the cab,
paying the driver a hefty tip. I watched him for a long time out the
back window as I rode away, his dark, still figure growing smaller, and
finally dissolving into the New York night."

Lennon's complex sexual appetite revealed itself as far back as
1960. In Hamburg, as the youthful Beatles indulged themselves in
the city's raucous atmosphere, John set the standard for wild behavior. His antics, often alcohol-fueled, had him acting out childishly, like the time he urinated on several passing nuns from his
perch on a *Reeperbahn* balcony. Off stage, his powerful sex drive
was satisfied by willing women in Hamburg, and the other Beatles
followed his lead.

One night, as the Beatles were due on stage, Lennon was off in a
bathroom having a sexual encounter. A furious Horst Fascher (the

group's occasional bodyguard) located his star guitarist. Intent on teaching John a lesson in responsibility, and armed with a water-filled basin, Horst stole into the adjoining stall and drenched the stunned Beatle. Lennon emerged, cursing and sputtering. When he did reach the stage, he was stone drunk, sporting a toilet seat for a collar, and thus was born the notorious "Hamburg toilet-seat legend."

Of all the sexual legends told of the young Beatles in Hamburg, few are as startling as Allan Williams's allegation in his memoirs that at least two of the boys were involved in frequent unions with a glamorous, six-foot-four transvestite they met in a nightclub. Although Williams never revealed which two members he was talking about, Lennon later noted that Williams's memoir was by far the most accurate book written about that time. Horst Fascher also corroborated Williams's story: "There was a transvestite who regularly used to give John blowjobs. When he found out she was a man, he was merely amused."

Stories like these gained momentum a couple of years later, when sexual innuendo blossomed regarding Lennon's relationship with Brian Epstein. During John's first brief visit with Julian in the hospital following his birth on April 8, 1963, he told Cynthia he was leaving for Spain with Brian for a quick holiday before the Beatles resumed their rigorous touring schedule. While she certainly was not happy about it, she knew he had been working hard, and felt he deserved a vacation.

Later, on the eve of Paul McCartney's twenty-first birthday party at his Aunt Jin's in Liverpool, Cavern owner Bob Wooler made the mistake of referring to the trip as Lennon and Epstein's "Spanish honeymoon." John's explosive response was to beat the poor man mercilessly. Wooler was one of his closest friends and, like John, had been drinking heavily. An ambulance was summoned and, with Brian riding along, Wooler was rushed to the hospital, where he stayed for two days, suffering from several badly broken ribs. After he came to his senses, John felt terrible and asked Brian to send a telegram apologizing to the battered man for the whole stupid mess.

Commenting on the incident to BBC journalist Andy Peebles in 1980, Lennon remarked, "The Beatles' first national coverage was me beating up Bob Wooler at Paul's birthday party, because he in-

timated I was homosexual. Actually, I had a fear that maybe I *was*
homosexual to attack him like that. It's very complicated reasoning.
But I was very drunk and I hit him. I could have really killed him,
and that scared me."

The piece, entitled "Beatle in Brawl," showed up in the *Daily
Mirror* the very next day. It read: "Guitarist John Lennon, 21-year-old
leader of the Beatles, said last night, 'Why did I have to go and punch
my best friend? I was so high I didn't know what I was doing.'"

"I don't know why he did it," said Bob Wooler. "I have been a friend
of the Beatles for a long time. I am terribly upset about this, physically and mentally."

A settlement of £200 put the matter to rest, but did not quell rumors of Lennon's occasional bisexuality. McCartney has steadfastly
denied the possibility, insisting that, having spent so many years in
John's company, he would have noticed were his friend homoeroti-
cally inclined.

But Lennon's close boyhood friend Pete Shotton insists the stories
were based on truth: "I visited John at Aunt Mimi's a few days after
his return to England, and when he started in about how much he enjoyed Spain, I could hardly resist taking the piss out of him. 'So you
had a good time with Brian, then?'

"John didn't so much as crack a smile. 'Oh, fuckin' hell,' he
groaned. 'Not you as well, Pete! They're all fucking going on about it.'

"'Actually Pete,' he said softly, 'something did happen.' John then
went on to confide the particulars to me. 'Eppy just kept on and on
at me. Until one night I finally pulled me trousers down and said to
him, "Oh, fuck it, Brian! Just stick it up me arse then."'

"'And he said to me, "Actually John, I don't do that kind of thing.
That's not what I like to do."

"'So I let him toss me off.'

"'That's all?' I said. 'Well, so what? What's the big fucking deal, then?'

"'Yeah, the poor bastard. He's having a fucking hard enough time
anyway.'" This was a reference to a savage assault Brian had recently
endured at the hands of a dockworker, who responded to his advances by beating him to a bloody pulp.

"'So what harm did it do then, Pete?' John asked me. 'The poor
bastard can't help the way he is.'

"'What's a fucking wank between friends?' I said."

Although Pete's version of the story has been challenged over the years, in a mid-1980s interview Shotton insisted he told the truth. "I know what happened. John told me! John wouldn't have wanted to gloss anything over. He was the last person who would have wanted that. This particular incident highlights the compassionate side of John. They can stop making it up. They can stop having fantasies about what happened. It's in my book what happened, from John's mouth to me. I don't think it's dirty. I don't think it's smutty. I think it was a nice thing John did, showing his compassion. It shows him in a very good light. John had a very, very strong sexual urge. This followed him through life. He was a very sexually oriented person. But I mean he didn't go, 'God, I gotta have sex!' He had a good appetite when the food was on the table, so to speak."

Years after the notorious Spanish holiday, Lennon himself commented on the interlude with Epstein and how it actually inspired a song. "'Bad to Me' I wrote specifically for Billy J. Kramer. I was on holiday with Brian in Spain, where the rumors went around he and I were having a love affair. Well, it was *almost* a love affair, but not quite. It was never *really* consummated. But it was certainly a pretty intense relationship.

"It was my first experience with a homosexual I was conscious was homosexual. He admitted it to me. Cyn was pregnant so I went [with him] to Spain. We used to sit in a café in Torremolinos looking at all the boys, and I'd say, 'Do you fancy that one, do you like this one?' I was rather enjoying the experience thinking like a writer all the time. And while he was out on the tiles one night, or lying asleep with a hangover one afternoon, I remember playing him 'Bad to Me.'"

Lennon's equivocations notwithstanding, Sandra Shevy offered still another take on the relationship: "Contrary to the opinion that Brian was on the make for John, I believe it was John who attempted to involve himself with Brian, believing, as he did, that he was irresistible to both sexes, and more importantly needing the confidence of Brian to maintain his supremacy as founder of the Beatles."

Another twist in the tale was offered recently by former McCartney girlfriend Francie Swartz, who remembers finding a passionate love letter to Paul from Brian in the glove box of McCartney's car while visiting in Liverpool in 1968. Brian's love for his boys, it seemed, went far deeper than merely acting as the group's business manager.

John's relationship with his mother Julia too often confused him. One afternoon John stumbled onto a sexual tryst between Julia and her lover, Bobby Dykins. The couple was hunkered down beneath the covers in their bedroom when a stunned Lennon witnessed his mother performing oral sex. Recalling the incident in 1979, John was initially startled, although—having experienced a few similar encounters himself—he was not exactly unprepared. What Lennon found far more disturbing was the idea of his mother giving a blowjob to the stepfather he dubbed Twitchy. John described the diminutive waiter (known as Spive to his mates) as a raunchy character who was constantly clearing his throat and slicking back his sparse hair with butter from the kitchen table. A resentful John would often nick the tips his stepdad stored atop the kitchen cupboard, even though Dykins would inevitably accuse poor Julia. As John saw it, they owed him that much.

Seventies disco king Tony Manaro, the inspiration for the New York magazine story that later became the film *Saturday Night Fever*, offered the most convincing evidence that Lennon was indeed bisexual.

In May 1974, Manaro was walking alone through Greenwich Village when he spotted Lennon, singer Harry Nilsson, and another fellow strolling down a street.

"John was my idol. I walked up to him and said, 'I know a lot of people hassle you, but I just want to thank you for your music. You've helped me through a lot of bad times.' Outside Jimmy's Bar he said, 'Why don't you come inside for a drink?'

"After we ordered, John switched seats to sit next to me. He said to me, 'Are you gay?' When I told him I wasn't, he looked really disappointed. He could have been joking, but he wasn't. My initial reaction was fear. And yet I wouldn't leave because it was John Lennon. I said to him, 'No, man, I don't go that way.'

"'Are you sure?' he said, 'give me head.' I remember Harry was 'borrowing' $100 bills off him.

"At one stage I went out and when I came back, he was talking to this woman and he said, 'Pauly.' I thought he meant Paul, meaning McCartney. So John turns around and says, 'No, he's much prettier than Pauly. He's got a nicer mouth than McCartney. Paul's got a small mouth.'

"Then he turned to me and said, 'Let's go out and get some chicks.' This man was giving me a dream to pay millions for. John almost admitted his gay tendencies. So anyway, we went out walking and he put his arm around me. He said, 'It feels good to hold someone. You know what I mean?' Prior to that, he said, 'There is nothing wrong in being gay. Two people exchanging feelings is not wrong. Did you ever try it?'

"People were following us. We were wasted, and he put his arm around one girl and said, 'Suck my cock.' He stuck his tongue down her throat. We were loaded. Somebody stole the hat right off his head."

Lennon and company meandered over to the Pierre Hotel, where he and Nilsson shared three adjoining suites, rooms 1608, 9, and 10. Manaro continued: "There was Harry's bedroom, John's, and a living room with a keyboard. He gave me a guitar, but it was later stolen. [After we returned to the hotel] he propositioned me again. After he died, I wish I'd done it. He tried to kiss me. He put his arm around me. John was making moves on me like a guy would a chick. When I said 'Halt,' it was finished, and we laid down together on the couch.

"I love the guy. I never asked him if he'd had sex with a man, but it was obvious to me he had. I stayed at the hotel sleeping on a sparc bed next to his for about a week, but he never attempted it again. There were feelings and looks, though. He was very loving, like when a guy is very lonely. The man was bisexual. There are no two ways about it. He was feeling me out."

Fred Seaman, Lennon's personal assistant and close friend at the end of his life, has said, "I knew Tony when he was on drugs and very weirded out. But I feel he's telling the truth." Seaman himself has also described Lennon as bisexual.

Yoko's longtime assistant and friend Elliot Mintz commented on the fray: "Manaro keeps changing his story. If John were alive today, he would have scratched his head at the Alice in Wonderland [stories]. There seems no end to people's fantasies."

But Manaro himself remains adamant: "John did come on to me. He *did* try to make love to me. He asked me to perform a lewd act and that's the truth. The man was bisexual. There are no two ways about it. Any of his fans who can't dig that, I'm sorry, because if you listen to his music, sensitivity is what it's all about. I'm sorry, you closed-minded little people!"

Other indications suggest that, at the very least, Lennon wasn't in any way homophobic. He was comfortable enough with the concept to engage in occasional gay impersonations that were friendly rather than demeaning. During *Magical Mystery Tour* he portrayed an obviously gay wizard, and later commented it was his favorite film role.

Pauline Lennon, Fred Lennon's young second wife, recalls her first impression of her famous stepson in 1967: "He appeared much more delicate and gentle than the solidly tough, macho image he projected on stage. Tall and surprisingly narrow-framed, John walked with a mincing shuffle, always in stocking feet, and it immediately struck me there was something very feminine about him when he was relaxed."

Pete Shotton, too, tells a story indicating that Lennon often assumed that people thought he might be gay. After the two dropped acid one night in 1967, they ended up in Lennon's Kenwood attic, where they both passed out on the floor. The next morning they were awakened by the maid trudging up the long, narrow stairwell. John suddenly shot to his feet saying, "Oh Christ, she'll think we've been fucking!"

Finally, a story told to this author offers further confirmation. The anecdote was related during a London dinner party in 1993 at the home of British radio and television broadcaster Gloria Hunniford. Hunniford's friend (who asked not to be identified) was a guest at a London bash in 1965 when she and a friend happened to pass by a bedroom door. They peered inside and found John Lennon passively engaged in anal sex with a well-known male celebrity photographer. The door was quickly slammed shut and the secret, likewise, kept all these years. Finally, in the mid-seventies Lennon penned a short piece for something call *The Gay Liberation Book* in which he muses, "Why make it sad to be gay?"

While these examples arguably point to a pronounced homosexual element in Lennon's makeup, it was only one side of his complex personality. John wrestled with these inclinations, sometimes angrily, as in the Wooler episode, other times with sarcasm, once quipping to a journalist who asked if he'd ever had a homosexual encounter, "I haven't met a fellow recently I fancy enough!"

John's uncontrollable libido got him into hot water on more than one occasion. On December 21, 1967 he propositioned George Harrison's wife Pattie at a party to launch the *Magical Mystery Tour* film. John was drinking heavily. By the party's end Lennon, who had been noticing Mrs. Harrison throughout the evening, flirted with her in the presence of George and John's long-suffering wife Cynthia. His behavior was excessive enough to provoke the ire of another guest, pop singer Lulu. Appalled by John's actions, and concerned about the effect on Cynthia, the fiery singer took matters into her own hands, suggesting pointedly to Lennon, "Tend to your own wife before you make an even bigger fool of yourself!"

In 1983 George Speerin, a former Lennon aide, recounted yet another anecdote about John in New York. Further, John himself referred to the incident in an unfinished handwritten note to himself, seen by this author, which was probably intended for inclusion in his diaries. During the *Abbey Road* sessions over the summer of 1969, the Beatles often used McCartney's North London townhouse as a pit stop during recording dates. Close to the studio, it provided the opportunity for them to rehearse, grab a shower, have a bite, watch some television, or smoke a few joints. Lennon was comfortable at Cavendish Avenue, as he had spent time there when he and Yoko first got together. If the imposing iron gate happened to be locked when he arrived, John would merely climb over it.

During this period John and Yoko were enduring a rough patch in their new-but-already-prickly union. They were also recovering from the effects of an auto accident that had occurred in July while they were on holiday in Scotland. To complicate matters, Ono was in the early stages of a delicate pregnancy that would end in a miscarriage by October. Lennon was also trying to quit heroin, and the resulting withdrawal caused a great deal of tension. When things became too heated, Lennon would often roar off to St. John's Wood, leaving his wife alone in their empty sixteen-room mansion. This was especially galling to Yoko, since Linda McCartney was a near-constant fixture at the sessions.

Once, Lennon had forgotten the appointed time of a session, and stopped by Paul's to confirm the studio schedule. Upon his arrival he discovered that Paul had already left for the studio. Linda was home alone, nursing a headache in the aftermath of a heated argument with Paul. Grateful for the company, she invited John in. After sharing a bottle of wine, a large joint, and some conversation with the bespectacled Beatle, she excused herself and returned to the bedroom, where she had been making the bed prior to John's unexpected visit. Lennon promptly offered her a hand. In the course of spreading the sheets their hands touched briefly. Linda paid the contact no mind, but as she reached over to tuck in the top sheet, Lennon caught her arm and kissed her. A gentle, awkward embrace evolved into caresses and a quick interlude of sexual intimacy. According to John's account, Linda deeply regretted the indiscretion and never told a soul. He, on the other hand, found it rather amusing.

In a recently discovered 1968 taped conversation John interrogated his new girlfriend, Yoko Ono, about her sexual history. The ensuing dialogue lifts the veil on their complex partnership, and reveals a ruthlessly inquisitive Lennon who was often disturbed by his discoveries.

No mere pillow talk, this was rather an aggressive inquisition, with a determined Lennon driven to ferret out the intimate details of Ono's previous encounters. John was clearly caught up in the salacious details of her past bedroom trysts, pushing her to compare the penis sizes of her two previous husbands, Japanese composer Toshi Ichiyanagi and New York filmmaker Tony Cox. He reminded her that she termed one lover's penis miniscule and discolored. Whenever Ono tried to change the subject, he pressed her not to feed him evasive responses.

He then berated her about her numerous past lovers and accused her of hypocrisy. When she tried to explain her conduct as simple artistic experimentation, he retorted that the truth was she slept around for the hell of it.

Yoko defended herself by attacking the typical male approach to sex, branding it mechanical and devoid of emotion. John shot back that he had discussed sexual attitudes with many men and that wasn't the way they felt at all.

John and Yoko, more than most couples, have told the world, in seemingly frank terms, exactly what they were thinking. From "open love letters" to the autobiographical songs that fill their records, the Lennons never shied away from saying what they thought or how they felt. Yet much of these public expressions were censored, muted, or shaped by circumstance. The truth was often fitted to the marketing reality. Cynthia Lennon notes: "As his wife, I had to be prepared to take the full impact of his unreasonable rages. . . . I would be accused of not being loving enough, of being unfaithful, of looking or talking to a member of the opposite sex for too long. John's possessiveness was at times unbearable and I found myself a quaking, nervous wreck on many occasions." Later, while he was with May Pang, the song remained the same. During Lennon's "Lost Weekend" fling with the patient and giving Pang, he accused her of cheating on him, and flew into a rage, trashing the room and trampling her eyeglasses. Lennon himself admitted toward the end of his life: "I was a very jealous, possessive guy. A very insecure male. A guy who wants to put his woman in a little box and only bring her out when he feels like playing with her. She's not allowed to communicate with the outside world because it makes me feel very insecure."

Lennon's many unresolved sexual issues were symptomatic of his position in life: a rich, gifted, respected pop icon, at whose feet men and women endlessly cast themselves. But he had no perspective, nothing to check the rage of the child bruised by Oedipal confusion and blatant abandonment. Certainly, John hailed from a family of five fiery "Amazon Aunties," from his permissive mother to Aunt Mimi. The men in his life, from his ineffectual father to his mother's carousing boyfriend, offered no real role models. John was left to his own devices when it came to both forming and informing himself.

On the 1968 audio tape Lennon ruthlessly zeros in on Ono's relationship with a Sarah Lawrence classmate with whom she shared a New York City brownstone in the early sixties. Yoko tried to brush it off, claiming that if that was the relationship she wanted she would have searched out other lesbian lovers. But in fact, she asserted, even the thought of it made her nauseous.

But Lennon would have none of it, pointing out that this was no casual one night stand, but rather, an extended relationship that lasted a year and a half, clearly indicating that, at least at that juncture of her life, Yoko obviously preferred female intimacy.

Yoko then posed the theory that if she brought a woman into her relationship with John it might backfire should he fall in love with her. Lennon shot back that she was probably more afraid of falling for the theoretical lover herself.

John then got down to what was really bothering him: that Ono felt he was ready to sleep with any woman he found attractive. He asserted that there were no attractive women he knew that he would truly consider sleeping with, and challenged her to say the same thing.

Lennon's reactions suggest he was unprepared for the blunt truth of Ono's rejoinders. And regarding Tony Cox, Yoko's second husband, she was even more blunt on another occasion: "I divorced him because there was nothing more in him for me to take."

Like Yoko, Julia represented a riddle wrapped within an enigma for Lennon. Despite the fact that he professed love for her and sang publicly of missing her, Lennon's feelings for his mother were deeply conflicted. Pauline Lennon, Fred's insightful younger wife, recalled telling John, "You can't put all the blame on your dad. Your mother was just as much to blame for your problems." John didn't defend Julia. The mere mention of her name, noted Pauline, "triggered a vicious verbal attack on [his mother], whom he reviled in the most obscene language I had ever heard, referring to her repeatedly as a 'fucking, cock-sucking whore'!"

This conflicted memory of his sensuous mother was an image that was seared into John's mind as he continued his interrogation, the injurious memories of the past linked to the pain of the present triggering the infamous Lennon temper. He cited Ono's recent performance in London, where he felt she was trying to flirt with everyone in the house.

Even two years later—while publicly proclaiming, "Yoko saved me!"—John was growing ever more paranoid. Certainly, there were other factors, such as the pressure brought on by the breakup of the Beatles, the steady decline of Apple's fortunes, and his heroin addiction. In this context it was understandable that John and Yoko, together 24 hours a day, were often at each other's throats.

When John sought escape by partying with old friends like George Harrison, Yoko felt abandoned, and saw his actions as the first cracks in their mutual armor. She labeled such behavior as uncaring, and accused John of behaving like an unmarried man. She found him becoming increasingly anxious, confrontational, and hostile. John had become so tense that he often wouldn't let Ono touch him. Strange, when one considers the content of Lennon's little-known book, *John Lennon's 1969 London Diary*, which was filled with repetitive entries such as "Got up, fucked the wife, went to work."

Lennon also seemed to be searching for a father figure to ease his loneliness and confusion. Candidates included the Beatles' technical wizard "Magic" Alex Mardas, Primal Therapy advocate Dr. Arthur Janov, and even Yoko's ex-husband Tony Cox, about whom she grew envious, later categorizing their relationship as something akin to a "spiritual bond."

Lennon's perpetual search for a father figure was further evidenced by his brief fascination with the Maharishi Mahesh Yogi during the Beatles' notorious 1967 visit to the yogi's Rishikesh compound. John, however, quickly grew disillusioned with the giggly guru. The extent of his disappointment came to light in a recently discovered demo tape he recorded, entitled simply "Maharishi." Lennon revealed that he took the lectures seriously, hoping to acquire a higher spiritual understanding, but found them to be of no real comfort. John also admitted he was initially entranced by the yogi because he was charming and avuncular.

But he soon realized all was not right at the meditation academy when he discovered the yogi's right-hand man was a former CIA operative and the spiritual atmosphere he expected had turned lascivious. Lennon zeroed in on a pretty middle-aged woman resembling actress Jean Simmons who had several private meetings with the Maharishi. "She came in with the tailor and could sit at his feet, while the rest had to wait like good American people in line to see the master walking on the petals who lived in a million-dollar house overlooking the Himalayas."

On yet another secret tape recorded in 1970, John and Yoko discussed intimate details of their fragile relationship during a time the couple was undergoing therapy at the Primal Institute, a former private club in Bel Air, California.

Dr. Janov reported that his new patient was in rough shape when the doctor first encountered him. "John was simply not functioning. He really needed help." It seems that Lennon and Los Angeles were a harmful combination for the Beatle. He often got himself into deep personal crises there.

In 1980, a decade removed from his Primal Therapy experience, Lennon compared it to being hooked on drugs, once the high was gone you'd quickly need another dose. Easy fixes seemed to be

Lennon's method of dealing with many of the problems he faced near the end of his life.

The therapy did address his problems with erectile dysfunction: John, despite a seeming obsession with sex, battled impotence. Yoko felt the cause was psychological rather than physical, "like he's afraid of something," she ventured on the tape.

John eventually confessed to several dark sexual impulses: he wanted to be spanked or whipped and he was drawn to the notion of having a spiked boot heel driven into him. Outside of his fantasies, however, Lennon was hardly a hardcore masochist in matters of the flesh. Later in his life, John gathered together a collection of S&M-inspired manikins, which he kept tucked away in the bowels of the Dakota. These dummies, adorned with whips and chains, also had their hands and feet manacled.

John's violent sexual impulses troubled Yoko. She was deeply concerned that his therapy was merely a substitute for these behaviors, simply another drug. She didn't want him risking their marriage by bringing other partners into it.

Yoko contended that John—rather than honestly experiencing the pain released by the therapy and truly trying to understand himself—was reveling in the physical excesses of the treatment. The officially sanctioned caterwauling, weeping, and rolling-on-the-floor hysterics, which were enacted under the strict eye of Janov, was a form of mental torture for Yoko, one from which John drew perverse pleasure. Ono worried that the therapy would simply indulge, rather than cure, Lennon's sado-masochistic tendencies.

Lennon's well-known abuse of women was an issue he dealt with all his adult life. He once admitted to Fred Seaman that during the height of Beatlemania he frequently availed himself of a "quickie" right before concerts. "I was always obsessed with sex. I'd run after girls and feel them up, shove them up against a wall, that sort of thing." One night before a concert, he grabbed the first young woman he saw, heaved her against a wall, tore off her underwear, and virtually raped her on the floor. Because he was a Beatle, the woman raised no protest, filed no complaint.

May Pang tells a similarly disturbing story. She and John were relaxing one afternoon in a jacuzzi in Los Angeles. John, who had been drinking, suddenly turned vicious. He began to strangle her. A terrified Pang raced for her life into the hotel room, where he followed. Upon catching her, he threw her across the room and into the wall. The incident left her badly bruised and shaken.

Trying to explain his behavior, Lennon once said, "The big He-Man was always supposed to smack his woman across the face. In all the movies they propagate the slap in the face, right? She succumbs in tears and you make love. Most of guys I knew in Liverpool thought that is what it was all about. If she didn't lie down, first you smacked her and then you got what you wanted. That was the Tough Guy."

John didn't have to look much farther than Blomfield Road for examples of male violence in the sexual arena. Bobby Dykins, given to frequent alcoholic rages, battered Julia with impunity, once even forcing her into the yard stripped naked, in plain view of the neighbors. On another occasion Lennon recalled his mother turning up at Mendips with her face covered in blood, claiming she'd had an accident. "I couldn't face it," John recalled. "I thought, 'That's my mother in there bleeding.' I went out in the garden. I loved her, but I didn't want to get involved. I suppose I was a moral coward. I wanted to hide all my feelings." With his mother's death, a bitter and disillusioned John labeled all women as traitors and occasionally entertained grisly visions about lethally brutalizing women. Lennon further admitted in 1980 that, despite all the therapy he underwent, he was still plagued by these disturbing thoughts.

On another occasion he confided to a friend, "I've always wondered what it would be like to kill a woman, many women! It was only becoming a Beatle that saved me from actually doing it. Can you imagine, a Beatle serial killer?"

Lennon further confessed toward the end of his life, "I was a hitter. I couldn't express myself and I hit. I fought men and I beat women." It was a sentiment he expressed, of course, in the song "Getting Better." "I used to be cruel to my woman, I beat her and kept her apart from the things that she loved. Man I was mean but I'm changing my scene. . . ."

John often argued with Yoko's assertion that women were helpless pawns in the hands of lustful, stone-hearted men. Men had the advantage of size and strength, making them far more capable of barbaric acts. Having been raised by five dominant women, John felt the female sex was far stronger, enjoyed a longer life expectancy, and could easily rule men should they so choose. Men, he felt, were basically a fragile, self-obsessed sorry lot.

It was ironic that a man who campaigned so passionately for world peace was himself so often guilty of inflicting pain and injury on others. Lennon spoke directly to the dichotomy between his grand words and his actions. "That is why I'm always on about peace, you see," he explained. "It is the most violent people who go for love and peace. Everything's the opposite of what it is!"

WHO LOVES A KING [1]
Revolution For The Hell Of It

1971

There was something oddly portentous about the way John Lennon departed England for the last time. His rambling 74-acre Ascot estate, Tittenhurst Park, lay in shambles. The white Georgian mansion resembled a crumbling mausoleum. When he all but gave it to Ringo in 1973 for payment of back taxes and the sizable repair tab, the formerly easygoing drummer-turned-lord-of-the-manor suddenly became a changed man: now volatile and moody, a heavy drinker and unfeeling womanizer. Unceremoniously dumping his loyal wife Maureen, Starr fled abruptly to Los Angeles. It seemed as if Tittenhurst had a negative influence on those who lived there.

In reality the internal, bookish Beatle was not at all made for America. Arriving in the United States, Lennon wasted no time choosing a new home. As he later recalled, "It was Yoko who sold me on New York. She'd been poor here and knew every inch. She made me walk around the streets, parks, squares, and examine every nook and cranny. In fact, you could say I fell in love with New York on a street corner. . . . Not only was Yoko educated here, but she spent fifteen years living in New York, so, as far as I was concerned, it was just like returning to your wife's hometown."

John's departure from England was given a significant push from Yoko. While Lennon loved the old estate and had for a time considered it his final home, the place was a constant reminder to Ono of how irrevocably tied she was to her husband's overwhelming success.

While she had hoped to springboard her own dubious "career" on John's popularity, it hadn't quite worked out that way. Frankly, Yoko's mile-high ambitions could not be satisfied by hiding out in rural Berkshire. So she set to work convincing John to emigrate, goading him with her tales of glory as the "Queen of the Happening," hoping to retrace her early steps in New York's burgeoning avant-garde. There are certainly mixed views as to how influential an artist she was in those days. Lauded by some, condemned by others, Ono's enduring legacy as a conceptual artist depends on to whom you speak.

Furthermore, in England, Yoko was also faced with the issue of access to her husband. Their lavish and spacious Ascot showplace gave family and friends an ample excuse to visit. There was John's faithful cousin Leila, whose close kinship with the eccentric Beatle proved difficult to undermine. George Harrison and Ringo Starr also enjoyed hanging out at Tittenhurst, and thus came around frequently. Most problematic, of course, was the reintroduction of John's estranged son Julian, at six years old no longer a baby to be shunted out of mind. Yoko was secretly worried that any close contact with the boy might bring her new spouse closer to Cynthia, whom she despised.

In luring John to America, Yoko utilized two major factors to her advantage. The first was his vulnerability to heroin, which Yoko admittedly introduced to his life. She encouraged the move by pointing out that they could both escape the long shadow of John's 1968 drug conviction and enjoy greater freedom to experiment with various pharmaceuticals. Besides, the drugs were purported to be much more potent in America. Overnight, John's eagerness to depart for the "Promised Land" increased significantly.

The second draw was the recently completed *Imagine* album and its documentary companion (both produced at Tittenhurst), which required active promotion in the States. "*Imagine* is a big hit almost everywhere," said John at the time. "An anti-religious, anti-nationalistic, anti-conventional, anti-capitalistic song, but because it's sugar-coated, it's accepted. Now I understand what you have to do. Put your political message across with a little honey. This is what we do, Jerry [Rubin], Yoko, and the others, to try to change the apathy of young people. The apathy which exists in America (but which is infiltrating everywhere because everyone follows the American pattern), above all because of the music. The lifestyle of this century has been fashioned by America. Young people are so apathetic. They think there is nothing worthwhile to do and everything is finished. They want to take refuge in drugs and destroy themselves. Our work is to tell them there is still hope and still a lot to do. We have to change their minds; we have to tell them it's okay. Things can change and just because flower-power didn't work, it doesn't mean everything is finished. It is only the beginning. The revolution has only just begun. It is just the beginning of big changes!"

Drummer Alan White remembers the "Imagine" sessions at Tittenhurst: "I spent about ten days down there. We all slept in the house, which was being heavily remodeled. John wanted to watch a particular program and the only telly was up in one of the bedrooms. I remember Clapton, John, Yoko, and myself all lying on the bed watching the telly after a session!

"George Harrison kept poppin' in, different people were coming in from town, and we'd all sit around a big oak table in the kitchen with the builders working around us. It was very close. Being around John and George, having a couple of Beatles in the room, is very hard as they're the axis of everything that goes on. Especially a person as strong-willed as John, who always knew exactly what he wanted. He had that sound in his head. John played us 'Imagine' before we started the album. He gave us a set of lyrics for every song and said, 'This is what you're about to be saying to the world.'"

According to photographer Kieron Murphy, also on hand for the sessions, Phil Spector garnered the most respect, especially from John, who treated the legendary producer like royalty. Their collaboration had begun with Lennon's infectious 1970 hit, "Instant Karma," and continued with the Plastic Ono Band. "It was almost as if he'd come out of the floor in a puff of smoke," said Murphy of Spector. "He had a very strong presence. Phil seemed to arrive without even coming into the room. Lennon was almost as in awe of Spector as I was of John. He leapt up to give him his chair, fussed around him, and got him tea. Everybody else was being a bunch of boisterous lads, swapping football stories, but Spector just sat there. Then Phil says to him very quietly, 'John, I think we should make a start.' Whereupon Lennon leapt to his feet and literally took the cups of tea out of people's hands, frog marching them into the studio: 'Phil wants us *now!*' I was amazed to see that John Lennon was willing to obey anybody!"

Lennon offered rare insights into the recording of *Imagine* via an only recently discovered unpublished overview he wrote in 1971. The blistering "I Don't Want to Be a Soldier," for example, hailed from his "Working Class Hero" period. John praised its odd beat, but pointed out that many of the final lyrics were either lost or wrong. His wandering off-key vocals, reminiscent of Yoko's quirky deliveries, drew high praise from his wife.

Lennon's moody treatise on self-doubt, "How," was George Harrison's favorite. While the verses were penned in 1970, the middle-eight—George's favorite part—was knocked off during the session. Lennon conceded the vocal could have been better, but was pleased overall with the number. He also noted that the guitar breaks were a challenge.

The lengthy piece went on to discuss "How Do You Sleep?"—his stinging telegram launched at McCartney in response to Paul's cutting volleys on his *Ram* LP. John deemed it Harrison's finest guitar work and was especially proud of his own searing guitar riffs, although Lennon was critical of his rather strident vocals.

Murphy recalls John writing the tune with Yoko at his feet taking down the lyrics. "He was literally making the album up as he went along and was teaching it to them. I thought at first it was a slag off to the fans because the first line is, 'so Sgt. Pepper took you by surprise.' But it began to click when he sang 'The only thing you done was "Yesterday"' and so on.'"

Artistically, when Lennon left his homeland for America, he was at the top of his game. Following the stark emotional purge of his complex Plastic Ono period, he now returned to more familiar poetic musings with the just completed *Imagine* (released in October 1971), his most successful solo work. The bittersweet holiday single "Happy Xmas (War Is Over)" would become a perennial holiday favorite. Lennon was also on the verge of making important social and political contributions, speaking out on leftist issues in venues such as Tariq Ali's Marxist popular manifesto, *Red*, and supporting the landmark British miners' strike. But in his private life Lennon desperately sought an escape from fame and its oppressive trappings. He had also grown angry and weary of the media's relentless assaults upon Yoko. Thus, America afforded a real solution on several fronts. Wild and woolly, open-all-night *America*, the birthplace of rock and a haven for the downtrodden. But America was also the place where everything was for sale, including innocence and the very fame from which he had fled. As John's tragic karma rolled on, America would play a major part in his undoing. Still, John was very optimistic upon his arrival, as he noted, "I know there are rough areas in New York, but I don't visit them often. The district can change abruptly within one block, but I find I can walk the streets quite freely. People recognize me, but they don't trouble me too much. Sometimes they want to audition right there on the street, which can be a bit embarrassing. But they don't recognize me as much since I shaved my beard off. I shaved it off because I was finding it difficult to eat.

"The cab drivers treat me almost as one of the locals. The younger, hippie types still regard me as a rock superstar; they're always turning right round to ask questions and terrifying me.

"I like New Yorkers because they have no time for the niceties of life. They're like me in this regard. They're naturally aggressive, they don't believe in wasting time."

During this period Yoko initiated an extended custody battle for her daughter Kyoko.* It was an abrupt change of attitude considering her previous indifference to her daughter. Yoko, who had once referred to her pregnancy as a "tumor," had a history of dumping her child on anyone willing to take her. At one point she left her one-year-old daughter in Tokyo with her husband Tony Cox to travel to New York to pursue her "art." When Cox finally joined her, Ono left the toddler with Tony's relatives for some nine months, even arranging an adoption with Tony's aunt before her husband put a last-minute stop to it. When she migrated to London in 1966, she virtually abandoned Kyoko to pursue her affair with Lennon, only rarely spending time with her daughter. As longtime associate Jon Hendricks once put it, "Yoko *never* put her child before her career."

In the wake of the Lennon's Primal Therapy, Yoko's third miscarriage, and the awareness that John's son Julian was growing up, Ono had a change of heart and decided in April 1971 that she wanted her daughter back. The resulting custody battle was so tenacious, acrimonious, and confusing that at one point both Tony and Yoko had legal custody in several different jurisdictions.

---

*Born August 8, 1963 in Tokyo.

For John the battle was particularly wrenching. Lennon's hot and cold relationship with Cox was revealed in a letter "welcoming" Tony to London: After telling Yoko's ex that Kyoko wanted her dad to visit, John none too tactfully exposed his jealous insecurity. Yoko was the only woman for him, he stressed, and he didn't want anything or anyone, particularly her former hubby, to rock the boat. John begged Cox to make his excuses that he couldn't get away and come see them after all. John made it clear he could hardly even abide speaking with Tony on the telephone.

The court fight quickly became intensely personal when a judge asked Kyoko to choose between her parents. It brought back anguished memories of the day John was confronted with a similar choice: "I remember when it was happening to me. I was shattered." In Lennon's turbulent life everything seemed framed by the torment of his own fragmented childhood.

Eventually, Lennon enlisted a regiment of top detectives, headed by a $50,000 Pinkerton investigator, in a full-blown, two-year search that ranged over the Virgin Islands, Texas, and California. Lennon gave Jon Hendricks some money to snoop around Houston and Sausalito, where Cox had been sighted, and Hendricks often had to jump into action at a moment's notice whenever a frazzled Yoko swore she'd seen her daughter.

Another key figure in these activities was Ken Dewey, a talented performance artist from the wealthy New York Dewey family, and a former intimate of Ono, who had been tapped to become director of the New York Art Council. Tragically, while searching for Kyoko, he died in a small plane crash in Connecticut in August 1971. A memorial service was held at the family's estate in Sommerville, New York. Dressed entirely in black, a pale-faced Lennon appeared sombre and agitated as he and Yoko gave a silent concert, with John playing air guitar and Yoko an imaginary piano. When a photographer snapped a photo during the proceedings, Lennon exploded. He grabbed the camera, confiscated the film, and tossed the photographer a wad of money, screaming "I don't want you taking pictures!" After the service, Lennon hosted an exhibit of his drawings and writings in the Deweys' barn. The tribute further included an embarrassing John-and-Yoko blood-brothers ritual. Those close to the rocker say guilt over the young man's death eventually convinced John to call off the worldwide search.

Another player in the extended custody drama was the ubiqui-
tous Allen Klein, the ballsy business manager who eventually bul-
lied his way into the case. Cox and his wife Melinda, along with
eight-year-old Kyoko, were on the isle of Majorca attending a meditation seminar being taught by Lennon's former guru, the Maharishi Mahesh Yogi. Finding the girl alone in a playground in Palma
in April 1971, Klein and Lennon whisked her off to their hotel, the
Melia Mallorca. Cornered by the local police, the Lennons were
detained some fourteen hours pending a possible kidnapping
charge. They were eventually released.

In the interim, Cox spirited away the confused little girl once again.
John found the whole matter extremely distasteful, as if he were pursuing "an escaped convict." "It was a classic case of big boys playing
macho. It turned into me and Klein trying to dominate Tony Cox. Tony's
attitude was, 'You got my wife, but you won't get my kid!' I'll always feel
badly about it. It became a case of the Shootout at the OK Corral: Cox
fled to the hills, hid out, and the sheriff and I tracked him down."

Later John again flew to the States to pursue yet another lead, this
one claiming that Cox had been spotted at his parents' home on Long
Island. According to Tony's brother Larry, Klein dispatched a burly
detective to bully his way into Larry's home to flush out Cox, who was
nowhere to be found. An infuriated John was said to have erupted, "It
would be easier for me to have him killed than take any more of his
fuckin' shit!"

Perhaps the most absurd and desperate episode occurred in July
1972 when the Lennons returned to California, this time San Francisco, once more trying to smoke out the wily Cox. They drafted Craig
Pyes, editor of a hippie magazine called *Sundance*, to escort them
around the Bay area in his old VW, hoping to spot Kyoko. One day a
hysterical Yoko, certain she'd spotted Cox going into an apartment
complex, ordered Pyes to go door-to-door so John and Yoko could
stake out the rear windows, hoping to catch Cox stealing out the back.
Imagine catching sight of the great John Lennon and his Japanese
consort racing around one's backyard, and you get a sense of the deep
absurdity of the endeavor.

In a calmer moment Lennon eventually issued a truce to Cox:
"We'd like to stop the war (whatever it is) and be sensible about this,
without detectives, FBI, guns, and people jumping on them in the
middle of the night. It is like a divorce. It's as if war has been declared.

It gets unreal, particularly with a child involved. It should happen friendly and mutually without lawyers, courts, agents, or detectives."

For his part, Cox defended his actions in an obscure, strangely conciliatory 1981 interview. He painted an initially rosy picture of his relationship with Lennon, with the two men discussing everything from fish recipes for their cats to various philosophical dogmas. Cox revealed that Lennon's mystically fueled "Instant Karma" was the result of a profound talk with his wife Melinda. "One thing," said Cox, "that was really evident was that John wanted to escape from the prison of his fame. And despite our worst moments he always wanted to be friends. As a gesture of friendship he gave me a guitar that had been given him by the Beatles Fan Club of America on his first United States tour.

"Yoko wanted access to Kyoko and we weren't against that. In fact, we had just sent her to the Lennons for what was to have been a six-month visit prior to their visit on our farm. In their hearts they wanted to be friends, and there were several occasions when we all tried to work and live near each other. But Melinda and I would find such havoc introduced into our lives, we would have to withdraw. It was also very expensive as well as nerve-racking. Keep in mind that this was John and Yoko's most unstable period, and like everything else they did, it was larger than life. As it turned out, it took them another five years before they even began to stabilize. Prior to that, any contact with them was like touching some high-voltage machine.

"As part of their trying to gain custody of Kyoko, I was hounded by an army of private detectives and even thrown in jail. I should add, however, that this was the final straw in what was already an exceedingly heavy situation. I had now experienced almost total financial ruin on two occasions with considerable losses in between."

Despite pouring over $250,000 into the search, the Lennons were consistently outfoxed, always just one small step behind the clever Cox. The distressing situation reached its nadir over Christmas 1971. Although Cox had been awarded temporary custody of the child, Ono was granted generous visitation rights that included an initial ten-day visit. Upon arriving in Houston on Christmas Eve, John and Yoko, with the law on their side, at last anticipated seeing the youngster. First came Kyoko's not-so-merry yuletide greeting over the phone: "Mummy, I don't want to see you!" Next, despite being thrown in jail on a five-day sentence for contempt, Cox still managed to steal away with the girl, fleeing underground to a fundamentalist Christian group. A distraught Lennon cried, "I'm living with a woman who is screaming for her child every night. We've got so desperate we've been putting messages on our records. We've got a Christmas song out that begins with 'Happy Christmas, Kyoko.'*

"We've done everything we can to come to an amicable agreement with the father," he continued. "In all, it's cost us a lot of money and a shaft of broken promises. Yoko loves her daughter and I can't let her suffer like this any longer. What effect can all this be having on poor Kyoko?"

In fact, both baby-sitters and relatives described the eight-year-old as a defensive, often arrogant "mini adult" with daggerlike eyes and a habit of speaking like a stoned hippie. Insiders say she was often famished from a Yoko-imposed macrobiotic diet and encouraged to watch television constantly by her chronically absentee, fame-seeking mother.

Even in March 1972, when Ono was officially awarded sole custody, it was a Pyrrhic victory, as Cox blatantly refused to comply with the court order. Lennon was reduced to writing Kyoko a desperate birthday letter: "Happy birthday Kyoko, we want peace, no police, no FBI, no detectives. We understand the problem. Please get in touch with us through any group or media you trust. We are making no moves. We will wait for your call or letter. War is over if you want it. Give us a chance. Love and Peace, John Lennon."

In 1974 Cox phoned John, saying Kyoko could visit John and Yoko over Christmas in exchange for Lennon's promise to produce a film by Cox. John sent tickets for father and daughter to fly to New York, but they never appeared.

With the Lennons' frequent trips back and forth across the Atlantic, they decided that only by staying in the United States could they effectively conduct their search. Due to immigration problems John was advised to enter the country via St. Thomas. The troubled rock star managed to keep his sense of humor, as evidenced by the BOAC airlines questionnaire he filled out during the

---

*"Happy Xmas (War Is Over)," backed by "Listen, The Snow Is Falling," issued on Apple Records. The green vinyl see-through single is now a much sought-after collectors item.

flight: "Occupation: Artist. Reasons for making trip: World Peace. Additional comments: Why no films?" Ono blithely added, "A bed and bath would also be convenient."

On August 13, 1971, America's newest immigrants swept into Manhattan's premier bastion of wealth and propriety, John Astor's St. Regis Hotel. They took over three suites on the seventeenth floor bringing with them some eighteen trunks of belongings. Initially, Lennon was preoccupied with several ongoing projects he had begun in London, foremost being the publicity junket for *Imagine*, and the accompanying documentary of the same title. But the larger push was actually for Yoko, with the Lennons plugging her book *Grapefruit*, her far-out films *Fly* and *Up Your Legs Forever*, and the release of her haunting single "Mrs. Lennon." When the press coverage became venomous, John played the concerned husband, constantly issuing damage control to fortify his wife's besieged image. Together, they held carefully orchestrated interviews and appeared on public access television to promote the, by now, fairly tired John-and-Yoko love fest in the New World. Lennon's secretary, May Pang, noted that when together the two rarely displayed any physical intimacy. Although Pang didn't doubt their love, she observed no outward show of intimacy between them, unlike other rock couples she had known. "They behaved more like children snuggling against each other to ward off any demons that might be loose in the night," Pang observed. Interestingly enough, super groupie Jo Jo Laine made the very same observation about the relationship of Paul and Linda McCartney.

Unfortunately, efforts to promote Yoko as a solo artist were largely fruitless. Neither the public nor the media had any real interest in her off-key caterwauling or disappearing artworks. Lennon was compelled to defend her at every turn, as demonstrated in a public letter he wrote to *Melody Maker*, dated October 6, 1971, in response to an article the magazine had recently run: "1) We were seeing the press specifically to plug *Grapefruit*. Nothing else was going on. Communication breakdown? 2) The Joe Jones Tone Deaf Music Co. is on Yoko's album *Fly*, not mine. 3) Yoko never wears clogs on her most divine and beautiful little feet!" The postscript noted, "Except for the inevitable sneers we enjoyed your article."

At this time Lennon also felt betrayed by another hip magazine, *Rolling Stone*. He had granted Jann Wenner an exclusive and extensive interview in December 1970 on the condition it would run only in that periodical. Wenner, eager to launch *Rolling Stone*'s Straight Arrow Press, promptly published the now legendary compilation *Lennon Remembers* in the fall of 1971. An enraged John fired back this missive to Wenner: "As your company was failing (again) and as a special favor (*Two Virgins* was the first), I gave you an interview which was to be run *one time only* with all rights belonging to me. You saw fit to publish a book of my work without my consent and against my wishes. I told you many times on the phone and in writing that I did *not* want a book, album, or anything else made from it!" John was adamant and withdrew Apple's advertising from the magazine for a year. Lennon and Wenner eventually, however, made their peace.

Ono's primary artistic goal in coming to the States was to re-establish herself in New York's avant-garde scene. Once again, Ono's star was supposed to shine with her ambitious *This Is Not Here* retrospective at the Everson Museum of Art in Syracuse, New York. Yoko wasted little time in launching the elaborate showcase, which would prove to be her first and last major exhibition during her years with John. Tapping Lennon as "guest artist" (his contribution was a pink plastic bag labeled "Napoleon's Bladder"), she scheduled it on October 9th, John's thirty-first birthday, in an attempt to capitalize on the auspicious date. There is no definitive way of judging the event's success on the basis of Ono's art alone, but it seems doubtful that the administration of Syracuse University would have hosted a ten-day retrospective of Yoko Ono's work were it not for the presence of John Lennon. It seems equally dubious that 8,000 young people (including this author) would stand in line to view a running toilet, or a rotting apple on a pedestal, displayed by Mrs. Lennon, without the added attraction of glimpsing her famous spouse.

As for John, he was falling in love with New York City, a vibrant metropolis that fed his kinetic, insomniac nature. "I love New York. It's the hottest city going! I haven't been everywhere, but it's the fastest city on earth. The difference between New York and London is the difference between London and Liverpool.

"Slaves were brought to Liverpool and then shipped out to America. On the riverfront in Liverpool you can still see the rings in the side where they were chained. We got the records, the blues and rock, right off the boats and that's why we were so advanced musically. In Liverpool, when you stood on the edge of the water, you knew the next place was America." He added, "It's the only place I've found that can keep up with me." And later he admitted, "I'm sort of fascinated by it, like a fucking monster."

November opened with a memorable session for the single "Happy Xmas (War Is Over)," which John would later reference in his frustration about the search for Kyoko. This session was also co-produced by Phil Spector. John declared he penned the tune "because I was thoroughly sick of 'White Christmas.'" Spector wasted no time informing John that the opening lines were lifted from the 1960s tune "I Love How You Love Me," a hit for Bobby Vinton. Lennon admitted occasionally pilfering from the old classics, noting the pitfalls of possible copyright infringement. (It was a lesson he would painfully learn just a few years down the road during the *Rock 'n' Roll* debacle, which would pit him against notorious producer Morris Levy.)

The session reunited Jim Keltner on drums and pianist Nicky Hopkins with guitarist Hugh McCracken, who also played on Paul McCartney's *Ram*. Lennon couldn't resist quipping, "So you were just auditioning on *Ram*, were you?"

The subject of Paul hit a nerve when Phil asked John if he'd heard McCartney's latest LP. Spector told him, "It's really bad, just four musicians and it's awful."

"Don't talk about it. It depresses me."

"Don't worry, John," consoled Phil. "*Imagine* is number one and this will be number one, too. That's all that matters."

"No, it's not that. It's just that whenever anybody mentions his name, I don't think about the music. I think about all the old business crap. So please don't talk about him."

With the session under way Lennon and Spector worked together intuitively, generating a productive give-and-take. John would begin a sentence with, "I like ones that sound like records" and Phil would complete the thought "before you've made 'em." Bassist Klaus Voorman confirmed their natural rapport, noting that each appreciated the other's musical vision. "There were never any problems. No fights or arguments. Phil was very easy to get on with."

One thing that did draw Spector's ire was Lennon's constant chain-smoking, which naturally affected his voice. Phil shouted the ultimate indictment, "Yoko's outsinging you, John!" while muttering to those in the control booth, "He's smoking his ass off while he's fucking!"

A few sour moments ensued when Yoko made a vain bid to dominate the sessions. First she argued with John over his refusal to play organ, then tried to dictate the tempo to pianist Hopkins, and ultimately chastised the band for its impromptu jams between takes. Still, the final result was the inspirational Christmas classic.

Reasoning that they couldn't live forever in a hotel, the Lennons moved to a permanent dwelling that fall. John, particularly, had been growing uncomfortable with the hotel's decadent opulence. On November 1st the couple left the St. Regis to settle on Bank Street, a quiet cobblestone street in New York's West Village, Yoko's old stomping ground. The tiny, stark, two-room-plus-kitchenette basement apartment, with its beige walls trimmed in green, was distinguished by a large American flag and an open, iron spiral staircase leading to a skylight. An enormous bed, its headboard fashioned from an antique church pew, dominated the main room. This new downsizing was right in character for chameleon Lennon's next persona—that of millionaire hippie revolutionary.

The transformation happened so swiftly that Lennon didn't realize until years later he had been "conned" by the rabble-rousing "Mork and Mindy of the New Left," Jerry Rubin and Abbie Hoffman. The outrageous pair first swooped down on Lennon during a June trip to New York, and anointed him their savior in a ragtag parade in Washington Square Park. David Peel, a street musician with a silly novelty tune called "The Pope Smokes Dope," led the march.

Lennon recalled: "I got off the boat, only it was an aeroplane, and landed in New York and the first people who got in touch with me were Jerry Rubin and Abbie Hoffman. It's as simple as that. It's those two famous guys from America who's calling, 'Hey, what's happenin', what's going on?' The next thing you know I'm doing John Sinclair benefits and one thing and another. I'm pretty movable as an artist, you know. They almost grabbed me off the plane and the next minute I'm *involved*."

By this time, Rubin's counterculture hero mantle as one of 1968's notorious Chicago Seven was wearing thin. Furthermore, his idiotic rhetoric of "acid for everyone and fuck the establishment" hadn't succeeded in moving the masses any more than his platform to legalize marijuana. Rubin was constantly engaging in infantile "guerrilla theater" antics to attract attention: tossing soot bombs at Con Ed, mailing joints to 3,000 people chosen at random from the phone book, and blowing bubbles before the House Committee on UnAmerican Activities. Even his own Yippie party soon split over Rubin's puerile behavior, breaking off into the Zippies. What Jerry badly needed was a megadose of good publicity. John, a trusted pop icon, was the perfect addition to rally the youth around the flagging Yippie political agenda.

But Lennon should have had his antenna out. This wasn't the first time he stuck his neck out to support a controversial figure. In the past there had been Michael X, known at various times as Michael de Frietas or Michael Abdul Malik, who was nothing more than a pale British imitation of Malcolm X. Michael X was eventually tried, convicted, and hanged in 1975 for the murder of two associates. He was a highly controversial figure, either a peace-loving martyr for the black movement (according to Dick Gregory) or a cold-blooded killer (according to Tariq Ali). Lennon funneled considerable funds into Michael's legal defense and supported him personally until the very end.

From his smart headquarters on Bank Street, John held court from his huge bed, planning rallies and benefits with militant Black Panthers Huey Newton and Bobby Seale, as well as hanging with pacifist-poet Allen Ginsberg. Lennon would think nothing of cavorting about the apartment stark naked among this varied company. He was also entranced with the idea of learning to type, repeatedly pecking out his favorite line: "I'm sucking Yoko's pussy." Heady stuff indeed.

At Bank Street John began his great obsession with American television, which was always left on with the sound muted. "TV is what the fireplace used to be," he explained. "You always get these surreal things happening. I used to watch fires as a kid, but since they took those away, I've decided TV is it. It's like a window only the picture continually changes. You see China and the moon all in ten minutes. You'll see real, surreal, strange, psychedelic, *everything*." The irony was that nothing could have been as strange and surreal as what was occurring in real life in Lennon's very own living room.

David Peel, the off-the-wall Lennon zealot whom John found to be a convenient, amusing companion, often accompanied him and his bodyguards on "walkabouts" through the Village. Peel was among the first at Apple to view John as "cynical, mistrustful, and paranoid." Peel provoked the nocturnal bad boy in Lennon's nature: "I brought out the side of John that just wanted to go crazy and party all night."

During this period, the lion's share of Lennon's time was spent smoking marijuana, drinking, and indulging in socialist "Power to the

People" chat with his new compatriots. Although Rubin pronounced his newfound friend "far more radical than I," Lennon's recent activism was merely his latest *cause du jour*. The fact was, the ex-Beatle, by his own admission, was no political animal. John was far too intimidated by authority figures and lacked "the kind of gut" to stick his pacifist iron into the often chaotic revolutionary fire.

The differences between Rubin and Lennon were best summed up one evening when the pair stopped by an East Village deli for pancakes. As they were eating, a young devotee of Parsi Avatar Meher Baba silently approached their table and handed Lennon a card with the phrase "Don't Worry, Be Happy" inscribed on it. The insolent and insensitive Rubin grabbed the card, scribbled a swastika on it, and threw it back to the shaken boy. John quickly stepped in, telling Rubin it was hardly the best way to win converts or change consciousness. When put to the test, Lennon's basic Church of England decency often came shining through.

From Lennon's perspective there was "a whisper campaign going around against us. Some of the most extraordinary things were being said about us by people with no basis in fact, usually to do with Jerry Rubin or John Sinclair, who we only ever met once or twice at the most. But this big story is going around about what we're doing with them, financing revolutions and all that, and we ain't. The only thing we ever intended to do was to do some concerts, but we just didn't take the money. We gave it to some poor kids or prisoners. That was about it, but the story got so enlarged and out of proportion, they thought we were gonna go to San Diego and have a prison riot or something. I don't wanna be involved in any of those things that turn into riots."

Lennon's brand of chic radicalism seemed to be an extension of Primal Therapy, an opportunity to vent his vehement "us-against-them" bravado. At the heart of his angst were most likely memories of individuals who, like his Aunt Mimi, had hurt or disappointed him. After the repressive atmosphere of England, Lennon was like an outlaw in the Wild West, never stopping to consider the havoc his actions might create for him just down the road.

Energized by this latest kick, John spent the next six months feigning the snarling rock militant: demonstrating on behalf of Native Americans in Syracuse; financing the IRA (though he was careful to point out that he was contributing to a nonviolent organization, the Irish Civil Rights Movement); and headlining a controversial concert at Harlem's Apollo Theater for relatives of prisoners killed in the Attica uprising.

The centerpiece of these activities, and the one that would wreak devastating consequences, was the "Free John Sinclair" rally held in December in Ann Arbor, Michigan. Here was someone Lennon believed he could really relate to: the wild activist sentenced to ten years in prison for buying two joints from an undercover officer. But before committing himself, Lennon should have dug deeper into the party line regarding Sinclair. The charismatic White Panther promoted a cynical and pernicious agenda: "With our music and economic genius we plunder the unsuspecting straight world for money and the means to revolutionize its children. We will use guns if we have to. We have no illusions." Sinclair further advocated a "total assault of the culture program of rock 'n' roll, dope and what Eldridge Cleaver and Huey P. Newton called 'the mother country radical movement.' We will fuck their daughters in dressing rooms while their mothers whimper in front of their television sets."

John and his cohorts felt that a proposed White Panther event was the perfect vehicle, not only to unveil the newly formed Rock Liberation Front, but also to expose the Nixon administration for persecuting Sinclair. "Tomorrow," vowed Rubin at the rally, "the name John Sinclair will be a fucking household word!"

A capacity crowd of 15,000 filled Michigan University's Chrysler Arena for a seven-hour rally that boasted an impressive lineup of the New Left's high priests, such as David Dellinger and Rennie Davis as well as musical giants Stevie Wonder and John Lennon.

But when the smoke, along with the rhetoric, cleared, a solemn reality kicked in: the event had been atrociously organized. Broad gaps between musical numbers killed any momentum. The brilliant revolutionary minds offered the same uninspired, self-motivated, anarchist bottom-line rhetoric. Even Lennon's appearance dampened, rather than ignited, the rally's purpose. From the moment he was announced, the show's energy was driven not by the politically dedicated in the audience but by a throng of beer-guzzling college kids eager to boogie with Lennon, the rockstar Beatle barking out "Revolution" and "Instant Karma." As the price of admission, a restless crowd endured the mental maze of political sermonizing but booed David Peel and his tatty Lower East Side Friends Chorus.

To make matters worse, Lennon didn't take the stage until after 3:00 in the morning. Peel's musicians backed him for a mere fifteen-minute, three-song set of unfamiliar protest songs he'd just written: "Attica," "Luck of the Irish," and "John Sinclair." For her part, Yoko bellowed out her strident women's liberation anthem, "Sisters O Sisters." After a few pat words of encouragement Lennon made a quick exit, leaving the audience deflated, confused, and generally disappointed.

Even when, three days later, Sinclair was released on bail pending appeal, it had nothing to do with the rally. The Michigan legislature passed a law three days prior to the event reducing the maximum sentence for marijuana possession to one year.

Proclaiming victory nonetheless, Lennon dovetailed his activism into his unlucky seventh solo album, *Some Time in New York City*, released on June 12, 1972. It was an effort doomed to almost universal critical, commercial, and artistic failure. *Melody Maker* called it "mindless overkill, cheap rhetoric with appallingly bad lyrics." *Rolling Stone* summed it up tersely as "embarrassingly puerile and witless." It limped to number 48 on the charts and sold an abysmal 164,000 copies. John teamed up with Elephant's Memory, the backing band on the soundtrack for *Midnight Cowboy*. Guitarist Wayne "Tex" Barrett remembers the John Lennon he knew: "My mother had just died and John had a bad experience with his mom's death, so he helped me through a very bad period and gave me a lot of encouragement. I remember his words exactly: 'Death is only a dream.' You could see the depression on his face when he talked about her. You know, sometimes you can talk to someone and help them, but you can't help yourself. That was the impression I got of him. I felt he was in a lot of pain all the time."

Predictably, the album collapsed under the weight of its heavy-handed political clichés. Wrought by Phil Spector, the package reflected its hasty production, recorded over nineteen stoned days. There were some moments of energy, anchored by saxophonist Stan Bernstein's blistering licks, and Barret's impressive bluesy slide guitar. But the lyrics, usually Lennon's strength, were fraught with ham-handed propaganda: "Was he jailed for what he done/Or representing everyone/Free John now if we can/From the clutches of the

Man." Only the Ono-inspired "Woman Is Nigger of the World" was
built on an intriguing concept.

Interestingly, both Lennon and McCartney released albums at the
same time that featured similar protest songs, John with "Luck of the
Irish" and Paul's "Give Ireland Back to the Irish." Both were controversial, but met with similar lukewarm reviews. The BBC banned
Paul's song; John's didn't even inspire that much of a response. His
album was padded with material from his 1971 Fillmore East show
and the 1969 Live Jam for UNICEF, held at London's Lyceum Ballroom, where half the audience walked out when Yoko performed
"Don't Worry Kyoko."

By the new year Lennon's passion for the cause was beginning to
wane. February 5th marked John's last truly activist stand as he joined
400 demonstrators boycotting British exports to protest British policy
in Northern Ireland. By his April 22nd appearance at the National
Peace Rally on Fifth Avenue, leading the crowd in a chorus of "Give
Peace a Chance," Lennon did what he did best—inspiring his audience while uniting and raising a positive consciousness with a memorable lyric and an unforgettable hook.

By mid-year Lennon's last major concert put him back where he
belonged, on stage. The *One to One* concert on August 30, 1972 was
conceived with future talk-show host Geraldo Rivera, then a fledgling
New York television journalist. Rivera made his first mark as an in-
vestigative journalist with a dramatic exposé of the appalling treatment dispensed to mentally challenged children at Staten Island's
Willowbrook Hospital.

The Lennon who took the stage at midnight in Madison Square
Garden was the Beatle of the raw Cavern Club and Hamburg days.
Outfitted in tattered army fatigues, cowboy boots, and blue-tinted
shades, this was the John Lennon of old, the master of good-time rock
'n' roll. Backed by the pile-driving energy of Elephant's Memory,
John held the audience in his palm, delivering searing renditions of
"Come Together," "Mother," and "Cold Turkey." One audience member observed, "His voice became unnatural with torment, like he was
being sick. It creased your ears. How his jugular vein kept pumping
without exploding was a miracle."

It proved a memorable event for a great cause. The concert proceeds raised nearly $250,000 and, supplemented by government
funds, a total of $1.5 million. The money went directly to a trio of

charities to construct proper facilities to aid mentally challenged children. This was a prime example of Lennon joining forces with the establishment to use his talent for the greater good. As rock critic Simon Frith put it, "The energy of Lennon's music had always come from the tension between the private use of song (as a way of handling emotion, a celebration of personal powers) and a sense of public duty." Curiously, in the aftermath of Lennon's death, Yoko re-edited and then released the concert video, leaving much of John's footage on the cutting room floor while inserting several shots of herself pounding away at a keyboard that, according to several witnesses, wasn't even plugged in.

Years later, looking back on his stint as a counterculture revolutionary, Lennon dismissed it all as guilt-driven phoniness: "I'd always felt guilty I made money, so I had to give it away or lose it. I don't mean I was a hypocrite. What I believe, I believe right down to the roots. But being a chameleon, I *became* whoever I was with. When you stop and think, what the hell was I doing fighting the American government so Jerry Rubin could get what he always wanted—a nice cushy job?" He later went even further, saying it actually "ruined" his career. Instead of sloganeering, he should have stuck to his primary function. "My role in society is to try and express what we all feel. Not to tell people *how* to feel. Not as a preacher, not as a leader, but as a reflection of us all." Lennon's was yet another case of an intellect, overridden by foolhardy gullibility and impulsiveness, inviting the vultures to feed on its generosity.

As Roy Carr, author of *A Century of Jazz*, observed, "Lennon was living in a New York radical-chic ghetto surrounded by committed political figures and a fair percentage of the usual big-city cultural vampires. Having deliberately rejected world leadership as a Beatle, Lennon freely allowed himself to be manipulated as John Lennon, ex-Beatle."

Foremost among these manipulators was Jerry Rubin, the aging rebel with a lost cause. Through Lennon he managed a week-long stint on the *Mike Douglas Show*, where he was able to force-feed his own nonsensical agenda at a host of rallies, and even played congas in John's band.*

Similarly, David Peel used his access to Lennon to gain national exposure through various television and concert appearances, as well as by

---

*All the shows were later released on home video in 1998 by the Rhino company.

persuading John to produce his album *The Pope Smokes Dope* on the Apple label. John was reportedly a rather detached supporter of Peel's own label, Orange Records, which issued the less-than-memorable albums *Bring Back the Beatles* and *John Lennon for President*.

Despite these opportunities, Peel soon soured on Lennon, and labeled him "a millionaire trendy." Peel quickly and conveniently forgot the support he had received from Apple via John. "As soon as the carriage turned back to a pumpkin," Peel complained, "Cinderella was a housemaid. When you're with John Lennon, you're a prince. When his trendy thing is over, you go home a pumpkin. Twelve midnight, you're back in your rags doing what you did before. Like me."

John Sinclair was perhaps the most amnesiac in his condemnation of Lennon. Although he had been a stranger, John had freely given his time and money to help spring Sinclair from prison. In 1980 Sinclair eulogized Lennon as "one beautiful cat," yet previously Sinclair was whining that Lennon didn't compensate him for his appearance on the rally video, and that the proceeds weren't really going to legalize marijuana. Lennon replied, "We always insisted on keeping physical and legal control over any film footage which included us. John Sinclair threatened to sue us, even after we helped get him out of prison!"

Even Tariq Ali, as late as 1973, was looking for a handout to subsidize his overtly Marxist propaganda. But John felt disappointed by what he perceived as Ali's sexism. In a letter dated April 26th Lennon deemed Ali a chauvinist, and accused him of being very far off track, and out of touch. John urged him to get with the times and back causes worth fighting for.

This phase in Lennon's life may have turned out differently had he remained in Britain. His abrupt departure in the midst of the defining British mining strike at the Upper Clydeside Shipbuilders in Scotland has been cited by those involved as a crucial turning point in workers' rights. It was very much Lennon's involvement, his enormous stature, that finally gave this historically repressed class a voice and brought this serious issue to the forefront. According to socialist writer Robin Blackburn, "The miners would have radicalized John even further and would have drawn a direct link between his own humble origins and the class struggle in Britain." Lennon's opportunity to truly become a working-class hero might have springboarded him into a major leadership role. Significantly, it was only the British who successfully fused rock with politics. Consider Bob Geldoff with Live Aid, Peter Gabriel and Sting with Amnesty International, and the Rock Against Racism campaign. These artists learned to work within the establishment, to utilize the great power of corporations, and even to deal with the leadership of governments to effect change. Take the example of Pete Townshend, who cooperated with the conservative Tories to adopt an extraordinarily effective war on drugs that included life sentences for pushers and generous grants for rehab units. But Lennon recklessly aligned himself with several rather suspect characters who only wanted their fifteen minutes of fame. "It took a long time and a lot of good magic to get rid of the stench of our lost virginity," he once lamented.

On the musical front Lennon also lost a prime opportunity to be a leader for the punk/new-wave craze that erupted in the seventies. Yoko's impact on the new music of bands like the B-52s is well documented and may be her most important contribution to pop art. In turn, the At-lanta-based band inspired Lennon to compose and record again in 1980 with *Double Fantasy* via their breakthrough "Rock Lobster."

While others basked in the reflected glory of Lennon's perpetual spotlight, his own turn at revolutionary politics brought him troubling consequences. He was being watched. "I'd open the door and there'd be guys standing on the other side of the street," he has said. "I'd get in the car and they'd be following me. Not hiding. They wanted me to see I was being followed." Lennon further reported he was receiving numerous unsolicited visits from the phone company, allegedly to repair the phones. John was convinced his lines were being tapped as part of the government's ongoing surveillance. At some point a local drug dealer told him about a number that one could call to see if a phone was bugged. If it was, it would ring with a busy signal when the number was dialed. It did.

John Lennon was a target of surveillance and persecution from almost the moment he stepped onto American soil in the late summer of 1971. Suddenly, the ex-Beatle was Public Enemy Number One, cracking the Top Ten list of President Richard Nixon's "Political Enemies." Lennon was branded a dangerous radical before he penned a single protest lyric, attended a demonstration, or funded a political rally. In the eyes of the government, his friendships with the Chicago Seven made him guilty by association.

J. Edgar Hoover's FBI maintained a huge file on John, recording his every move, which over the next four years would swell to an astounding 26 pounds. It read like an impossibly bad spy novel: "Over drinks Lennon gave Abbie Hoffman and Jerry Rubin an envelope containing fifty $100 bills for the 'cause.'" Another entry recounted, "the subject has been offered a teaching position at New York University during the summer, and officials presume subject will accept." "Lennon is reportedly a heavy user of narcotics known as 'downers.' This information should be emphasized to local law enforcement agencies with regards to subject being arrested if at all possible on possession of narcotics charge."

John's eventual immigration woes were exacerbated by plans for him to head a major rock tour slated for early 1972. The details of the tour further unnerved the authorities. Lennon envisioned a kind of traveling caravan, "a mobile, political Plastic Ono Band show," with his band joining up with local groups in the towns in which they played. His idea to free political prisoners across America was, in his mind, "one way of paying the people back." He even contemplated a worldwide expedition to the far corners of the globe to distribute this "freedom music." His grand plan included an ambitious, large-scale cruise of the South Pacific he termed "Easy Rider at Sea."

John even wrote a lengthy, animated letter to Eric Clapton, dated September 29, 1971, asking the guitarist to jump on board. He opened by stroking Clapton's ego, telling him what fans he and Yoko were, and that Eric's style of music was exactly where he was headed. He explained that missing out on the Concert for Bangladesh whetted his and Yoko's appetite for heading out on tour. John was envisioning a much slower, easier pace, almost like a touring vacation where everyone could do some sight-seeing. Certainly not like that hellish nightmare experience during the old Fab Four days, he emphasized.

The first order of business, wrote John, was to get a band together. He'd already tapped old mates: pianist Nicky Hopkins, bassist Klaus Voorman, Jim Keltner on drums, plus producer Phil Spector, if he would come. This would make up the core ensemble and together they would choose additional musicians to fill out the band, like brass players, backup singers, and so on.

One of the perks of this tour, noted Lennon, was suggested by Nicky Hopkins. When he was on the Rolling Stones tours, Hopkins wasn't permitted to bring his wife along. But for these gigs, wives, girlfriends, even kids would be welcomed, even to join in on stage. The idea was one of total harmony and contentment. There would be no pressures on anyone, Lennon continued, and he wouldn't be handing out contracts to be signed either.

The real kicker, enthused John, was the mode of travel. How 'bout if they went by sea on their own ship, and got a major movie company to foot the bill! The film crew would shoot the band in rehearsal, while recording and during performance, a kind of seafaring rock 'n' roll documentary. Wouldn't it be great, exhorted John, to shove off from Los Angeles, sail to the South Seas, cruise around the islands for a while, play a few gigs, and even edit the footage *on board*? John was on a filmmaking kick, he explained, since he and Yoko had recently completed some terrific avant-garde footage to accompany their new releases *Fly* and *Imagine*. Now they were setting their sights on a feature film.

Lennon had thought of everything. He'd be sure to take along a physician for emergencies and would allow everyone who wanted to "jump ship" to fly back and forth whenever they liked. After all, they wouldn't be straying too far from terra firma. And for those who didn't like the ocean, the boat adventure wouldn't even be a requirement to be in the group.

Although he and Yoko weren't into the gigs for the money, John certainly didn't expect the others to play without compensation, and he made it clear everyone would have to be monetarily satisfied before they signed on. Lennon reckoned the tour would last anywhere from three to six months.

The rocker then went on to make clear the underlying purpose of this global junket. This was a tour with a message—to make the world a better place to live through pounding, searing, radical, in-your-face rock 'n' roll. It certainly wasn't necessary to share their own political tenets, Lennon offered, only a belief that music was the path to worldwide liberation. This was to be a tour for ordinary people to speak out and interact at will, a rock 'n' roll circus for the common man.

For Lennon, the Sinclair rally was conceived as a prototype, a trial run for his proposed grand tour. To the FBI it had all the makings of a sinister anti-government plot. Undercover agents were sprinkled throughout the Chrysler Arena taking careful notes of the proceedings. These agents, who ultimately reported back to old man Hoover, even ventured into music criticism in their reports: "'John Sinclair' will become a million seller but it is lacking in John's usual standards. Yoko Ono can't remain on key." Lyrics to "John Sinclair," readily available on the album jacket, were nonetheless labeled "classified" and sent to six regional branch offices across the country.

Lennon's association with Jerry Rubin was especially damning. It was Rubin who implicated Lennon in his own ambitious plans to disrupt the San Diego Republican National Convention (later moved to Miami), which he saw as an opportunity similar to the Chicago convention a few years before. At the Sinclair rally Rubin challenged the audience, urging "a million of you to turn up at the Republican National Convention in San Diego next summer." That, coupled with a more detailed itinerary he gave to *Rolling Stone*, placed John squarely in the thick of things.

Lennon believed that the seeds of his problems in this area were planted earlier on in a meeting with Rubin, Hoffman, and others at Bank Street where they met to discuss tactics. He was certain the conversation had been recorded. His compatriot's agenda shocked and appalled John. "We said, 'We ain't buying this. We're not going to draw children into a situation to create violence. So you can overthrow what, and replace it with what?'"

"I felt the Yippies were the Beatles music put to politics, and John was the most politically aware of the Beatles," Rubin commented later. "On his *Working Class Hero** album, John was singing to my soul. I found him to be a good friend, honest, loving, and brilliant. He eased me over my age hurdle by telling me how proud he was to be 31—the 'Best age of all!'"

Jerry spoke about his many visits to the Lennons' West Village flat, where he usually found John and Yoko working from "headquarters" in their gargantuan bed. He learned firsthand the enormous and rabid swell of their celebrity. He often followed the pair down the New York streets as they were crushed with fans all wanting a piece of the superstar, John feebly attempting to shoo people away. When they stopped for lunch, the waitresses were so flustered that plates and glasses tumbled out of their hands. Despite this kind of massive adulation and worldwide fame, Rubin observed that Lennon wasn't a contented man.

---

*Actually, *John Lennon/Plastic Ono Band*, Apple Records, 1970.

Jerry pointed to John's penetrating lyrics of late, and concluded the artist was on a mission to dig out the private, inner, *real* John Lennon.

Rubin further spoke of arranging lively meetings at John's pad with the celebrated radicals of the day, including Bobby Seale, Rennie Davis, Huey Newton, and Dave Dellinger. One particular evening Jerry, Abbie Hoffman, John, and Yoko slit their fingers together in a blood-brother oath and rubbed their hands on the Ram Dass early seventies manifesto, *Be Here Now.*

Rubin further recalled John's invitation to join Lennon's band even though he possessed no musical talent whatsoever. The move was a PR stunt designed to soften his image as an out-of-the-loop hippie radical. The next thing Jerry knew, he was playing drums on "Imagine" and picking up a tambourine for the band's Attica show at New York's Apollo Theater. "When John and Yoko hosted the *Mike Douglas Show* I helped them back up Chuck Berry, doing 'School Days,' stated Rubin. "This, the culmination of every musical fantasy I'd ever had, was possible only because every musician had amplification but me!"

Things began to sour, however, when the Feds moved in on Lennon. "He got paranoid," said Jerry. "For a time he even considered the possibility I was a CIA agent who had snuggled close, seduced them into a rock tour, and then nabbed them. He didn't really mean it, but the hot breath of the U.S. government complicated our friendship."

Surely it must have been evident to Lennon that here was not the kinder, gentler, England of bed-ins, bagism, and acorns for peace. This was America, where kids were shot on college campuses and soldiers annihilated daily on the killing fields of Vietnam: a nation deeply divided along political lines and racked by longtime racial tensions. But instead of heeding the warning signs, Lennon did nothing to distance himself from the waning radical left. For some months more John continued to ride the runaway leftist train, headed on a collison course with disaster.

LIFTING THE VEIL $\boxed{2}$
Beyond The Lost Weekend

1972–1974

By January 1972, the United States government was convinced that John Lennon was at the heart of a plot to wreak havoc at the upcoming Republican National Convention, a "political Woodstock" as Rubin coined it, designed to deny Richard Nixon a second term in the White House. On February 4th, Senator Strom Thurmond penned a top-secret memorandum to Attorney General John Mitchell, informing him of the proposed rock tour with its five-pronged agenda: to obtain access to college campuses; to register young people to vote; to campaign to legalize marijuana; to finance their activities; and, above all, to recruit followers to descend upon San Diego to stir up the convention. "Rennie Davis and his cohorts intend to use John Lennon as a drawing card to promote their success. If Lennon's visa is terminated, it would be a strategy counter-measure," advised the senator from South Carolina.

Apparently, the FBI didn't merely want to keep an eye on the potential troublemaker; they wanted him out of the country. The problem was they had no proof. Lennon was a model citizen, simply exercising his right to free speech and assembly. The FBI, therefore, had to reach back into the past to find an excuse to oust him: his 1968 conviction for possession of marijuana. The arrest had been a blatant frame-up, designed and executed by infamous British detective Sgt. Norman Pilcher. Pilcher had made a career of planting drugs on musicians, notably Rolling Stones' Brian Jones, whose personal problems and legal difficulties were made appreciably worse by the shady detective's relentless hounding. Officers who stormed Lennon's sparse London flat at 34 Montague Square found a mere half-ounce of black hash inside a binocular case. John duly pled guilty, paid the £150 fine, and thought that was the end of it.

According to American law, Lennon now fell under the class of "excludable alien." The code made ineligible for permanent residence "any alien who has been convicted of a violation of any law or regulation relating to the illicit possession of marijuana."

The February 4th memo, issued just weeks before Lennon's visa was due to run out on February 29th, ensnared the Beatle in a hellish three-and-a-half-year legal battle that had devastating emotional and financial consequences. Battling back, John retained Leon Wildes, a shrewd immigration specialist who had never lost a case. Wildes fought for a series of waivers under the very "loophole" that gave Lennon a temporary visa in the first place: the exception given to "qualified immigrants who, because of their exceptional ability in the sciences or arts, will substantially benefit prospectively the national economy, cultural interests, or welfare of the United States." The law was so lenient it even stated that such an alien could apply for permanent residence any time after the visa expired.

Even though John had the letter of the law on his side, the government was determined to deport him. The Immigration and Naturalization Service put their top litigator, the flamboyant Vincent Schiano, on the case. Schiano was a courthouse pit bull who spearheaded New York's most notorious deportation cases: alleged mobster Carlo Gambino, Nazi Hermine Braunsteiner Ryan, and Irish revolutionary Joe Cahill. So began a vicious campaign fueled by a web of lies, harassment, and conspiracy, the trail of which led all the way back to the Oval Office. New York journalist Al Aronowitz reported that it was the "offensive" Yoko the government was really after. By kicking John out, he argued, they would also be rid of her.

With his keen sense of public relations Lennon had the good sense to take his case to the people, lobbying for his freedom on the *Dick Cavett Show*, writing articles for underground magazines like *Oz*, and even authoring a piece for the *New York Times*. The composer also drew sympathy with his conceptual country "Nutopia," a territory of "no boundaries, no passports, only people." The support that followed his efforts was remarkable. At the hearings even the British ambassador to the United States, Lord Harlech, stated, "If John Lennon were a painter, he would be hanging in the Metropolitan." Celebrities from all of the arts flocked to his defense, signing petitions against the deportation. Among John's supporters were Willem de Kooning, Kurt Vonnegut Jr., and even Jack Lemmon. Mayor John Lindsay said, "This town always had a very important history of welcoming contributing talent. I could see no compelling reason to get rid of this kind of artist. John Lennon was a major force as we saw it, far more good than bad." Even as the government dug in its heels, it hadn't counted on this wellspring of celebrity support.

Lennon's immigration problems became an issue in the already draining custody battle. John wore his emotions on his sleeve on the *Cavett* show when commenting, "Yoko's daughter is not allowed to visit us because her ex-husband won't let her see her own daughter. All Yoko wishes is that now and again Kyoko could be brought to Tittenhurst to spend some time. That's the house waiting for her, if you're watching, Kyoko."

The INS countered these efforts by trying to use Kyoko against John and Yoko, inferring that the child wanted no part of the Lennons, and resented and feared the private investigators tracking her. The INS also went so far as to attempt a divide-and-conquer strategy in 1973 by offering Ono a permanent visa, thereby trying to force her to choose between returning to England with John or staying in the States to search for her daughter.

A desperate John tearfully told the court, "I don't know if there's any mercy to plead for as this isn't a federal court, but if there is, I'd like it, please."

The year 1972 brought additional pressures. Lennon and McCartney were feuding both in the media and on their records over the bitter dissolution of Apple. McCartney, eager to extricate himself from the Beatles to explore his own solo career, forced the issue by taking the three other Beatles to court and placing the corporation in receivership. The resulting complex legal entanglements pitted Paul and his father-in-law, manager Lee Eastman, against Allen Klein and John. The bad blood, in Lennon's view, could be traced all the way back to differences over the 1968 *White Album*, a work that, according to John, wasn't enough of a "Paul album" for McCartney's liking.

Their vitriolic exchange soon went public in Britain's music press:

Paul: I just want the four of us to get together somewhere and sign a piece of paper saying it's all over and we want to divide the money four ways. . . . But John won't do it. Everybody thinks I'm the aggressor, but I'm not. I just want out.

John:

1. We give you *money* for your bits of Apple.

2. We give you *more money* in the form of royalties which legally belong to Apple (I know we're Apple, but on the other hand we're not).

Maybe there's an answer there somewhere . . . but for the millionth time in these past few years I repeat, *What about the* TAX? It's all very well, playing "simple, honest ole Paul" in the *Melody Maker* but you know damn well we can't just sign a bit of paper.

You say, "John won't do it." I will if you'll *indemnify* us against the tax man! Anyway, you know that after we have our meeting, the fucking lawyers will have to implement whatever we agree on—right? If you're not the aggressor (as you claim) who took us to court and shit all over us in public?

Paul: John and Yoko are not cool in what they're doing.

John: If we're not cool, what does that make *you*?

Paul: I like . . . *Imagine*, but there was too much political stuff on the other albums.

John: As I've said before—have you ever thought that you might *possibly* be wrong about something? Your conceit about us and Klein is incredible—you say you "made the mistake of trying to advise them against him [Klein] and that pissed them off" and we secretly feel that you're right! Good God! You must *know we're right about Eastman* . . . So you think *Imagine* ain't political, it's WORKING CLASS HERO with sugar on it for conservatives like yourself!! You obviously didn't *dig the words*. Imagine! You took "How Do You Sleep?" so literally (read my own review of the album in *Crawdaddy*). *Your* politics are very similar to Mary Whitehouse's—saying *nothing* is as loud as saying *something*.

Over this long winter John was also in the grip of a nasty drug habit. After periods of profound heroin addiction Lennon was now hooked on government-prescribed methadone. "I got off heroin cold turkey in three days," John lamented, "but I've been trying to shake methadone for five months." To escape the stress of legal troubles, Lennon and Ono hopped into an old Rambler station wagon and drove cross-country to California in an effort to conquer the addiction. Their San Francisco friend Craig Pyes put them in touch with

Dr. Hong, an Asian practitioner who used then-illegal acupuncture in his practice. Hong advised Lennon that his method could cure his cravings, and within a week John was weaned off the drug. (Later Dr. Hong was instrumental in helping them conceive Sean.)

But the ongoing deportation woes and the sluggish sales of *Some Time in New York City* took its toll. Throughout the remainder of 1972 Lennon locked himself in his bedroom, staring at television and receiving no visitors. Mired in an agoraphobic funk, he seldom left the Bank Street apartment. Ono, meanwhile, had begun working on her latest opus, *Approximately Infinite Universe*, due for release early in the new year.

Around this time the media began targeting the noticeable fissures in the famous couple's marriage. The *Sunday Mirror* called them "one of the saddest, loneliest couples in the world. Sure they have an abundance of fame, money, talent, and a magnificent obsession for each other. But one has only to glimpse a few scenes from their new full-length documentary *Imagine* to see a picture of two people who have everything that adds up to nothing."

At the beginning of 1973 Lennon had yet another monkey on his back, Allen Klein. Finding a kinship in the bearish agent from the New York streets who had diligently cultivated John's goodwill by committing all of Lennon's lyrics to memory, Lennon first hired him as the Beatles' business manager on February 3, 1969. Once Klein had his foot in the door, however, he was monumentally difficult to get rid of. The Rolling Stones had a similar experience with Klein, who is by most accounts almost universally feared and despised in the music industry.

Klein "was an orphan," said Lennon. "He never had his parents. His mother died when he was a kid and he's as neurotic as me or any other person that's got no parents. He's a capitalist, but that's really all. That's his worst sin. I think that's a bad enough sin, but that's it."

Another factor that bonded the pair was their hatred of Lee Eastman. In Paul's father-in-law Lennon found everything he'd always hated: the humorless, unapproachable, corporate authority figure who interfered in the Beatles' business affairs and seemed forever poised to take over. Lennon cheered like a rebellious schoolboy when the maverick Klein vowed to "roast McCartney's fuckin' ass!"

Although the crafty, charismatic Klein was instrumental in negotiating large deals for his clients, he also made a great deal of money
for himself. "DeKlein," as Lennon began calling him, showed his
fangs when he sued the three Beatles for breach of contract in early
1973. In November of that year Lennon countersued, just as the
Stones had done, for misrepresentation. Ultimately he had to admit
that hiring Klein had been a mistake. It must have galled Lennon to
give McCartney the deep satisfaction of being right.

Meanwhile, John snapped out of his lethargy in February 1973 with
a major move. The Lennons took over actor Robert Ryan's apartment
in the century-old Dakota building on 72nd Street and Central Park
West. The foreboding Gothic design, with its creaking water-powered
elevators, was a prestigious fortress for the rich and famous of New York
City. The couple spread out over twelve rooms, the apartment anchored
by the famous White Room with its stunning view of Central Park.

John immediately went to work composing material for *Mind
Games*. Although a vast improvement over *Some Time in New York
City*, it reached only number eighteen on the charts, and was certainly
not John Lennon at his best. "Like an interim record between being a
maniac political lunatic and back to being a musician again," he said at
the time. "There's no deep message about it. I very rarely consciously
sit down and write a song with a deep message. Usually, whatever lyrics
I write are about what I've been thinking over the past few months."
Politically, John was no longer obsessed with issues and causes and
backed away from taking sides: "We don't care what flag you're wearing, we don't even want to know your name," he sang in "Bring on the
Lucie (Freeda Peeple)." It was as close as he ventured to a political
statement; most critics considered it one of the better tracks.

Lennon's categorization of the album, "rock at several different
speeds," had a definite early Beatles feel to it, from the funky fifties-
sounding "Tight A$" to the McCartneyish "One Day at a Time." This
was Lennon's first real effort at producing and arranging. An attempt
to emulate his hero Spector's famous "Wall of Sound," without Spector's production savvy, *Mind Games* fell short of the mark. John's com-
positions were often buried beneath schoolgirl choruses and bloated
orchestrations.

Toward the end of his life Lennon decried the work. He dismissed
"Out of the Blue" as "nothing special," "Tight A$" as "a throwaway,"
and "I Know (I Know)" as "a piece of nothing."

He did, however, enjoy the title tune with its inventive middle-eight reggae. John was among the first to incorporate Jamaican rhythms into rock. "That was a fun track because the voice is in stereo and the seeming orchestra on it is just me playing three notes with a slide guitar. . . . I'm glad it's played, it ain't bad."

The irony of "You Are Here," John's tender love poem to Yoko with its symbolic merging of East with West, was that their marriage was foundering. All of their efforts, from communal living to Primal Therapy, failed to address their crumbling sex life or Ono's deep distress over her stagnant career.

Predictably, Yoko was the one who took the reins and decided she needed some space. The first step was finding a solution to her husband's seemingly inexhaustible sexual appetite. The key factor in her decision for a separation had been a disturbing episode, exemplifying John's boorish and cruel behavior, on Election Night in 1972 at Jerry Rubin's apartment. Upset by Nixon's re-election and harried by his legal woes, John loaded himself with drugs and fondled a woman's breasts in Yoko's presence. According to Rubin, "Their relationship really ended right there."

According to Sean Lennon the incident inspired "Death of Samantha," a track on Ono's 1973 *Approximately Infinite Universe.* "That's all about dad having sex with some girl at a party where my mom was. When I think back on those events, I think of my dad as a huge asshole. He was a macho pig in a lot of ways and he knew it. The only thing that made it okay was that he could admit it. That was his saving grace. He tried to overcome it."

Ono's solution to John's swelling sex drive was certainly unusual: she provided him with a lover. The obvious choice was May Pang, the young Chinese American secretary employed by the Lennons since their move to the States. John had always been attracted to Asian women, and he admitted to Pang that he found her very attractive. Yoko simply had to push them together, hoping the inexperienced young girl wouldn't be able to resist her famous boss.

Lennon soon plunged into the affair without the slightest apparent concern for either May or Yoko. In fact, when Ono left town for a week-long feminist convention in Chicago in October, Lennon took the opportunity to steal away with his new mistress to Los Angeles. He boldly told Pang, "I'm walking away from Yoko," blissfully ignorant that his wife was simply keeping him on a very long leash. The story he later told the press, that Yoko had kicked him out, was invented by Ono to maintain her stony image of absolute control.

As soon as John and May settled in at record producer Lou Adler's Bel Air estate on Stone Canyon Road, Lennon's behavior degenerated to that of a college freshman away from home for the first time. Suddenly New York's brooding Dr. Jekyll turned into Los Angeles' Mr. Hyde. John avidly indulged in a savage social life, clubbing at the Troubadour, the Roxy, and the Rainbow. He was seen shopping on Rodeo Drive, bunny watching at the Playboy Mansion, and even patronizing a gay cabaret in Las Vegas. Far from his days as a homebound New Yorker, John socialized with celebrities like Elizabeth Taylor, Cher, and the openly gay Sal Mineo.

Lennon soon gathered together like-minded people: Mal Evans, the down-on-his-luck former Beatles roadie who was every bit as unstable as John; Jesse Ed Davis, the strapping Kiowa Native American guitarist and a partner in drug abuse; and the hard-living Harry Nilsson, who became so destructive on alcohol that he often had to be locked in his room for his own protection.

Out from under Yoko's thumb, John frequently used LSD, cocaine, and dope, and began to drink heavily "for security," as he told May. His booze of choice, vodka, soon turned into a new favorite, Brandy Alexanders.

One evening, Lennon, along with May Pang and Harry Nilsson, arrived at the Troubadour around midnight to catch the opening night of the Smothers Brothers act. Already overloaded on Brandy Alexanders, John became immediately disruptive, joining Harry in a cacophonous songfest and hurling a stream of obscenities at the Smothers. Events took a nasty turn when the duo's manager Ken Fritz confronted an out-of-control John and hauled him from his seat. Lennon exploded, overturning the table and the pair exchanged a few halfhearted fisticuffs. Lennon and company were literally thrown out the door where they tumbled into a party of incoming patrons, touching off a full-blown street brawl. The incident made worldwide headlines the following day.

"I picked up a Kotex in a restaurant in the toilet," Lennon later remembered. "It was clean and just for a gag I came back to the table with it on me head. It just stayed there till it fell off. I asked the waitress, 'Do you know who I am?' And she said, 'Yeah, you're some asshole with a Kotex on your head,' and I think it's a good remark, and so what? I was with Harry Nilsson, who was no help at all.

"Ask any rock star about lawsuits. The more money there is, the more lawsuits there are. The bigger the artist, the more lawsuits. People sue me for anything. That bloody fan with the Instamatic who sued me for hitting her. I never touched her, never went near the girl in the Troubadour.

"I had to pay her off to shut her up. That happens all the time. She just wanted money. People sue you if you bump into them on the street. I do admit to chasing some weird people around, but she was not in the scene.

"I was not in the best frame of mind and I was wildly drunk. But I was nowhere near this chick; she's got no photographs of me near her. It was my first night on Brandy Alexanders and they tasted like milkshakes. The first thing I knew, I was out of me gourd.

"Of course, Harry was no help, feeding them to me, saying, 'Go ahead, John!' It is true I was wildly obnoxious, but I definitely didn't hit this woman, who just wanted to get her name in the papers and [make] a few dollars."

Subsequent episodes became even uglier. One night Lennon was wandering in a stupor in Bel Air, and in a drunken delusion mistook May for Yoko. He began by abusing her verbally but then got physical, striking her while whining that "no one ever loved me." On another occasion, John was banished from Adler's mansion for deliberately breaking several valuable antiques. Investigating an unrelated complaint, the police found Lennon at attorney Harold Seider's apartment where he and Pang were now staying. John and Jesse Davis, loaded on heroin and vodka, were becoming rowdy when the police arrived. Once John heard the cops outside, he went berserk, hurling a chair out the window, smashing mirrors, heaving a TV against the wall, and screaming nonsense about film director Roman Polanski being to blame. "My goal was to obliterate my mind so I wouldn't be conscious," Lennon later said of those days. "I think I was suicidal on some kind of subconscious level."

Although May tried desperately to cajole her companion out of his darkness, an inexperienced girl barely out of her teens was ill-equipped to deal with such mountain-high self-destructiveness. But in some ways May did a remarkable job in keeping him on an even keel. Without her compassion and patience the situation might have been much worse. And Lennon *had* come to life: productive, enthusiastic, and eager to compose again.

Even in the professional arena Lennon's decisions were often hasty and ill-advised. Whereas *Mind Games* harkened back to the security of the Beatles, he then took another step further back, to fifties rock 'n' roll. Perhaps John sought a musical safety net with such proven classics.

If his choice of material was suspect, Lennon's selection of producer Phil Spector was ominous. While the pair's previous collaborations had been successful, their last effort, the doomed *Some Time in New York City*, badly missed the mark. This time Lennon, driven either by severe self-doubt or by an unshakable belief in Spector, unwisely placed himself totally in Phil's hands, giving him full control over the ill-fated *Rock 'n' Roll* project.

In a letter John lavishly praised the producer's genius, recalling he'd first met Spector on board the flight that launched the Beatles' initial invasion of the United States. His words seemed to refer as much to himself as to the famous producer. "It seems that talented people of stature must always be in great pain," John wrote. "Their extreme sensitivity is what makes them great artists, but what a price they pay! How quick people were to say 'now he's finished'; only Phil himself could ever decide when the party's over."

The sessions were a disaster right from the start. Like John, Phil was battling serious personal problems. The composed and accommodating producer of old had become a volatile megalomaniac whose demand for control had all but ruined his celebrity marriage to recording star Ronnie and badly damaged his professional reputation. Dressed, at varying times, as a kung fu fighter or a doctor, complete with surgical gown and stethoscope, Spector would come to the studio with a bottle of Courvoisier in one hand and a loaded revolver in the other. Embroiled in a bitter custody battle with his wife for their adopted son, Spector was moody and unpredictable. One day, while he was drinking heavily, a scuffle broke out between Phil and Mal Evans. Whipping out his pistol, Spector fired into the air. Afterwards, Evans retrieved a bullet from the ceiling. An intrigued Lennon, examining the unwelcome projectile, exclaimed, "I think it's a real fuckin' bullet!"

The relationship soon began to break down with a clash over Spector's meticulous, extensive, and exhausting production methods. He would rehearse the band section by section, often for hours at a time. Meanwhile, the other musicians, including Lennon, waited around with nothing to do. For John, used to working very quickly, this frustratingly slow pace agitated his already fragile nerves. He began to openly resent Spector's heavy-handed authority and mistrust his motives. Finally, one night Lennon exploded, "When are you gonna get to me?" In a drunken rage he derided the unpredictable producer, calling him "a Jew bastard."

As he was driven home, Lennon was so out of control he began to kick the windows out of the car and later trashed the house. Even Spector's bodyguard couldn't contain him, and his wrists and ankles had to be bound to a bed with neckties. Lennon remained in these makeshift restraints until he cooled off. Afterwards, John professed to remembering nothing but was profusely apologetic nonetheless.

The *Rock 'n' Roll* project soon ground to a halt due to a lack of usable material. When the musicians were scheduled to start working on the sessions again, Spector refused to let John have the tapes, inventing several incredible excuses. At one point he claimed the studio burned down; at another time Spector claimed he'd been in a horrible automobile accident. In reality, Lennon was badly used by Spector. According to insiders the producer dangled his collaboration with Lennon as bait to seal a blockbuster deal with Warner Brothers. Without telling Lennon, he charged the recording expenses to Warner's, knowing well that Lennon was signed to Capitol. The resourceful Spector netted a tidy $90,000 fee for the return of the tapes, and it wasn't until much later that John finally got his hands on them. The quality was so poor that Lennon was forced to rework the entire lot.

Although soured by the horrific experience, Lennon was determined to make the definitive fifties album. In yet another ill-considered move he decided to produce Harry Nilsson's *Pussycats* LP, a whimsical and irreverent take on such classics as "Save the Last Dance for Me" and "Rock Around the Clock." Nilsson explained: "We were getting very bored at a Joni Mitchell session one night, peeing in ashtrays and that sort of thing, when John jumped up and said, 'I'm gonna produce Harry Nilsson!' I didn't know whether he was drunk or what, so a couple of days later he says to me, 'What do you think?' I said, 'If you're serious about it, man, you bet.'"

John and a few friends rented a five-bedroom bungalow on the beach at Santa Monica. It was a cast of characters tailor-made for misadventure: Ringo Starr, Harry Nilsson, Klaus Voorman, John, and, topped off by the ultimate merry prankster himself, the Who's drummer Keith Moon. Nilsson's reckless drinking and pill-popping finally caught up with him. At a session one day he began coughing up blood and his already gravelly voice gave out. The incident so alarmed John that he was forced to examine his own excessive lifestyle. Briefly scared straight, John became a model of responsibility, at least for a time. "It was just a madhouse," he later explained, "and I realized I was in charge. I wasn't just one of the boys. In fact, the bills were coming to me, and a company would be expecting me to produce this record out of this gang of drunken lunatics, Keith Moon, Harry, and me, all these people. So I just quit drinking, like that, and quit everything, and then I became the one that wasn't lying on the floor."

As Harry Nilsson recalled, "We just lived a normal, reasonable life. We'd wake up in the morning—well, about one o'clock actually—and eat breakfast prepared by this couple we had serving us. Klaus Voorman went out for a swim in the ocean quite a lot. My wife Una used to take long walks on the beach. John and May would sleep late. I'd sleep later, and then at six o'clock the limos would show up and we'd drive over to Warner Brothers to record, finishing about two o'clock in the morning. Then we'd come home, open up the brandy bottles, and listen to the tapes very loudly, get drunk, and tell each other how wonderful we were."

Dougal Butler, Keith Moon's full-time minder, also remembered the scene in Santa Monica. "The house was extremely well appointed and comfortable. It once belonged to the Kennedys and it is apparently where they invited Marilyn Monroe, among others, to view their etchings and indulge in private pleasures.

"For me, to meet John Lennon was similar to a devout Catholic meeting the Pope. I was nervous at first, though it soon turns out that he is a nice, relaxed sort of bloke and quite one of the lads. I personally never saw him awkward or hoity-toity, such as people claim he is. Far from it, he was a great laugh in the studio and a considerable hand in partying afterwards. He loved Moonie's drumming and rated Keith as one of the all-time greats. In fact, he and Keith struck up quite a friendship and spent a lot of time together."

Meanwhile the McCartneys had also come to town and sought out John and Harry at the studio. John and Paul vacillated between the comfortable banter of old buddies and the tentative, awkward preliminaries of strangers. Suddenly Paul eyed Ringo's kit and made a beeline, shouting "Let's play!" An inspired John grabbed a guitar, followed McCartney's lead, and the former partners launched into a driving version of "Midnight Special," backed by Danny Kotchmar, Jesse Davis, and Harry Nilsson. Stevie Wonder, recording down the hall, stopped by to join in on electric piano. Aside from John's jab at Linda (he untactfully requested that she turn down her keyboards), the mood was light and friendly. The old Liverpool magic was still there. The tape of that event, the last time Lennon and McCartney ever recorded together, is reportedly still floating around among serious Beatles collectors.

Dougal Butler later joined John for another night of partying, this time back in New York. "When the Who played New York, he intended to attend the gig. But then he rung to say he cannot make it, but can we meet later, which we do. We go round to his hotel suite and there we met Chris Charlesworth, the *Melody Maker* journalist. That night is very special because Lennon spent much of the time talking about the early days of the Beatles in Liverpool and Germany."

In a late 1997 interview, Charlesworth himself remembered that evening. "I was with Keith Moon and Dougal Butler, when we stopped by the Pierre to call up to the suite John shared with May Pang. He told us to come on up. When we got there, he said, 'What can I offer you to drink? All I've got is this bottle of wine, Rothschild 1845 or something, that [Allen] Klein sent me for my birthday. However, as I'm in a lawsuit with him at the moment, it might not be safe to drink! It could be poisoned! I certainly don't want to drink it because I'm a world-famous millionaire Beatle, and I don't want May to drink it because I'm in love with her at the moment. And Keith, I don't really think you should drink it, because you're famous as well and you obviously need your bodyguard, so Chris, it looks like you're the most expendable!' I said, 'Well, thanks a lot, John,' and I drank a glass as they waited to see if I'd drop dead or not. Then I said, 'I better try some more' (Only because it was absolutely the best wine I'd ever had). It was the most incredible wine! It had to have cost about $1,000. I drank about a third of the bottle before I told them I thought it was okay!"

Tiring of the high-gear lifestyle he was living in Los Angeles, Lennon decided to return permanently to Manhattan in May. In June of 1974, in a move that suggested to Pang at least a hint of commitment, she and John moved to their own $750-per-month apartment at 434 East 52nd Street, known as Sutton Place. The small but cozy one-bedroom penthouse featured a wood-burning fireplace and a patio overlooking the East River. Pang made it inviting by opening up the living room with mirrors and an exquisite white rug shipped over from Tittenhurst. Lennon's famous white piano was likewise sent over from the Dakota. The couple entertained guests like Elton John, Mick and Bianca Jagger, and Paul and Linda McCartney, whose unannounced visits always stirred up John's competitive juices. Yet, what appeared to friends as a cozy domestic scene was, in reality, only May and John playing house.

That June, Lennon booked time at the Record Plant and began work on *Walls and Bridges*, its title implying a life in transition with all its inherent instability. On the positive side, Lennon eschewed the failed experiments of the past three years and returned to his own musical and personal search, exploring the loss of love, youth, and innocence, all keyed by his conflicted attitude toward Yoko.

The LP's blatant distress signals made Pang uneasy. "Bless You," a bleak lethargic track, seemed to be an open letter to Yoko's close friend guitarist David Spinozza that he was only on loan to her because Ono's true love would always be Lennon. As a sidelight, Lennon suggested Mick Jagger took "Bless You" and turned it into the Stones' 1983 hit "Miss You." He harbored no ill feelings, however, admitting he found it a vast improvement over the original tune.

The disturbing and tormented "Scared" was Lennon's ode to aging: "I'm tired of being so alone/No place to call my own/Like a rolling stone" obviously suggested anything but the settled, contented companion Pang had hoped would emerge over the past nine months.

The forgettable "Surprise, Surprise (Sweet Bird of Paradox)" was written for Pang. The words "I was blind/she blew my mind/I love her" were certainly a testament to the couple's intense physical bliss, but suggested nothing deeper. It must have hurt Pang terribly when Lennon later termed it "a piece of garbage."

The album soared on the strength of its two hit singles. The first, the raucous "Whatever Gets You Through the Night," with Elton John guest-spotting on piano, organ, and vocals, was John's least favorite on the album. Although *Rolling Stone* reviewer Ben Gerson observed that saxophonist Bobby Keyes's "off-key blowing" weakened the production, it was precisely that element which gave the tune its raw rock 'n' blues flavor. The second top ten single, "#9 Dream," was a misty, tranquil floater: John's luminescent tribute to his always rich inner nature. *Walls and Bridges* illustrated how Lennon's stubborn naïveté, that Achilles' heel in his personal life, became an element of strength in his work.

Critics, however, hailed the vindictive "Steel and Glass" as the real jewel of the record. With caustic lyrics like "Your mother left you when you were small/But you're gonna wish you weren't born at all," it was widely assumed he was referring to Allen Klein, whose mother died of cancer when Klein was a child. But Lennon hinted it was actually an amalgamation of three or four people, including himself and McCartney, both their mothers having suffered tragically early deaths.

The album also had its share of throwaways: "Old Dirt Road"; the Sinatraesque "Nobody Loves You (When You're Down and Out)"; and "Ya Ya," featuring a young Julian on drums. "Beef Jerky" was remarkable only as one of John's rare instrumentals.

Released on September 26, 1974, *Walls and Bridges* went platinum within a month and returned Lennon to the top of the musical heap. Not surprisingly, John's comments were as contradictory as the material itself. On one hand, he praised its craftsmanship and conceded it was something positive that emerged from a "schizophrenic year." On the other, he claimed, "It gave off an aura of misery because I was miserable. I was trapped and saw no way out." Lennon, like many exceptional artists, produced his finest work from his deepest pain. The album cover, a collage of John's boyhood artwork, proved that his fractured childhood was never really far from his thoughts.

Meanwhile, as autumn approached, what Pang clung to as a new life was actually the beginning of the end. Temporarily distracted by plans for an October engagement at Kenny's Castaways in Greenwich Village, Ono neglected her usual daily checkup on her wayward spouse. May and John mistakenly took her silence as a signal that she was finally letting go. Yoko's talk of a possible divorce enhanced this misperception. Ono stated publicly to Japanese reporter Masako Togawa that her feelings toward her husband had changed significantly and John would have to accept it was "over." Moreover, Lennon related to Pang how his wife was telling him things weren't really working out and that he'd be a free man before long.

Yet even when she sent over a lawyer to discuss separation details, it was difficult to believe Ono was really serious. It wasn't the first time Yoko toyed with the idea of a split. Back in 1970, while going through Primal Therapy, Yoko declared she had no intention of maintaining a relationship with someone who acted like a pal. What she wanted and deserved from a mate was a deep, romantic connection, both physically and emotionally.

The hard evidence, however, indicated she was lulling Pang into a false sense of security before pulling the rug out from under her. After all, Ono had few options. Anything that had been brewing with David Spinozza was now definitely off, and her disastrous stint at Kenny's Castaways killed any hope he could ever go it alone as a solo artist. For Ono John Lennon was the only game in town. By informing John of Pang's past lovers, knowing it would spark his jealousy, Yoko made the first step toward retrieving her marriage.

So as May and John hung suspended in the eye of the hurricane, their fortunes began to turn on the Elton John concert at Madison Square Garden in November. Lennon found himself having to make good on a bet that if their collaboration "Whatever Gets You Through the Night" reached number one, he'd join his friend on stage for the Thanksgiving performance.

Despite the cozy tale of a spontaneous reconciliation later spun by the media, Ono told John in advance that she planned to attend the show. The night before the concert Lennon went on a major champagne-and-cocaine binge while partying in Elton's suite. Afterwards, he collapsed in Pang's arms, repeatedly saying that he didn't want to hurt her, and begging her forgiveness. It was as if Lennon somehow knew his holiday from Ono was about to come to an end.

In his final public appearance, however, John did himself proud. He and Elton were absolutely electric, their voices a perfect blend on "Lucy in the Sky with Diamonds." "I'd like to do a number from an old estranged fiancé of mine called Paul," John announced, and ripped into "I Saw Her Standing There" to a wildly charged audience. He praised the event as "a great high night, a really high night."

As promised, the calculating Yoko was in the audience. From her perspective, John had enjoyed his freedom long enough. The Lost Weekend was over, and with it, John's last pathetic gasp at independence. It was now time to permanently reel him back in.

KALEIDOSCOPE EYES 3
Apple And Isolation
1975

At no time was John's course more crucial than in the pivotal year of 1975, his thirty-fifth. Lennon's life was in a constant state of flux, rumbling with changes that would forever alter his course. One such turn was the official breakup of the Beatles via Apple Corps' extended, highly complex dissolution. While on the surface it appeared to be a cause for celebration after three wrenching years of bitter negotiation, Lennon charged that instead of freeing the band it created just the opposite effect, binding the group even more tightly.

"Everybody has said now that the Beatles have signed this paper, they're no longer tied in any way," Lennon told the press. "That's bullshit! We still own this thing called Apple, which you can explain as a bank; all the money goes into it. But there's also still an entity known as the Beatles. The product, the name, the likeness, *the Apple thing,* still exists and we have to communicate, make decisions, decide who's to run Apple and who's to do what. It's not at all as cut-and-dried as the papers have said."

One prominent factor in Lennon's resistance was the fact he owed Uncle Sam an immediate cool million in back taxes. While all the Beatles' assets were frozen due to the Apple litigation, John avoided the tax man. Lennon conveniently forgot he had borrowed heavily from Apple to finance various money-losing film and art projects, many of them Yoko's. This debt included a massive $400,000 renovation of Tittenhurst Park, a property he would never again set foot in. Another factor was a clause that tied up John's access to his foreign money, which represented a significant portion of his income. Lennon surmised that Paul McCartney's father-in-law and attorney, Lee Eastman, propelled by his own personal agenda, had a prominent hand in the proceedings. In fact, Eastman did have much to gain. As Paul's attorney he indirectly controlled the rights to much of the group's work. Also, none of the band seemed to realize that, with the breakup of the Beatles, they were perhaps forfeiting millions of dollars in future related merchandise, shows, and events.

Beyond that, the mere notion that Paul so badly wanted out was enough to stimulate John's rather spiteful sense of competition: if McCartney wanted it, it couldn't possibly be good. But according to May, Lennon's funk over the breakup ran far deeper. When it came down to it, he really didn't want the group, his group, to disband. Pang indicated that all the heated speculation over the years was true: it *had* been Yoko's idea for John to say good-bye to the Beatles.

All this time the other three Beatles pressured Lennon to sign the papers. Aside from the obvious financial considerations, they were all being courted by various record companies. McCartney, Harrison, and Starr wanted to be free of Apple to pursue other offers; George, in particular, needed to attend to his own floundering Dark Horse label.

John, however, desperately needed money. For months he'd been forced to survive on borrowed funds, living far below his usual grand standard. With legal fees skyrocketing, and still deeply embroiled in a critical immigration battle, Lennon simply couldn't afford to hold out any longer.

The 202-page document that Lennon once referred to as "The Famous Beatles Agreement" caused even more fallout, specifically between John and George. At the last minute John even reneged on his commitment to play Harrison's Madison Square Garden concert on December 19th. "George and I are still very good pals," Lennon said later, "and always will be, but I was supposed to sign this thing the day of his concert. He was pretty weird because he was in the middle of that tour and we hadn't communicated for a while, as he doesn't live here. I've seen Paul because he comes to New York, and I'm always seeing Ringo in Los Angeles. Anyway, I was a bit nervous about going on stage, but I agreed because it would have been mean not to go on with George after I'd gone on with Elton. I didn't sign the document that day because my astrologer told me it wasn't the right time, tee hee! In the end I signed it at Disney World in Florida with my son Julian. I thought it suited the occasion.

"George was furious because I hadn't signed when I was 'supposed to' and somehow or other I was informed I needn't bother to attend his show. I was actually quite relieved because there wasn't any time for rehearsal and I didn't want it to be a case of the great John Lennon jumping up and just banging out a few chords."

According to Pang, Harrison had every right to be angry with John's seemingly cavalier attitude about such an important matter. The pressures swirling around the dissolution of Apple had taken an enormous toll on the quiet Beatle. There were the endless protracted and unproductive meetings—Lee Eastman doing his best to drive a wedge between the parties, chiding Lennon, "George doesn't even like you anymore; George is never going to forgive you for this." John reacted by threatening not to ever sign the pact. Exhausted, in ragged voice and mired in a critically disastrous tour, who could blame Harrison for throwing up his hands and erupting, "Tell John I'm gonna go on alone and that's it!"

Yet it was all just agitation in the heat of the moment. Pang knew there was an extraordinary bond between the two old friends. "I finally saw how much George really looked up to John. I saw the love. . . . That's what I was trying to explain to people. There was so much love amongst the four guys, they had a love you couldn't believe." Finally, with young Julian acting as intercessor, Lennon made peace with his old guitarist mate following the concert, and after an exchange of hugs all was forgiven. Said Pang, "All four guys really do care about one another whether or not you read in print how much they hate. . . . It was only business, it was not a personal vendetta, ever. Paul was always at our house. The fans out there thought that John and Paul didn't talk for years, but he was always over."

Also symptomatic of Lennon's turbulent new year was his shaky relationship with his eleven-year-old son Julian. As with his own long-lost father Fred, the sins of the father were visited upon the son. That Lennon had any contact at all with the boy was really only through May Pang and Cynthia Lennon's determined efforts. From the beginning of their relationship, May drew everyone together, and even helped bring Julian over from England after a three-year absence. John and May threw two Christmases for the insecure preteen, the first at music publisher Morris Levy's Palm Beach condominium. It was an experience John deplored, a holiday even more hellish than his darkest days in Los Angeles. As they moved on to Disney World, Lennon spent most of the holiday penned up in his suite staring at television, stewing over the Beatles' dissolution, complaining of jet lag and constipation. Tellingly, it was around this time that Lennon started referring to himself as Greta Hughes (a reference to celebrity recluses Greta Garbo and Howard Hughes).

Back in his New York comfort zone, the Dakota, Lennon recovered, watching old Beatles films with his son, but he was unable to grasp the notion that it had actually been an entire decade since *A Hard Day's Night*. John found himself wondering what the next ten years would bring, not realizing he would live to see only five more.

Having already drummed on "Ya Ya," from John's *Walls and Bridges* album, Julian now showed evidence of genuine musical talent. As father and son shared a jam with Julian picking electric guitar, Lennon proudly viewed his offspring as a quick study whose skills were rapidly improving. John also fretted over the photospreads of his son in recent magazines, because he feared too much exposure for the shy boy.

Although Lennon felt Julian adjusted admirably on his visit, even making friends with a neighbor child, he found his presence exhausting. This was, frankly, a product of his anemic parenting skills, exacerbated by John's childish impatience and painfully short attention span. Not surprisingly, May oversaw the eleven-year-old and kept him entertained. She taught Julian backgammon, cooked him big English breakfasts, and acted as a discreet buffer between father and son.

On one occasion John and May were making love when Julian accidentally barged in on them, but they were able to continue their romantic interlude an hour or so later.

When, following the three-week visit, Julian returned to England, John admitted ambivalent feelings, relief tinged with deep regret. It certainly didn't help that he'd pulled several muscles lifting the boy's Christmas gifts.

Professionally Lennon was enjoying a very productive stretch, and was setting his sights on producing a new album. He ushered in the new year by completing the witty, infectious, and still-unreleased

"Popcorn," and his melancholy homage to playwright Tennessee Williams, titled simply "Tennessee."

Lennon also worked on a number with the strange name of "Big Hurt Answer," with Lori Burton (wife of recording engineer and friend Roy Cicala) supplying vocals. Lennon got a real kick out of the project, layering the backing track with a dreamy montage of violins. John worked quickly, only to learn that the obviously perfectionist engineer wanted a remix. When the tape was finally delivered, Cicala pronounced it worthless. John's further attempts fared no better. The discerning Cicala openly criticized John's efforts. Lennon replied that he couldn't care less, joking that his engagement with the perfectionist young producer was off.

That month also saw the pairing of Lennon with David Bowie when the latter asked him to sit in on a session at Electric Lady Studios. One of the earliest examples of techno funk, their collaboration, the now classic "Fame," became Bowie's first number one record. Lennon called it "an incredible bluff that worked. I'm really knocked out that people actually dance to my records, because let's be honest, my rhythm and blues are thoroughly plastic!"

Bowie also asked his idol to perform on his cover of John's wistful Beatle-era ballad, "Across the Universe." "David told me he was going to do 'Across the Universe,' which I thought was great because I'd never done a good version of the song myself. It's one of my favorite songs, but I didn't particularly like my version of it. So I went down and played rhythm on the track." Lennon also lent his talents to the Ben E. King standard "Stand By Me," along with "Catch Me Slipping." John was thrilled with the final product, calling it electrifying.

In the midst of all this activity, Lennon was dutifully going off to the Record Plant to mix the perpetually troubled *Rock 'n' Roll,* due out in March. Early word from Apple's public relations man in Los Angeles, Tony King, predicted the record was a potential gold mine. Industry insiders were so excited that there was already talk of a second volume. As always, the media were eager to court Lennon: *Newsweek* and the *Washington Star* wanted interviews, as did WNEW, Radio Luxembourg, and Alan Froeman of the BBC. Lennon also obliged respected rock journalists Lisa Robinson and Pete Hamill with exclusive chats.

Almost prophetic was John's breezy banter on the album's final track: "I'm just going to have to let you go. . . . Saying good night from the Record Plant East, New York. We hope you had a swell time. Everybody here says hi. Good-bye."

Lennon admitted later he couldn't quite shake the feeling that he was saying good-bye to the recording industry altogether. The album, though hardly a sizzler, did manage to peak briefly at number six on the American charts and sold a slim 340,000 copies. Lennon complained that May and Harold Seider seemed too concerned about the sales figures, which John himself believed to be quite respectable. Nonetheless, Lennon admitted he found their doubts troubling.

It was ironic that royalties from John's cover of the Buddy Holly classic "Peggy Sue" would contribute to Paul McCartney's already bursting coffers. Businessman McCartney had shrewdly acquired the publishing rights to the entire Holly catalog. "What a move that was," John diplomatically told the press. "I hope he gives me a good deal! With Paul it's cool 'cause we're pals. I'm not really gonna make much money from this album anyway." As if that weren't enough, royalties from Sam Cooke's "Bring It on Home" would go to Allen Klein, who owned the Cooke catalog. Lennon was still too deeply immersed in the ongoing lawsuit to rid himself of the notorious manager.

Fresh from the Apple settlement, John cautiously renewed contact with his cohorts, phoning Starr and McCartney and corresponding with Harrison, while preparing one of his famous handmade collages for George's coming birthday. All told, Lennon created some thirty of these unique gifts—each a meticulous, stylish combination of news and magazine clippings and photos tailored to the recipient. Sometimes he also created audio collages, weaving together snippets of songs, TV commercials, and his own witty Peter Sellers–type characters. Some of these imaginative works ran a full sixty minutes. These John reserved for his closest friends, such as Elton John. Although it seems out of character for the caustic Beatle, Lennon kept precise track of birthdays, not just family and close friends but also business associates and many neighbors at the Dakota. Sometimes he even made birthday cards for special friends. Tellingly, the one birthday he chronically forgot was that of his poor Aunt Mimi.

Now that the outstanding Apple issues had been resolved, the inevitable rumors of a reunion cropped up. When asked the tired question about the "future" of the long-dead Beatles, Lennon told *Melody Maker*, "Let's just say we're good friends. At least we're all happy with each other. If we got back together, it wouldn't be for one last show, right? If we ever do, my instincts tell me it would be more sensible to sit in a studio, get relaxed, and make some music before stomping out on dates. I'm not saying that's in the offing, though."

In many ways Lennon's high spirits could be directly linked to his always active sex life. As recorded in his diaries, he and his partner often made love several times a day, with Lennon taking special delight in having oral sex performed on him. At one point, his athletic antics caused him to wrench his back, spawning several new creative maneuvers. Almost anything aroused Lennon, from pornographic magazines to the adolescent fantasies that played endlessly in his head. In one favorite he was in a crowd and inserted his penis into a woman's behind simply to watch her startled reaction. One evening John and May were dining at a Mexican restaurant. John experienced a spontaneous erection, which he satisfied later that night. So important were these pleasurable episodes to the former Beatle that he kept a daily record of them all—in handwritten and taped diaries that he assiduously maintained to the end of his life.

Rather untypically, Lennon also enjoyed an active social life. He loved exploring the Village, stopping at favorite record shops, visiting Chinatown, and lunching at Ruskeys or some other familiar restaurant. John often purchased vintage clothing at a trendy boutique called Jezebel. Other favorite pastimes included strolling around the city and dining out at landmark restaurants like La Crepe, Emanuel, the Plaza, or Riverside. He enjoyed buying presents for friends, although he wasn't above recycling a gift now and then: once he pawned off a book, which his friend Richard Ross had given him, on an unsuspecting cohort. At one point John bought a bicycle for his wife, though it's difficult to imagine the dour Yoko pedaling around town.

Lennon's wide circle of friends included lawyer Michael Graham and Bob Mercer, an A&R man at EMI. Mercer and Lennon sometimes lunched together at Dew, where the former kept the latter laughing the entire time. John often dropped in on a couple who lived in the West Village, his old hunting grounds. After the expensive Dakota, Lennon appreciated the low cost of living but admitted he wouldn't care to reside in that neighborhood again. John also socialized with Warner and Kaye Leroy, owners of Manhattan's world-famous Tavern on the Green. While they possessed an impressive and expensive art collection, Lennon secretly questioned their often tacky taste.

During this time John spent a great deal of time with Mick Jagger and David Bowie, who had long harbored a serious case of hero worship for the former Beatle. The pair showed up at Led Zepplin's Madison Square Garden show, which featured Rod Stewart and the Faces as the opening act. Rather than going to enjoy the music, David made it clear to John that what he really wanted was simply a bit of cheap publicity. Bowie later called Lennon to report that he and Jagger had caroused around Harlem until the early morning.

Mick Jagger visited Lennon one day accompanied by Todd Rundgren's wife. John had feuded recently with Rundgren in the press. He noted in his diary that Jagger wanted to be more than just friends with Mrs. Rundgren, but, much to Jagger's disappointment, she considered the friendship strictly platonic. On another occasion, he and John did some serious partying that left the latter so ill he passed out soon after Jagger departed.

In early January 1975, Paul and Linda McCartney stopped by while en route to New Orleans, where they would record Wings' powderpuff *Venus and Mars*. (Lennon later panned the work, intimating McCartney got away with murder in producing such a pathetically thin effort.) Sharing an intimate dinner at Nartells, Lennon grew impatient with the McCartneys' relentless business patter. But John's ears pricked up with talk of their new album, and he seriously considered going south to watch Paul record. Afterwards, Lennon took them around to see Bowie, who phoned later and asked to stop by Lennon's Sutton Place apartment. John joked that Bowie obviously didn't want to miss anything.

Always a committed film buff, Lennon and Pang took in Mel Brooks's *Young Frankenstein*. John, a well-known skinflint, was intensely proud of Pang for retrieving their money when the projector broke. On another evening he and May caught a movie with actor Peter Boyle and his live-in love, Lorraine Alterman. Afterwards, they had dinner at the Cuban eatery, Victor's Cafe, followed by an uptown soiree that included guests like Mike Nichols, Jules Feiffer, Richard Avedon, and Jacqueline Onassis.

Incredibly, the chronically shy Lennon even attended a youth question-and-answer encounter session called the Friend's Seminar. Amazingly, he also appeared at a local school and spoke with students whose ages ranged from four to seventeen. He was pleasantly surprised at the warm reception and how genuinely in tune the students were with his music.

Around this time Apple executive Neil Aspinall phoned to arrange an emergency meeting at the Beatles' London office. John, protesting that he was unable to leave America, requested that Aspinall wire him the results. Like all business matters that intimidated him, John simply wanted to blow it off as painlessly as possible.

Due to the recent collapse of the Nixon administration, Lennon was at last making inroads with his protracted immigration battle. He was so confident that he began speaking out boldly. He described his entanglement, "a teeny Watergate." "I think things are looking up," he said, "because the old guard have left and there's been a change in politics. But it's still down to a political decision from the White House to let me off the hook.

"There's a lot people who've gotten into this country because there's a special bill put through for them, and there's a chance it may happen with me. They do it for Pakistani maids, and for that matter, there are known Nazis living here who're not being harassed. There are also many drug dealers here. My lawyer has a list of people who've committed rape, murder, and drug dealing—and they're hassling *me*!"

Troubling news came that winter: John's long-standing wiretap case against the government was now pretty much a lost cause. A September 18, 1973 FBI memo stated: "Such a review failed to indicate that Lennon, or any premises in which he had a proprietary interest, have been subjected to any unlawful electronic surveillance."

On the positive side, John's attorney Leon Wildes won the right to investigate crucial, previously barred government files on the case. Lennon sarcastically explained that it was all to be done under wraps because Uncle Sam mustn't be made to look bad. Although John was at last able to confront New York immigration director Sol Marks and government lawyer Vincent Schiano, he was really after Attorney General John Mitchell.

Still, the door was slowly beginning to open. Regarding a key element of the complaint, Lennon's alleged intention to disrupt the 1972 Republican National Convention, an FBI memo stated: "The subject did not travel to Miami for the RNC as he had previously planned." It went on to affirm that "there has been *no* information received to indicate the subject is active in the New Left." As for his being a bona fide anarchist, the FBI apparently had a curious set of criteria: one could apparently *not* be a junkie. "Lennon appears to be radically oriented," quoted a memorandum. "However, he does not give the impression he is a true revolutionist since he is constantly under the influence of narcotics." The government's prudishness reached the absurd with an opinion expressed about the cover of the nude 1968 *Two Virgins* album, which authorities called "a most discolored and vulgar display of garbage."

As Lennon suspected, the conspiracy against him reached the highest levels of the administration. Sol Marks conceded that he had "received orders from Washington not to ever give this man a break." As January wound down, there was no hint that either Lennon's lifestyle or his plans for the immediate future were about to change. He had been planning a ten-day trip to New England, hoping to stay at a Vermont cabin loaned to him by a friend of attorney Harold Seider. John was also quietly planning to purchase a stone house on the tip of Long Island. Although the Montauk property was in a state of marked disrepair, John had his heart set on it. He had fallen in love with the place when he first spotted it during the previous summer's trip to Montauk with the Jaggers. John had taken Julian and Harold Seider to see the house over Christmas. The place was tiny, with two small bedrooms and a kitchen, all in very poor condition. Moreover, the owner was asking an absurd $250,000. Conceding that it was shamelessly overpriced, Lennon was nonetheless prepared to meet the offer.

Lurking behind John's best-laid plans, however, was Yoko, the skilled puppet master who was about to orchestrate an abrupt, confounding turnabout in his life. Much had been made of their so-called reunion at Elton John's Thanksgiving Day concert at Madison Square Garden. Yoko, for her part, played up her appearance as spontaneous. In truth, her presence had been planned long in advance. Little by little she was weaving her master plan to win Lennon back. It had actually begun the previous September, when Ono returned from a disastrous tour of Japan. In contrast to her own career, John's was highly successful. "Whatever Gets You Through the Night," driven by Elton John's searing piano, shot quickly to number one. On the home front John and May were apparently getting a little too cozy for Ono's comfort. For the first time Lennon was refusing to take Yoko's numerous phone calls. John and May's extensive house hunting finally brought it home to Mrs. Lennon that things were getting seriously out of hand.

That's when Ono began to really take charge. Once, when Julian was in town, she barged into John and May's flat to fawn over the lonely boy whom she had always assiduously ignored. Then she made certain that John just happened to run into her at Lincoln Center for a Carmen Moore exhibition. Ono maneuvered her way into joining John, along with Lorraine Alterman and the Lennons' assistant Jon Hendricks, for dinner at the Red Baron. Ironically, John awoke in the night deathly ill from the meal.

Ono's scheme swirled around the mysterious final Friday in January. May seemed to realize that deep trouble was brewing. She felt that if she could get John to Louisiana, he and Paul might actually record together. But Lennon wasn't going to New Orleans or anywhere else. Ono allegedly lured her estranged spouse to the Dakota with a secret treatment to stop smoking, but kept insisting the planets weren't yet in proper alignment. Slowly, skillfully, Yoko began to reel John in with the lure that an amazing cure had allowed her to quit smoking cold turkey, playing on his childlike curiosity. She also engineered a high-stakes cat-and-mouse game with the inexperienced Pang, causing deep friction between May and John.

When he arrived at the Dakota that weekend, thinking he'd be miraculously cured of his nearly lifelong nicotine addiction and then would return to Pang, his days of freedom were over. Yoko refused to let May contact him. It wasn't until the following Monday that a distraught Pang finally caught up with him at the dentist's office. What she saw was Lennon groggy to the point of stupor, certainly not the aftereffects of any hypnotic she was familiar with. John's zombie-like demeanor was later confirmed by journalist Pete Hamill, who had scheduled a chat with the musician. The New York journalist found him so disoriented he wasn't even sure what year it was, and the interview had to be rescheduled. As Hamill put it, John resembled "a man recovering from a *very* serious illness."

Even more perplexing, Yoko insisted to her tarot guru and new confidant John Green that her husband had been poisoned. This statement suggests that the alleged cure was furnished by a Manhattan hypnotist well known for his potent black magic concoctions. Had the treatment been one of his Dominican-rooted cock-tails gone terribly awry? John confessed he had been alternately vomiting and passing out throughout the roller-coaster weekend. Lennon repeatedly lost consciousness, and when he came to, he'd be given another dose of the powerful brew. One clue could per-haps be found in the farewell gift Yoko had John pass along to May, a repulsive potion consisting of sulfur, arrowroot, and chili powder concocted to be given to one's enemy. Another clue had John com-paring the treatment to Primal Therapy, suggesting that Yoko used the ultimate weakness, his ever-present childhood trauma, to fi-nally rope him back. Whatever the cause, photographer David Nutter certainly thought it an unfortunate turn of events. He be-lieved John's partnership with May both liberated and greatly re-laxed the musician. Nutter was often a guest at the couple's East Side flat where a spirited Lennon had them roaring all evening with his hysterical takes on British culture. Then almost overnight he was back with Yoko. The photographer described Ono's influ-ence as almost hypnotic. When John reunited with his wife, Nutter noted that his friend just dropped out of their lives for a long time afterwards.

The unsuspecting Lennon was initially very excited about his re-turn home, hoping that he and Yoko were taking up where they had left off. But the reunion was carefully orchestrated. John was not yet permitted to move into their bedroom and had to be content with a courtship of sorts. Sexually, their initial attempts at reconciliation were on Ono's exacting terms. Getting reacquainted, the couple sailed down the Hudson River, got his-and-her haircuts and cleansing facials, and then went on a gourmet shopping spree that topped $600. Afterwards, they celebrated with the Boyles and the late Howard Cosell. Cosell eventually signed Lennon for his current ABC talk show, and the former Beatle appeared, noting that television was the power media of the future.*

For all its problems, John and Yoko's relationship still worked on many levels. Yoko was, quite simply, John's replacement for his

*In fact, John also appeared on ABC's *Monday Night Football,* which Cosell hosted. During the lively three-minute interview the crusty Cosell chided Lennon about his lack of knowledge concerning American football and, of course, getting the Beatles back together. Throughout it all, John remained remarkably good-humored.

beloved Julia, with whom no other woman could ever compete. "Yoko is mother, lover, daughter, and everything to me," he affirmed. "I can lean on her like I would on a mother when I'm in that kind of situation, and I can appreciate her. She is all women to me."

Elliot Mintz saw the reunion in more practical terms, calling it John's "sigh of relief. It was a reinstatement of his own manhood—that he was worthy of her. Because if John wasn't worthy of Yoko, he was only going to be worthy of having fleeting, meaningless relationships with women who said the right things to guys who used to be the Beatles. And that terrified him."

Overcome with childlike enthusiasm, John planned an elaborate celebration in honor of Yoko's forty-second birthday on February 18th. The night before, they attended a bash thrown by Ono's old friend, heiress, and avid art enthusiast Peggy Guggenheim. The couple apparently got a bit inebriated before officially marking the occasion with Yoko's thank-you blowjob, which, John happily noted in his diary, was his first from her that year. After snorting a few lines of heroin to get back to sleep, John awoke to a breakfast of psychedelic mushrooms. Lennon, apparently, had not yet chosen to give up the high life.

Meanwhile, the Lennons' reunion was hot copy and they were granting interviews to magazines like *Newsweek* and *Time*, which quoted them as saying "the separation didn't quite work out." But as the John-and-Yoko love myth rose from the ashes, Lennon continued to enjoy regular trysts with May. Over the next two months, the couple would meet twice a week, either at Richard Ross's place on 91st Street or sometimes at his apartment over the bar he owned, Home. While Pang had conflicting emotions regarding the romance, Lennon was quite content with the arrangement—an ideal situation with the matronly wife at home and the lovely, young mistress on the side. "Yoko gave me *permission*," he said, like an obedient schoolboy, a puzzling quality that made up such a large part of his adult character. As for Ono, it eased the nearly constant sexual pressure of living with John's libido, while giving her the peace of mind in knowing exactly whom he was with.

As the year headed into March, however, Yoko began slowly putting on the clamps. She was already taking control, dyeing John's hair red and overseeing a strenuous morning yoga routine, along with

supervising a strict diet consisting of brown rice and unseasoned vegetables. Yoko was certainly genuinely concerned for her husband's
health, but she also allowed him to indulge his taste for chocolates
and tobacco. As Lennon's nicotine habit swelled to twenty Gauloises
daily, Yoko informed him that he was entering the second stage. He
was now permitted to smoke only ten cigarettes a day, and had to
drink a glass of water before lighting up. During this period he attended a party at Rick Skylar's where he prided himself on having
only "one fag and zero booze."

"Yoko was a woman consistently interested in control," said Charlie Swan (the Lennons' nickname for John Green). "So this was very
comfortable because John didn't want to do it himself. Lennon was
always very afraid of rejection, so he accepted the idea that someone
else should set things up for him. Yoko assumed that role, I think, because she wanted control and also because from the Japanese tradition that was not as unusual as in our culture. Remember, too, having
this kind of liaison was advantageous over something that might develop emotionally."

‣One evening Lennon had dinner at a place called Gallager's with
plans to see a movie afterwards. Although he enjoyed the meal, the establishment's rather suspect clientele, which included an unruly group
of Canadians, quite upset him. The incident had such an adverse effect on him that, while stopping to browse in a bookstore, he was overcome by a sudden wave of diarrhea and forced to rush home. John was
so upset over the incident that he didn't fall asleep until dawn.

This was the start of the old Lennon paranoia reappearing. On
March 1st he was scheduled to present at the Grammy Awards with
Paul Simon. John was so anxious about the prospect of encounter-
ing May that he sternly warned her not to come. Despite his anxiety he decked himself out in a rumpled, ill-fitting tux topped with
a beret and white scarf, and he actually enjoyed the evening. Afterwards, John and Yoko went to a Motown party at the Jardin,
where he hung out with Stevie Wonder and the Temptations'
Eddie Kendricks. Back in Los Angeles, he soon reverted to his old
habits, chugging wine and smoking heavily. Interestingly, during
this period Yoko didn't touch a thing.

Returning to New York, Lennon began a questionable series of
medical appointments with a slew of doctors. The overhaul ran from

eye checkups to a rectal exam, prompting Lennon to joke that he had finally lost his innocence. An arduous series of dental work followed, as toothaches were constantly interfering with his sleep. Over the ensuing year he made several appointments for extensive root canal work, often three teeth at a time, as well as endless bridgework. Lennon complained that the dentist struck nerves that should have been numb from the novocaine. John's dental troubles were possibly the result of his prolonged heroin use, a narcotic notorious for the damage it does to one's teeth.

That spring the Lennons officially sealed their reunion by renewing their wedding vows on the couple's March 20th anniversary. Lennon devised a decidedly offbeat Druid motif for the ceremony. With the help of John Green, who performed the rite, John built an altar which held a silver chalice, sea salt, lamp oil, plus silver candles and a statue of St. Margaret. The Lennons' all-white wedding took place in the Dakota White Room. The couple solemnly promised to consecrate their vows by dunking their jade rings into the ocean. It was perhaps telling that Lennon later complained his ring was too tight!

With Charlie Swan now living at the Dakota, Lennon dove headlong into the wacky world of the occult. One of his favorite paperbacks addressed the Lost Spear of Destiny, the lance allegedly used to pierce the side of Christ at his crucifixion. Always fascinated by religious relics, John called on Green to try to divine the location of this coveted article. Lennon had visions of playing the adventurer and taking a bus tour of southeastern Europe (thought to be the site of the relic) to search for it. When Green asked what he would do with the spear, John responded that he could do anything in the universe. He'd always had brilliant ideas for action, he said, but only lacked the mystical force necessary to put them into action.

John was also fascinated by a couple he and Green dubbed "the Rabbits." As part of their new life, Ono arranged for Lennon to participate in a séance. She brought an elderly pair to the Dakota, "Peter and Bunny," who claimed to be mediums. The couple staged a rather silly show, making references to various friends and acquaintances, vague enough to apply to anyone and designed to keep John just slightly off guard. He was so amused by the pair that he wrote a witty story about them in *Skywriting by Word of Mouth* called "The Incredible Mediocre Rabbits."

Before long, John was not only listening to Green's readings, he was requesting them. The charming soothsayer counseled him on everything, from record and book contracts to his many legal battles, advising him, for instance, to carefully examine his record company's finances.

Lennon's real troubles began with Morris Levy, music publisher and Roulette Records executive, to whom John had given a rough demo of his *Rock 'n' Roll* album. It all went back to 1968 and the song "Come Together" from the *Abbey Road* album, where Lennon "borrowed" a couple of lines from Chuck Berry's "You Can't Catch Me." Levy, who at that time controlled the copyright through his Big Seven Publishing Company, slapped John with a plagiarism suit. Disaster ensued when Lennon agreed, as part of the settlement, to put three Big Seven "oldies" tunes on his next album. He should have sensed trouble when the next album was *not* the promised oldies collection, but rather *Walls and Bridges*. But Levy was his friend, after all, and to Lennon's naive way of thinking he'd certainly overlook a small discrepancy like that. Once again John demonstrated his abysmal business acumen when he handed over the demo and Levy promptly released the inferior version, naming it *Roots*, under his Adam VIII label.* Lennon claimed he was outraged at the maneuver, but the evidence strongly suggests otherwise. To hasten the album's progress, Levy arranged for Lennon to rehearse the numbers on his farm in upstate New York. John wasn't particularly surprised when he saw the television ad appear, pronouncing it not half bad and wondering what the package sounded like. Lennon nearly admitted that he and Morris had discussed the prospect of selling the LP via TV. He even hoped it might rake in a possible $25 million, but later formally denied any knowledge of Levy's intentions.

Meanwhile, Capitol was incensed over this brash invasion of its copyright. John decided to tell the company only at the last minute, sparking a vocal tirade by promotion head Al Cory. Capitol managed some quick damage control by rushing the polished version into mass release and placing an injunction against the bootleg product. Levy

---

*Levy's original version of Lennon's *Rock 'n' Roll* album is a prized collectors item these days, fetching upwards of $250. Not surprisingly, there are still literally thousands of near-perfect counterfeits flooding the market at about $75.

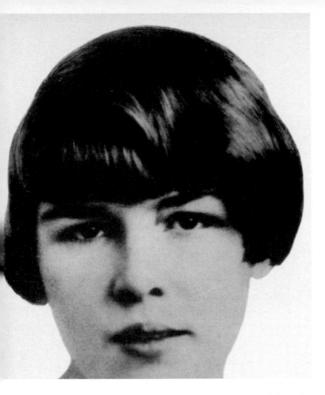

▲ John's beloved Mummy as a young girl. Her reckless life and tragic death shaped his life more than anything else. (1)

► The late Mary Smith, better known as Auntie Mimi. John's relationship with his often headstrong caregiver was turbulent to the very end. (2)

▼ A Stanley family gathering in the early sixties with John's aunts, Mimi, and Cynthia Lennon (*far right*) in Liverpool. (3)

▼ Alfred Lennon, John's wayward dad, relaxes in surburban London, January 1966. From this point on, John supported his father on and off until his death from cancer in 1976. (4)

▲ The senior Lennon promotes his one and only single on the Piccadilly label, "That's My Life," backed by "The Next Time You Feel Important." 1966. (5)

◄ Charlie Lennon, John's kindhearted uncle. Liverpool, 1990. Of all John's family, Charlie is the most honest and open with the fans. For the past several years he has lived in almost total poverty. (6)

◀ Beatle John, vaguely apprehensive prior to yet another raucous appearance by the Fab Four. London, 1964. (7)

▼ A picture important not for the three laid-back Beatles up front circa 1965, but rather for the absolute power behind the Fab's throne lined up in back. *Left to right*: manager Brian Epstein, publicist Derek Taylor, road manager Neil Aspinalli, and group gofer Mal Evans. (8)

▲ John and Cynthia on holiday in the islands, 1965. Despite the spin of recent years, they actually shared several happy years together. (9)

▲ Beatle John outside Abbey Road Studios, St. John's Wood, London, early 1968. (11)

▲ Hanging out at Brian Epstein's posh Belgravia townhouse, summer 1967. (10)

▲ "I don't love the Queen as much as I love Yoko." Lennon on Ono, London, January 7, 1968. (12)

▼ John and Yoko leaving court following their infamous pot bust in London, 1968. (13)

▲ With the charismatic and elusive Kyoko. London, 1969. (14)

◀ The Lennons accompany Kyoko Cox on a trip to Canada, 1969. John's love of the little girl was evident by the special attention he perpetually paid the troubled child. (15)

◀ A haunted-looking Lennon in 1970 while visiting the Jutland region of Denmark. (16)

◀ Just before leaving London forever, John appeared at a book signing to promote the paperback edition of Yoko's poetic book of Zen-inspired koans, *Grapefruit*. Try as he might, John was never really able to get his wife's sputtering career on track, a sad fact she never let him forget. (17)

▲ Arriving at London's Heathrow Airport during the couple's round-the-world search for Kyoko Cox, July 7, 1971. (18)

immediately cried foul, and after several failed attempts to serve the musician papers, Lennon found himself on the receiving end of yet another ugly lawsuit, this one a whopping $42 million action for breach of oral contract, antitrust violations, and fraud. John later summed up his reaction to the impending ordeal: "There's a jinx on that fucking album!"

From this point on, the pressures intensified. John was not sleeping well, sometimes unable to doze off until dawn. He was also experiencing disturbing nightmares from which he awoke in terror. One nightmare had him trapped in a maze full of giant spiders. In another he was about to dine on a lobster when it suddenly shrieked. In one particularly frightening dream John was encircled by several headless figures as he faced the gruesome task of slashing their heads in a garden where no one could find them. One reason for Lennon's increased dream state might be found in his intermittent indulgence in psychedelic mushrooms. The organic hallucinogens—similar to, but less potent than LSD—not only increase the essential REM period but tend to make dreams much more graphic.

John encountered further problems trying to get into the musician's union, which at first simply refused his request. Even here, politics loomed. Lennon noted that one of the questions on the membership application asked if he'd ever belonged to the Communist Party. The union was jumpy over his ongoing struggle with the INS, but Lennon demonstrated a persistence that finally paid off. Once he did get in, his stature greatly helped the union, allowing it to demand larger recording advances for its artists.

As the year progressed, John once again began isolating himself. Scheduled to fly to Los Angeles to film a spot for the *Rock 'n' Roll* album, he instead begged off. He even tried to cancel his appearance on Tom Snyder's *Tomorrow* show, but ultimately had to attend. The interview, which would be Lennon's last, aired on April 28, 1975. He felt the segment went well enough, but charged that it had no real teeth. Yet, when he saw the tightly edited interview, he changed his mind and felt he came over rather well. The main focus of the program was Lennon's ongoing immigration battle. He told the audience: "If it was up to Joe Doe on the street, he either doesn't care or would be happy to have an old Beatle living here." Snyder remarked he'd been prepared for the reputedly "difficult" Lennon, but found him accommodating and mild mannered. John responded, "If being an egomaniac means I believe in my art and music, then you can call me that. Otherwise, this is pretty much me."

More and more, the increasingly reclusive Lennon began to shun his friends. When chums like Bowie would telephone, John would hang up on them. Another time, when Bowie and Lennon often made plans to see Ken Russell's overblown adaptation of the Who's *Tommy*, Lennon canceled at the last minute. He also bowed out on playing on "Listen" and "Man in the Moon," feigning fatigue.

Other situations weren't quite so easy. Rod Stewart and a gang of his friends once tried to crash John's flat, and Lennon's assistant Jon Hendricks had a difficult time getting rid of them. There were also early morning tussles with pesky fans who somehow evaded the doorman. Another superstar nuisance was Neil Sedaka, who honored Lennon by naming his latest single "Immigrant," then begged him to appear at his upcoming New York show. Elton John received a similar request from Sedaka and also declined. John admitted he felt badly about turning Sedaka down, but he longed to get out of the city. Even his appearance at the annual Dakota party seemed forced. Next-door neighbor and film critic Rex Reed called his attitude "shlumpy" and observed that John always kept a low profile, not wanting to draw attention to himself.

Lennon was also estranged from Mick Jagger, who attempted to move into the Dakota, allegedly to pursue Yoko. According to her version, she went to the board of directors and persuaded them to reject Jagger on the basis of his wild lifestyle and reputation. Confiding in John Green, an overly dramatic Yoko claimed she feared that if she and Mick were neighbors, they might become more than just friends and thereby threaten her relationship with John.

Lennon apparently got wind of the situation. In the middle of an innocent conversation one night in the limousine with Jagger, John erupted, "That's a lot of middle-class bullshit!" and ordered Mick out of the car. The bad blood escalated in later years when Jagger told the British press how he felt that John was obsessing over Sean and locking himself away when he should have been making music. Perhaps Mick was right.

Lennon tried to rationalize his aloof behavior as fear of being once again lured into the nightlife that had gotten him in so much trouble in the past. He explained that he regularly blew off Jagger, Bowie, and even Elton John whenever they were in New York because he knew they would try and drag him to clubs and discos. Lennon knew he would probably succumb to temptation and didn't feel strong enough to say no to his buddies. Besides, he didn't want that kind of hassle in his life anymore. While there may have been some truth in that reasoning, the reality was that Lennon, back in Yoko's steely grip, was slowly losing his creative and social edge. It was therefore simply easier to hole up in his safe, homogenized cocoon.

When Lennon did socialize, it was usually with the predictable Boyles, dining out with the couple and enjoying their brand of offbeat conversation (and the pleasant buzz from a few glasses of wine). One night Lorraine discussed her personal experiences with ESP, which surprised John since he initially viewed her as a skeptic. Another time he and Peter attended a play by Richard Foreman. John also spent time at their place, where people like Albert Brooks would drop by. On one occasion the Boyles invited him to dinner along with Paul Simon. When Simon didn't show, Lennon was immensely relieved he wouldn't have to make small talk all night with the diminutive singer.

John seemed to prefer spending his time with the vintage jukebox, decorated with pulsing lips, that Capitol Records had sent over. Lennon installed it in the Black Room, loading it with fifties classics, only to discover it needed a costly repair. Elton John later bought the same jukebox, and Richard Ross also began to shop around for one.

Another favorite escape for Lennon was the movies. It was easy to be inconspicuous in the dark. John viewed films like *Shampoo* and *The Pink Panther*. Despite his love of movies he had an aversion to movie theaters, calling them smelly, raucous places that made him uneasy. One time, though, he did brave the public for a visit to Coney Island, even taking a turn on its notorious rollercoaster, the Tornado. The crowds made him edgy, however, and he didn't stay long.

Most of the time, John holed up in the Black Room with his beloved felines Major and Minor. Sometimes he would spend days reading for 24 hours at a sitting. His tastes ran from sleazy hard-core pornography to politics. Oddball television news briefs also caught his eye, like the one that reported that the individual who started the long-hair craze for men was now losing his locks. Absurdly, the fellow blamed his baldness on David Bowie's barber, who coincidentally also snipped John's hair. He also loved to scour the personals, especially the dating columns in the *Village Voice*. He even answered a few anonymously, although he never divulged his true identity. As for books, John read popular fiction, from the insufferable Clive Davis to the more satisfying Manson tale *Helter Skelter*, which he devoured in one night, pronouncing it astonishing. He also enjoyed a historical account of the Dakota, given to him by a friend, which focused on his own apartment, #72. Lennon would pick up anything from Alan Alda's memoirs to obscure novels like *Tros of Samothrace* by Talbot Mundy. John often took on scholarly material too, studying world religions and philosophies and with a particular passion for history, as evidenced by his interest in the Crusades and the Third Reich. He even waded through *Early Man and the Ocean: A Search for the Beginnings of Navigation and Seaborne Civilizations*. Elliot Mintz was certain John would have one day written historical nonfiction under a pseudonym.

John had also begun to write *Skywriting by Word of Mouth*, essentially a stream-of-consciousness collection of semi-autobiographical thoughts and episodes. At one point Lennon considered abandoning the work, as the prospect of allowing an editor to see it unnerved him. For the moment, he showed it only to Mintz, who gushed like an enthused Beatle groupie. Published posthumously in 1986, the book is certainly witty at times, but best when John sticks to autobiographical material, as his old familiar play on words had grown somewhat threadbare.

Along with his forays into reading, there was John's well-documented obsession with television, which ran 24 hours a day. He devoured the talk shows, especially Tom Snyder's (which ran a favorite topic: "UFOs Destroying Wildlife in America's Heartland") and old pal Dick Cavett's program. Lennon was also endlessly fascinated by Manhattan's PBS Channel 13, a catchall forum that featured a range of personalities, from shows featuring performers, gardeners, and chefs to profiles of obscure painters and artists. John and Yoko were even invited on by avant-garde filmmaker Jonas Mekas. As Ono gave demonstrations culled from the *Grapefruit* compilation, John, in the familiar role of assistant, cut up bits of string while she performed a piercing primal scream.

A typical night found Lennon alone, inhaling shepherd's pie and ice cream and watching films like *Jailhouse Rock*, *Rosemary's Baby*, or *The Conversation*. One evening he caught the *Cher Show* when Elton John appeared as her guest. John predicted an early demise for the show. He abhorred Cher, both personally and professionally. Lennon was thrilled when he finally received Home Box Office (HBO).

This was not to say that John didn't continue to have productive days, granting interviews with the BBC and filming a segment for *East Side Art*, which aired on French television. He also sat for an enjoyable photospread with photographer Bob Gruen for Bravo. Lennon worked on his still-unreleased docufilm, spending entire days carefully editing and perfecting the mix, and read countless scripts, usually by filmmakers wanting permission to use Beatles songs. One of these was *John, Paul, George, Ringo, and Bert*, the London stage show, which originally had plans to include Harrison's "Here Comes the Sun." When George withdrew permission, John agreed to let the producers use the Lennon/McCartney tune "Good Day Sunshine." He was also sent a political script about an American revolt, which he heartily applauded while wondering just what the filmmaker wanted from him. Lennon also spent time catching up with his family in Liverpool after a long absence, via phone calls and letters from his half-sisters Jacqui and Julia* and brother-in-law Allen Baird. He enjoyed hearing about his little nieces and nephews and all the old Liverpool gang. On occasion he'd even draw a little or play piano for no one in the shuttered White Room next to the apartment's imposing entrance. But, despite his intermittent bursts of activity, Lennon's life was, by all accounts, a fairly hapless, lazy, and directionless existence.

In a pivotal turn of events that spring, Yoko announced her pregnancy. According to his diary, she relayed her suspicions to her husband as early as March 3rd, which set the due date for sometime in November. An elated John was quickly cut down by her initial reaction: that she was considering an abortion. This was a radical divergence from her earlier pro-life stance that both she and John consid-

*Jacqui, unfortunately, was a longtime heroin addict, but is now clean and sober, and working as a shop girl in suburban London. She has one son called John. Julia is a retired French teacher, author, and divorced mother of three who has spent long periods traveling in India with her boyfriend and youngest son.

ered abortion murder. Apparently, just not in her case, it seemed. She feared that John would play the typical hands-off father, free to run off and pursue his career while saddling her with the total care of the child. "No matter how cooperative he is, I'm going to be the one going through it." This time, however, the normally weak-willed Lennon put his foot down and the pregnancy continued, but on Yoko's stringent terms.

When John phoned Aunt Mimi with the news, she promptly invited herself to visit. Not wanting to be bothered, he put her off until the baby was born. Aunt Mimi, of course, was thoroughly piqued. Meanwhile, a giddy John began to shop with Yoko for her maternity wardrobe, ironically at a boutique called Lady Madonna. John immersed himself in the upcoming event, pouring through baby books for names and participating in Lamaze classes. Yoko, however, accused him of being attracted to one of the instructors. The Lennons actively investigated revolutionary birthing options like the Bayer Method (developed at New York University), which included a controversial massage technique performed on infants. John dutifully interviewed obstetricians, including one doctor whom he described as caring but too overtly intellectual.

To his credit, Lennon never missed his beloved wife's medical appointments. During one procedure the doctors probed Yoko with a rather sharp instrument, resulting in a severe case of abdominal spasms. They discovered the baby was a boy (as Green predicted), although the *I Ching* indicated a girl.

Three months after their second honeymoon, Yoko was tiring of John's constant presence. The doctors had all but forbidden sexual intercourse. So, for sexual relief, Lennon frequented several Manhattan brothels. The most prominent of these was an upscale Korean house located on 23rd Street where Lennon satisfied his urges in every conceivable way: one on one, sometimes in groups, or enjoying one of his favorite sexual acts—to be masturbated by a bikini-clad woman.

In May a desperate Yoko packed John off to Philadelphia for a series of radio broadcasts in support of that city's local charities. Lennon was reportedly ecstatic, allegedly having cried, "Great! Yoko and I need some time apart." Although radio station manager Jaye Coolie tried to rope him in for a concert, John would only commit to radio and a brief appearance on television. He proved himself a real trooper, however, laboring nonstop on the airwaves from Saturday through Sunday night to the point of exhaustion. Lennon then rewarded himself by getting ripped at an all-night party. Later, on the train back to New York, he continued his bender, which culminated in an orgy with a trio of uninhibited passengers in an Amtrak compartment. It took Lennon a full week to recover, so bad was his hangover. He slept most of the time, managing only a little writing.

There seemed to be no satisfying his rapacious libido. If anything, it grew stronger. Lennon was now masturbating several times a day and keeping a strict written log of each and every interlude. If he couldn't have sex in the real world, he readily manufactured it in his dream life. Lennon's imaginary encounters ranged from rising star Madonna to the unlikely Barbara Walters, from Yoko's sister Setsuko to McCartney's kid sister Ruth. Another dream lover was his old friend Jill Richter. There was nothing sophisticated about these sophomoric daydreams: John played the naughty adolescent, slipping a hand inside someone's blouse or catching an unsuspecting stranger off guard with a quick grope.

Back in real life, June 13, 1975 marked John's final scheduled public performance on the live television broadcast *Salute to Sir Lew Grade*, the lauded British entertainment mogul and tyrannical chairman of ATV. Lennon eagerly anticipated the event with its stellar list that included Peter Sellers, Lord Snowden, and Elton John. Lennon's contribution to the tribute kept him awake at night as he conferred with Ringo and remixed the rhythm part on "Imagine." When John showed up for the rehearsal at the Hilton, the careless and sloppy conduct of the crew (some of whom fell asleep while the production overran by four hours) seriously dismayed him.

Lennon also complained that the program was a collection of hypocritical right-wingers shuttled in on the Concorde from Britain. John was received, in stark contrast, as a card-carrying Communist, or so he believed. In his diaries Lennon insinuated he wasn't the Beatle of choice, that indeed it was Mr. Showman himself, the ingratiating Paul McCartney, whom old man Grade would have obviously preferred. Perhaps Lennon still harbored some animosity toward Grade over ATV's aggressive 1969 acquisition of Northern Songs, the Beatles' publishing company, which he considered a betrayal. Lennon got a measure of revenge by hissing his performance of "Slippin' and

Slidin'" and "Imagine." During the show his only positive support came from Shirley MacLaine, New York Mayor John Lindsay, and Pete Hamill. Lennon was also touched by Gene Kelly's gesture of encouragement as he passed him backstage on the way to get changed for the encore. John and Yoko had a good chuckle about the events before going to bed. But deep down the rejection bothered him. That night he dreamed of being a helpless child in a building filled with unfamiliar faces, a child sliced with a knife by a woman for simply tugging on her hair.

As the trying year reached the halfway point, Lennon was suffocating under his various legal entanglements. For months he had given tedious depositions in the Levy case, which ended in a mistrial. A second trial was slated for 1976. Then there was the ongoing battle to rid himself of Allen Klein, who clung stubbornly to Lennon's back. John Green, who predicted Lennon would not lose the case, offered a scheme to help dump the troublesome manager. First, he suggested a bit of voodoo, having John create one of his collages for Klein and rubbing a certain herbal mixture on the portrait to "make him squirm." Green predicted the spell would make Klein lose his temper over a woman. The next suggestion was far more practical. He told John to go to Klein's office with a cock-and-bull story about a joint business venture guaranteed to make millions. In order to succeed he needed access to all his files, which required taking them home. John then stripped the files of any and all evidence, leaving Klein with virtually nothing to defend his case.

As summer began, the McCartneys came to town, eager to look up their old mate. Much to Lennon's consternation, Green predicted a visit from the couple. Ultimately, John ended up at dinner listening to their endless bragging about how wonderfully they were doing. In his diaries he termed them obnoxious, smug, and even downright stupid. Green also boldly predicted that the pair would go their separate ways in a year or two. Lennon admitted he'd wondered if the celebrated marriage really had legs. Even the owner of Nartells, the McCartneys' favorite restaurant, commented to John that Mrs. McCartney was terribly overbearing. Paul also called on the Boyles that trip, joining them and Lennon for dinner at John's apartment before returning to their place for a nightcap. Lennon reported it was actually a fairly nice evening for a change.

Shortly afterwards he was put on the spot by activist-comedian Dick Gregory, who wired his Beatle friend requesting a hefty $50,000 to pursue a plan to expose the CIA. Lennon had neither the heart nor the guts to personally decline the favor. Gregory was determined to get his point across, even if it took going to prison. It remains unclear if John ever accommodated him.

The summer of '75 delivered some singularly sad news: Lennon's close friend Richard Ross was admitted to Mount Sinai Hospital for treatment of Hodgkin's disease. John began paying regular visits to the handsome restauranteur, and advised him to consult his cousin, Dr. Leila Harvey, before undergoing surgery to remove his spleen. The pair discussed a mutual passion for sailing, delving into a nautical text that Ross's brother Jack had given him in the hospital. Lennon deemed the prospects of learning to sail difficult but challenging.

John's visits however, weren't entirely altruistic. May Pang (also a close friend of Ross, having steered several big-time musicians to his Home eatery) often showed up at Mount Sinai to lend support. For Lennon it was just too much of a temptation. He desperately missed the young, unassuming secretary since she'd left in April for a temporary job at London's Apple offices, and often dreamed of May in very lusty terms. An obliging Ross would excuse himself to go to the bathroom, leaving the couple to enjoy a quickie in the poor man's sick bed! These bold, bizarre trysts apparently went on with some regularity.

May's impact on John went far beyond mere sex. *Daily Mirror* reporter Don Short, who years before had forged a professional friendship with all the Beatles, saw an immediate difference now that Lennon returned to Ono. With Pang, John was content, confident, productive—"his own man," in Short's view. "When he got himself into Yoko's jet stream, he just couldn't shake free from it. . . . She seemed to restrict him in his thinking and what he was doing. Maybe some talent was lost there. He did write one or two nice songs, but I think there was so much more pure talent that simply went adrift."

Apparently Ono, now well into her pregnancy, found John's presence increasingly intolerable. She tried to get him out of the house as much as possible, to movies and dinners at places like the Russian Tea Room. The couple also made the rounds of popular Broadway plays like *Love and Death* and *Same Time Next Year*, featuring Ellen Burstyn and Charles Grodin, which John dismissed as mildly entertaining but ultimately pointless pap. Unfortunately, the theater's publicity department got wind of Lennon's intention to see the show and ran the item in a popular newspaper column. The notice drew a horde of fans, and the nervous rocker felt he was in the midst of an opening night bash. On a subsequent evening, he took in *Death of a Salesman*, and confessed he was too bashful to meet George C. Scott backstage. With Norman and Helen Seaman he also attended *Equus*, which he thoroughly enjoyed, no doubt intrigued by the plot of a man blinding a horse.

Lennon even braved his first ballet, *Swan Lake*, with the late Rudolph Nureyev (a Dakota resident). This time Lennon got up the courage to actually go backstage and say hello. As for future evenings at the ballet, Lennon declined, deeming it so stifling he even had a nightmare about being forever trapped in the second act!

Lennon's obsession with his weight (instigated, some say, by Yoko) started to get out of hand. Determined to rid himself of a tiny spare tire, he experimented with a juice diet mixed with nuts and fruit, supplemented with an occasional piece of dry chicken. He indulged himself on Sundays with small helpings of salmon and caviar. Pronouncing himself still too heavy, he switched to a strict juice-and-rice regimen, interrupted by periodic water fasts. One night he went to the French restaurant Le Busgue to eat his first real meal in some fourteen days. Certainly, Lennon didn't need to lose more than a few pounds, and his seesaw dieting resulted in easy tiring, and a lot of needless digestive problems. Often when John found himself overeating, he would hide in the master bathroom and force himself to vomit.

As for his wife's pregnancy, Lennon supervised her diet and pushed her about the Dakota in a wheelchair, lest something happen to the baby. His fears manifested themselves in a dream where he tried to escape from guests who poured into their house by perching on a cliff. John and Yoko were forced to jump off the edge into a river as his arms embraced her stomach in an attempt to protect their unborn baby.

Despite his concern, John was desperate for a break from his testy, always overbearing wife and was ready to explode from her nearly constant moodiness and irrational behavior. He doubted she was even aware of how she burdened him with her trivial upsets and baseless insecurities. The slightest thing could set her off, like a satirical piece in the *Daily News* that portrayed her as an operative for the CIA. She would regularly accuse John of trying to kill her and of hating their child.

Yoko, too, could not tolerate John's relentless fussing, and resented having to hide her chocolate. She couldn't abide either his restlessness or his mindlessly hanging about the apartment. So she sent him off to Long Island (the first of many such short trips) to scout out a house to rent. Accompanied by the Boyles one time, and Mike Graham on another occasion, John found a parcel of land he was interested in buying. These were welcome excursions. In his diary Lennon noted that on this jaunt he cheated on his diet, gorging on fried clams, which left him with a severe case of diarrhea for nearly a week.

Finally, John decided to rent the house he so admired in Montauk. Yoko, though, was doing her usual tarot-inspired tap dance, dickering over the *safest* time to go. While at the shore, Lennon practiced Hatha yoga, did some meditating, and tried his best to stay on Ono's relentlessly severe juice regimen.

No sooner did Lennon return than he was off again, this time to Connecticut, to explore the homes of the politically famous. This included the Rockefellers' $2 million private island and William F. Buckley Jr.'s lavish estate. Connecticut was also a convenient romantic getaway for him and Pang.

According to various diary entries, throughout August and September Lennon spent most of his time with Richard Ross and his pretty airline attendant wife Cynthia. John increased the frequency of his visits while his friend underwent intensive follow-up radiation therapy. The treatment's ravaging effects, following just two sessions, disheartened Lennon. Ross's hair was falling out and he looked haggard, almost skeletal. To get John out of the house and his mind off his friend's illness, the pair went for extended walks with Ross's dogs. They lunched together at Fool Lib and got haircuts, where John ran into comedian David Brenner. Another time they went to Soho to look at clocks (a favorite gift), followed by dinner at Nirvana, where Lennon consumed a meatless curry. He even took the restauranteur out to Long Island, where they looked at a jukebox Ross was thinking of buying. Lennon proclaimed it ten years old and grossly overpriced. One evening they went out for coffee, then caught a showing of Disney's *Fantasia*. John left halfway through the film, disturbed once again by a disruptive audience and the dingy surroundings.

As soon as Ross felt strong enough, the pair made good on their vow to go sailing. They had spent weeks pouring over how-to books, including a collection of yachting texts someone had discarded at the curb. Together they attended boat shows, one on City Island, another in New Rochelle, where John enthusiastically soaked up information from a seasoned sailing couple who owned a state-of-the-art, light-weight craft. He also discovered that Record Plant manager Eddie Germano had bought a 53-foot motorboat, and the two took it out for a spin. Perhaps it was a case of Lennon seeing his own mortality through Ross's brush with death, but neither music nor writing nor even the iron-willed Yoko inspired John like this new urge to get out on the water. He even stopped smoking, noting it was easier than he envisioned, and managed to keep up with his rigorous yoga practice. Furthermore, John and Ross took up swimming at the YMCA, doing some 25 lengths in the pool, followed by a long, recuperative sauna. Ignoring his absurd liquid diet, Lennon taught himself to make a pretty mean omelette. When distanced from the control-conscious Yoko, John inevitably soon sprang back to life.

But even Charlie Swan felt he would never really stick it out. Although Lennon, he stressed, wasn't heavily into drugs (though he indulged in his fair share of marijuana), John's real battle was with nicotine. He vowed, without lasting success, to quit at least once a month. John, for most of the time Swan knew him, believed there was a right way to live. The tarot reader stated, "This involved proper diet, proper behavior, proper attitudes, and when the strain of living in that false position would get a little too intense, he would naturally rebel against it. Part of that rebellion was 'I'll go out, I'll go to a bar, I'll smoke a lot of cigarettes, I'll talk to people and be flippant. I can be anyone I want.' It was pretty much the same thing you see in an adolescent obliged to go to high school and change seats every time the bell rings and study when he is told. Then when he goes out at night, he wants to drive the car very fast and drink beer."

After finding an instructor to take him out on the water, Lennon finally set sail in September. Gentleman singer Richie Havens tried to arrange a three-day boating trip, but John feared it would be a bore. As it turned out it was actually Lennon, Ross, and Elliot Mintz who sailed away on a bright, crisp day in New York Harbor. They were like three blind men taking turns at the helm, with John delighting in his chance to actually command the vessel. He was euphoric, comparing sailing to playing guitar, and noting it took the same amount of time to be competent at both. The perfect day came to a sour end, however, when he tagged along with Yoko and a friend to eat Japanese at Takabei. Lennon found it a dreadful experience, charging they were served a deliberately lousy meal.

Eager to get out on the water again, John took a solo excursion the next day when Ross and Mintz bowed out. Chauffeured to New Rochelle, Lennon temporarily lost direction to the marina. Once again, he reveled in the sailing experience, even though the winds didn't pick up and he got too much sun. Although exhausted from the unaccustomed labor, the fledgling mariner felt he was fast shaping up. Yoko, not wanting to be outdone, promised that she would take lessons as well, though she despised the water. Lennon was having so much fun that he almost failed to record he had gone seven days without a cigarette.

True to his habit of totally immersing himself in any new endeavor, Lennon was ready to test himself. He and Richard took off in Ross's sleek Maserati for Cape Cod, finding lodging in a run-down bed-and-breakfast with a minuscule, smelly kitchenette. John barely noticed, so caught up was he in his latest passion.

Moving on to Martha's Vineyard, Lennon suddenly found himself gazing into a remarkable face that took his breath away. Her name was Alexa Grace, a 25-year-old, stunningly beautiful commercial artist whose passion was sculpting ceramic figurines. For John it was like looking into a mirror and seeing the same painfully shy, withdrawn soul, lost and vulnerable. Alexa had just broken up with her boyfriend and faced the grim prospect of returning to New York alone.

Fascinated by the clay figures that peeked out of her carrying bag, Lennon asked if he could see them. Alexa, recognizing a kindred spirit, spilled out her collection, and the pair sat on the ground playing make-believe like blissful six-year-olds. Lennon let down his hair, making the figures move and interact, plunging everyone into hysterics by giving them all names and histories. John and Alexa drew out the child in one another: for him it was the most relaxed he had felt in years.

He persuaded the wholesome beauty to postpone her bus trip back to the city and to tag along with him and Richard. The unlikely band wheeled about Hyannis Port sight-seeing, antique hunting, and visiting the local health food store. Stopping at motels for the night, Grace was content to camp out on a cot, letting John and Ross take the beds. There was nothing sexual about the relationship, although Lennon did attempt a slight advance and was promptly rebuffed. It was his first platonic relationship with a woman in a long time and he found it very refreshing.

The trio went sailing, this time without a navigator, in a 17-foot, second-rate boat. While casting off posed no problem, maneuvering the small craft back to shore was another matter. Swells came up, rocking the vessel and carrying it out to sea. So much for Lennon's budding nautical prowess: the boat had to be towed back to shore.

Although Alexa shared John's fragility, she had none of her new friend's oddball insecurities. Anything unfamiliar would immediately spark his paranoia—whether exploring an old weathered building, wherein Lennon, fearing strangers lurking inside, wished he had a weapon, or going horseback riding, where John refused to climb into the saddle. Even something as benign and familiar as Ross's erratic driving would set him wailing in alarm and running off to phone Yoko (or "Mother," as he often called her).

Following a brief stay at Grace's grandmother's farm in the Catskills, the threesome's grand adventure ended and they returned to the city, where they dropped Alexa off at her fashionable East Side flat. If not for John's impending fatherhood, one can only guess what might have unfolded between him and the lovely, wistful artist. As it turned out, however, this would not be the last he'd hear of the charming Grace.

In October 1975, as the baby's arrival grew closer, Lennon accompanied Ono to her now weekly medical appointments. Although everything was progressing well and the baby was apparently healthy, John's insecurities about fatherhood were intensifying. These fears were channeled into his dream life, heavily laced with episodes of his own tortured childhood. John's dreams took him back to Liverpool and the familiar haunts of Penny Lane, Mendips, and Newcastle Road. His five "Amazon" aunts were also on hand, as was the occasional celebrity like Joan Crawford. In his dreams Julia was now heavier around the middle, perhaps indicating pregnancy, while Fred was inexplicably very elderly. John recalled strolling the grounds of Mendips with Rex Reed while Jagger, taking the place of Lennon's solid boyhood mate Ivan Vaughan, wandered through a favorite meadow.

For the past twelve months Lennon had been toying with the idea of dropping his career. At one point Lennon talked over his prospects with Apple man Tony King during breakfast at the St. Moritz. John told his old friend that he wanted to enjoy himself for once rather than jump back onto the fast track in an industry now run by lawyers, CPAs, and sycophants. The very next day he canceled all further recording sessions.

Lennon's anxieties were rapidly getting the better of him. A few lines of cocaine, or better yet heroin, generally took the edge off his growing depression. Lennon frequently felt unwell, plagued with headaches and alternating bouts of constipation and diarrhea. He was forever complaining of needing more sleep, even though he was actually getting far too much. John would invariably turn a simple cold into a major illness, taking to his bed for days at a time. A case of jumbled nerves could likewise arise at any time, causing John to miss doctors' appointments or a trip to the hairdressers. He fretted about either his dandruff or the growing bald spot on the back of his head. While walking home one time, John got caught in a rainstorm and had to hitch a ride with some nice young people, an uneasy adventure for the paranoid pop star. John even canceled a visit to the local library because he didn't "trust" the atmosphere.

Lennon couldn't handle simple household matters any better. Spotting a harmless insect, he once resorted to calling an exterminator. It took him days to get up the courage to dismiss Yoko's assistant Jon Hendricks,* and in a similar instance another Lennon employee requested a secretary and once again John wimped out, lacking the backbone to refuse.

He received a disquieting letter from the National Organization for Women, claiming that various medications Ono was receiving were potentially life threatening. Lennon dubbed the entire matter crazy, but he was clearly unnerved. In the wake of that troubling episode, someone left a black cross bearing a satanic motif with the doorman, only to come back days later asking to have the amulet returned, saying it belonged to a relative. This was not the first such incident, forcing a tense Lennon to order the doorman to say that such gifts had

---

*Amazingly, as recently as November 1997 Hendricks was still employed by the Lennon empire. In the end, it seems, he was able to escape John's apparently toothless enmity.

been immediately donated to the Salvation Army. Although he tried to be calm about incidents like these, Lennon was often unsettled, and he resorted to consulting Green about visitors to the Dakota and their possible motives. He wanted to avoid any negative confrontations at all costs in an attempt to revive his own good karma.

Weighing most heavily on Lennon's mind was the quality of his sex life with Ono following the birth of their child. He feared Yoko had glossed over the true cause of their initial separation, which was an essential bone of contention throughout their marriage. It took more than just love, declared Lennon, a reality he claimed Ono was reluctant to acknowledge. He was so sexually charged that he was terrified the old problem would once again divide them and destroy their always fragile relationship.

October 1975 was filled with various court appearances, in which Lennon had to face both Lee Eastman and Allen Klein. During one such appearance, the situation got a bit out of hand when the two bigwigs and Lennon erupted in a childish tantrum. On a more sedate note, John kept up his Lamaze classes with his wife and dined with Neil Aspinall. He also filled his time by attending boating exhibitions with Ross, and squired Yoko and her visiting sister Setsuko around town. At some point he decided to have the kitchen remodeled, a hefty $35,000 undertaking. But in general, these days were too often wasted with busywork like tidying up the library, sorting books, purchasing antiques for the Black Room, and John's seemingly fruitless battle to quit smoking for the sake of the baby.

During this time Lennon also mixed his disappointing compilation *Shaved Fish*, an anthology of singles released in late October. Roy Cicala's fiddling with the recording equipment in the control room—which Lennon pronounced sheer unproductive folly, the very type of showbiz crap he'd grown tired of—deeply upset him.

Lennon's record contract was due to expire in 1976, and John was quietly mulling over his options. Columbia offered him a lucrative deal, but Lennon was wary of the label's overly aggressive tactics and commercial attitude. He figured if he signed with them, it would only be for a brief partnership. By now his long-term relationship with EMI/ Capitol had grown stale, compounded by his escalating legal problems over the *Rock 'n' Roll* debacle. Capitol executives laid it out in black and white: their famous client was no longer the hot commodity he once was. With the exception of *Walls and Bridges*, Lennon's last few albums were poor sellers, and the extensive litigation surrounding his professional endeavors made him a serious liability. John appreciated their candor, but considered them only a last resort.

Lennon also decided he could no longer trust attorney Harold Seider, his unofficial scapegoat for the Levy predicament. On the surface the dismissal of his once-close confidant was both unexpected and baffling. Upon closer examination it appears the decision was Yoko's. She was planning to assert even more control over her husband's business affairs, making Seider expendable. John planned to keep the lawyer in his employ to work out any new record deal and let him go later. He would also phase out Seider's associates. John was thinking of bringing in Jon Landau, the former *Rolling Stone* writer who became Bruce Springsteen's manager. Lennon conceded the man was undoubtedly intelligent, yet in other ways fairly naive. He was finally forced to admit that Landau was not really a mate and couldn't be lured in.

But as the first week in October came to a close, all of that was delayed for the moment. On the evening of the 6th Yoko was admitted to New York Hospital following a series of worrisome blood tests earlier in the day. A concerned John helped his wife, now almost 36 weeks along, into their private suite overlooking the East River, the same room where Jacqueline Kennedy had delivered Caroline nearly twenty years earlier. John remained with her from 9:00 p.m. until early afternoon the next day.

While beginning the long wait, Lennon received some very unexpected news: his INS case was finally over. In a vote of two to one John won his right to live in the "land of the free." The decision was officially based on the obvious conclusion that he didn't fit the category of a "deportable alien." Circumstances were now certainly working in John's favor. Proceedings were being brought against his archenemy, Attorney General John Mitchell, in June. Then in July, England passed the Uniform Rehabilitation Act, and with it wiped out his 1968 drug conviction. By September he was granted yet another extension based on "humanitarian grounds" due to Yoko's pregnancy. Because the conspiracy against John was now out in the open, the three judges issued their ruling, declaring, "the court cannot condone selective deportation based upon secret political grounds." The United States Court of Appeals even called him an adopted patriot:

"Lennon's four-year battle to remain in our country is testimony to his faith in this particular American dream."

The elated father-to-be was struck by the irony that two judges of Jewish extraction voted for him, while his own countryman William Mulligan cast the lone dissenting vote. John joked to Lorraine that he would plant a seedling in the Holy Land in honor of the victory. Yoko instantly beckoned her lawyers to her hospital bed, demanding to go over every element of the decision. After the impromptu celebration, Lennon went home to pack some things so he could move into his wife's hospital room, where he spent hours watching the boats sail up and down the river.

The events swirling around the arrival of the baby were at once bizarre, incredible, and dangerous. Lennon couldn't even bring himself to speak about it until a full two years later. First, Yoko's determination to have the child born on October 9th, John's birthday, was problematic. She wanted the infant to "inherit" John's soul: she was convinced the baby would be a messiah who would one day change the world. "If a messiah were going to be reborn today," Ono had told John Green, "he would choose rock stars as parents so he could have access to the media. Everything is perfect for a new prophet. It's the right time and we are absolutely the right parents!"

Yoko later dismissed charges of the contrived birth date, insisting she entered the hospital on the eighth day of the month due to contractions, but records show that her admission was two days earlier. Even Lennon himself conceded this fact years later to Fred Seaman.

Although the Lennons expected a normal delivery, an examination discovered the child was in the breach position. Noting Yoko's age the doctors advised that a cesarean was warranted. At 2:00 a.m. Sean Ono Taro Lennon weighed in at a sturdy eight pounds, ten ounces. A euphoric Lennon could find no way to describe his elation, although he later offered his famous line, "I'm as high as the Empire State Building!"

In the middle of their celebration the infant began to experience muscle spasms and was rushed to the Intensive Care Unit. Doctors decided to run a routine urinalysis on Yoko. The doctor confronted her with test results showing traces of drugs in her system, which Ono heatedly claimed were merely the anesthetic. John flew into an immediate rage, "We weren't taking any fucking drugs! We were on a health food diet! We're taking our baby and getting the fuck out of here!"

The physician suddenly grew confrontational and threatened, "If you take the baby, we'll get a warrant to search your residence, and perhaps even a court order to take your baby away from you as unfit parents!"

Following that crisis, Yoko went into convulsions, which Lennon attributed to a transfusion of the wrong blood type. In a surrealistic scene he frantically tracked down a physician, dragging him into Yoko's room. The star-struck doctor, disregarding his suffering patient, rushed to shake the rock star's hand while gushing, "I've always wanted to meet you, Mr. Lennon! I've enjoyed your music for years."

An incredulous John started screaming, "My wife's dying and you wanna talk about fuckin' music!" Lennon later charged that Ono nearly died because of the incompetence of the hospital staff and their refusal to hear the truth.

Meanwhile, events grew even more harrowing as doctors performed a dangerous spinal tap on the newborn, so delicate a procedure that the slightest miscue could have left him permanently paralyzed. Lennon felt that, in their determination to search out illicit pharmaceuticals in his parents' systems, the doctors' misguided efforts could have cost Sean his life.

John suspected a conspiracy, later saying the medical staff kept his wife plied with barbiturates for several days, not allowing her to breastfeed or even to see the child. He further labeled them mad. After a week the couple were all but forced to kidnap their son from the nursery and spirit him out of the hospital, while a nurse scurried behind shouting, "You can't do that! He needs more blood tests!" John Green tells a completely different story, saying that Yoko—far from fleeing the hospital after a week—did not come home to the Dakota until a full two weeks following the birth, preferring the sedate confines of the hospital.

At home little Sean's violent spasms continued for several months. His worried parents concocted their own topical Chinese herbal treatment, which eventually succeeded in stopping the twitching.

For all the vaunted planning prior to the birth, when John took his son home, he didn't even have a crib for the infant. Ono explained this away by superstition: her last three pregnancies ended in miscarriages, and she didn't want to tempt fate. The question remains: did Yoko ever let her husband in on her intention to give birth in October? Everyone John spoke with confirmed the due date was definitely

November. Ringo even gave the newborn a ring engraved with the word "November." David Nutter, who photographed their 1969 Gibraltar wedding, was invited to the Dakota by Elton John, whom Lennon tapped to be his son's godfather. "John had the baby in a shoe box because it was so unexpected," Nutter revealed. "They didn't have anything to put the baby in. It was the afternoon. Elton had a day off from the show. Yoko had a woman there to serve tea. John was ever the proud father."

While Ono retired to bed, Lennon assumed his assigned role as sole caretaker, taking over feedings just as he had done every day in the hospital. (One doctor later admitted that John had been the most attentive and involved father he had ever seen.)

Although Lennon did take more of a hands-on approach than most dads, his intensive care lasted only a few weeks before he handed the baby over to a nanny. Typical of his short attention span, he was soon absorbed in his next project: a study of popular American culture through its television commercials.

Ono, meanwhile, fretted that the baby's head seemed too small for his body. Faced with the task of hiring a nanny for Sean, John settled on Yoko's choice, an efficient Japanese matron named Masako. John, finally able to relax a bit, threw Sean a homecoming party and even managed to pay a visit to his new wealthy neighbors, whom he regarded as a bit quirky.

The birth of Lennon's second son precipitated correspondence with his family in England. Leila promptly conveyed the immediate prickliness over his Liverpool family's impression that John had deserted them. John fired back that he could never win with his British kin. As a child they viewed him as a burden, difficult to control; as an adult they held his fame and fortune against him.

Lennon's exchanges with Aunt Mimi were as thorny as ever. John confessed he was still caught off guard by her frequent irrational outbursts followed by her equally emotional apologies. He told Mimi he'd penned a stinging response to her latest letter, but decided against mailing it, adding if they were face-to-face he probably wouldn't be able to contain himself.

When Lennon told his auntie he'd named the boy the Irish equivalent of John, Mimi pleaded not to saddle the boy with such a heavy mantle. To which her nephew curtly replied, it was a typical snooty,

English provincial viewpoint. He was damn proud to be a New York, living in a city esteemed for its divergent, tolerant cultural mix, perfectly suited for Sean's multiracial background.

In another note to Leila he also took a snipe at ex-wife Cynthia, whom he blamed for discouraging any contact with Julian as punishment for his reuniting with Yoko. It was plain to see Julian was simply being used. He told Mimi he feared what kind of games Cynthia would play now that he had a second son. Inevitably, John also spoke of his plans to return to his homeland, suggesting a big family reunion to reconcile ill feelings. Mostly, he wanted to show off his pride and joy, Sean. Sadly, the homecoming would never take place as Lennon would never again set foot in Britain.

In December Bob Gruen was summoned to the Dakota for the first shoot of the new family, with orders that snapshots be sent to Yoko's relatives in Japan. With John, Yoko, and even Sean decked out in kimonos, Gruen noted, "This was not the wise-cracking pop star, but the proud papa. He seemed able to express more love and caring than ever before. He was happier that day than I'd ever seen him."

But was he? As the world's most famous rock 'n' roller officially closed the door on his public life, a strange dream ended the year: John and Yoko were out for dinner when a chubby, bespectacled stranger approached their table. John asked him to prove he was not some nutcase. The man grew increasingly anxious because John did not treat him as he usually treated an admirer. The cops then informed the former Beatle that this fan had come to the restaurant armed with a loaded revolver. Lennon was very upset that he could not remember the rest of this portentous dream.

TWO VIRGINS $\boxed{4}$

The Conning Of A Beatle

1976

America was poised to commemorate its bicentennial in 1976, and John Lennon was ready to celebrate victory in his battle for citizenship. It should have been a time of great happiness and growth, yet John was withdrawing more and more into self-doubt and negativity. Everybody's working-class hero was sliding steadily into a morass of hopelessness and solemnity.

January delivered the first of several blows that would severely shake Lennon's psyche over the first half of the year: on the night of January 4th, Malcolm Evans lost his life. Mal had endured two painful separations: one from his long-suffering wife Lil, and the other from the Beatles during Apple's extended dissolution. During Lennon's "Lost Weekend" in L.A., he had been Mal's last tie to the happier days of the past. John's return to New York left Evans lost and alone. He began drinking heavily and brooding over his glory days with the band.

As the new year opened, Evans was finishing up work on his memoirs,* *Living the Beatles Legend,* for the publishing house Grosset and Dunlap. The end of the project, though, had a devastating impact on him, as if putting the finishing touches on the book somehow put an end to the purpose of his life.

The night of the fourth, a despairing Mal finally snapped. First, he phoned his writing collaborator John Hoernie, imploring him to make

---

*To this day, Evans's manuscript has never been published.

certain the book was delivered on its January 12th deadline. Next, he ordered his girlfriend Frances Hughes and her four-year-old daughter out of their Hollywood flat at gunpoint.

Evans, beyond despair, made his way to an upstairs bedroom, where he clutched a shotgun as police surrounded the home. Telephone records indicate that Evans made two calls during the crisis, one to an unknown L.A. exchange, and the other, a call of under one minute, to Lennon's residence in New York. The call was apparently never put through to the former Beatle. What followed next might have been very different had John spoken to his despondent friend. Ordered by police to give himself up, Evans refused, screaming, "You'll have to blow my fucking head off!"

The police then stormed the room, demanding he drop his weapon. Evans, cornered and desperate, leveled his shotgun at the officers, leaving them no choice. Four shots rang out, two fatal strikes to the chest, knocking the former Beatle roadie to the floor. Although Evans's girlfriend told authorities he'd been drinking heavily and ingesting pills, an autopsy revealed only a moderate amount of Valium and alcohol amounting to just one drink. Suicide by cops is what they call it these days.

Paul McCartney later commented that had he been at the scene that fateful night, Evans might still be alive. "Mal was a big lovable bear of a roadie," stated McCartney. "He'd go over the top occasionally, but we all knew him and never had any problems. Had I been there I would have been able to say, 'Mal, don't be silly.' In fact, any of his friends could have talked him out of it without any sweat because he was not a nutter."

Lennon's reaction upon hearing of the tragedy was hysterical laughter, not unlike his response to the death of Stuart Sutcliffe years before. When the roadie's ashes were somehow lost en route to Britain, Lennon morbidly observed that Mal probably ended up in the dead letter office.

Beneath Lennon's bravado, however, lay his awareness of troubling parallels to his own fragmented life. Both he and Mal were divorced, and both indulged, heavily at times, in drink and drugs. Both were certainly prisoners of the past, walking on very fragile psychological ground. Lennon's own haunting premonition that he would also suffer a violent end was again brought home to him by Mal's death.

Moreover, John had lost yet another important figure in his life. Evans might have been one of his last real friends. Mal was a regular working-class man and a link to his Liverpool roots. They shared a kind of blood-brother relationship. It was Mal who had his ribs broken while shielding John in a Manila riot during the Beatles' troubled visit to the Philippines. He had joined John's Greek holiday aboard a yacht in the Aegean during the latter's foray into transcendental meditation. Mal also played harmonica on "Being for the Benefit of Mr. Kite," and conceived the idea behind *Sgt. Pepper's Lonely Hearts Club Band*, a credit Paul McCartney still hotly contests.

Pete Shotton, however, seems to back up Evans's story, saying that Mal was the one who came up with the moniker *Sgt. Pepper's Lonely Hearts Club Band*. Furthermore, it was the roadie's idea to have the Beatles slip into these Victorian characters and have the album play like an uninterrupted performance by Sgt. Pepper's band.

Evans was at once John's baby-sitter, drug dealer, equipment manager, bodyguard, as well as a very broad shoulder to cry on. As Shotton once pointed out, the power behind the Beatles' throne, apart from Neil Aspinall, was in fact big, burly Mal.

"We always took it out on people like Mal," Lennon later commented. "He was ever faithful. He took a lot of shit from us because we were in such a shitty position. It was hard work and somebody had to take it. These things are left out you know, about what fucking bastards we were."

In the aftermath of the tragedy, John began a six-week juice fast. Perhaps this was his way of grieving, of washing away an ugly past. Or maybe he was trying to purge himself of any guilt. He and Evans's ex-wife had been involved in a sexual encounter during John's dark days in Los Angeles. Although the alleged trysts meant nothing to John, the betrayal enraged and deeply saddened Mal.

Paul McCartney later took Lil Evans to court when she tried to sell some of Mal's personal memorabilia related to his time with the Beatles. Accused of "widow bashing" by the British media, Paul soon gave up his suit and quietly settled with her.

On January 26, 1976, John's contract with Capitol/EMI expired. Over the years the Lennon spin has been that he had turned his back on music in order to focus fully on fatherhood. The truth, however, was vastly different. Record companies weren't exactly fighting each other to sign him. John's spotty sales record as a solo artist made them cautious, and the sales of his last two releases were downright poor. Record executives, looking at Paul McCartney's phenomenal success with Wings, wondered if Lennon was, in fact, washed up.

As a result, Lennon's fragile self-image was perpetually under siege. When, later that winter, John Green asked John if he had retired, Lennon snarled: "Retired hell, I'm dead! What chance do I have now? They've got me nailed in a coffin called the past. I'm a golden oldie now. The only thing I can do is Beatles stuff. Travel the circuit, play Vegas, and sing songs from the good old days to a bunch of good old boys who want to have a look at a real live Beatle. They've turned me into another Elvis, and I don't even own the rights to the fuckin' songs! I'd have to get permission and pay for the privilege of doing an impersonation of myself."

Something else was disturbing John. A quiet rage had been building up for some time. He had lost his confidence as a composer, and wouldn't write another complete song for some four years. Not until the end of his life did he concede that turning his back on his music only exacerbated his predicament. "Work is life, and without it there's nothing but fear and insecurity."

With John on the ropes, Yoko's influence was supreme. Her cadre of psychic advisers suggested that her husband should not resume his musical career until 1982. The idea of such a long layoff didn't seem to concern Lennon. He was susceptible to manipulation: having important decisions made for him gave him an excuse to forgo responsibility. When his problems grew worse, he used his naïveté like a shield or even a club. "I believe in everything until it's disproved," he once stated. "It all exists, even if it's in your mind. Who's to say that dreams and nightmares aren't as real as the here and now? Reality leaves quite a lot to the imagination."

It is doubtful, though, that these advisers were really speaking in John's best interest as their fortunes depended upon Ono's approval. She had always sought to connect her musical efforts to her husband's, and his recent failures worried her. She must have realized she had no chance to succeed as an artist on her own in the music industry. Now that the business arm of the Lennon empire was reaping rewards, the conceptual artist became a conceptual businesswoman.

This new world, which both baffled and intimidated John, was a natural arena for his spouse. Even as the media were dubbing the pair "the Robert and Elizabeth Barrett Browning of pop," the business instincts of the shrewd Ono were beginning to emerge in a meaningful way. What John was unable to do with Apple—build an empire—Yoko was accomplishing without him.

When the going got tough, Lennon, as was his custom, turned to heroin. His use of needles to administer the narcotic has often been alleged, though with little hard evidence to support the claim. But in late 1969, at the request of George Harrison, Lennon opened his home at Tittenhurst to several Hare Krishna devotees. Searching the office for supplies one day, a young Scot named Dhananjaya Dasa stumbled upon several used syringes tucked behind a file cabinet. Sources close to the singer insisted to this author that they belonged to Lennon. John himself wasn't above making a veiled reference to the use of needles. During the 1969 filming of the *Let It Be* recording sessions, John made insinuating references to the drug, comparing heroin to sex by cracking, "Shooting is good exercise."

By early 1976, Lennon was spending time with his old friend and all-around bad influence, guitarist Jesse Ed Davis. In late January the pair ended up at the Plaza Hotel, where Led Zeppelin were staying. When they visited the suite assigned to the group, they found drummer Jon Bonham hunched over a toilet in the bathroom, vomiting after ingesting some very potent heroin. Bonham, vowing he would never use the narcotic again, told them to help themselves. Lennon no sooner snorted a line of the high-quality contraband when he too began vomiting. Unfortunately, Bonham was unable to keep his resolution: he overdosed and died in 1980.

The architect of the Bonham misadventure that night was likely the underworld figure Thomas Cho, better known as "The Chinaman," who had a well-deserved reputation as a drug dealer to the stars. Many drug suppliers don't use what they sell, but Cho was an exception. He was known to have a heavy habit and renowned for making deliveries anywhere, anytime. Cho and John met for the first time that night. From that point on the diminutive, unassuming Cho became Lennon's most trusted and reliable supplier, serving him right up until the end of his life. According to Davis, Lennon's habit soon escalated to $700 per day. Where once he had been content to smoke hash and ingest psychedelic mushrooms, ex-Beatle John had become a true heroin addict with a prodigious appetite.

One of heroin's many insidious effects is a significant loss of libido. May Pang experienced this phenomenon, as her physical relationship with John dwindled from weekly trysts to once every two months. She also observed a listlessness and resignation in her lover, a lack of focus and drive. At times he would stare right through her, the familiar Lennon spark totally drained away.

Meanwhile, Yoko introduced John to a therapeutic regime involving self-hypnosis and "past-life regression." In one such session, he found himself a Neanderthal male, overseeing his clan from a cave near a forest. In yet another episode he traveled back to the Crusades. He was ordered to kill his compatriots, after which he loaded the dead onto a cart and disposed of them.

On a typical day during this time John awoke shortly after dawn, poured himself a cup of coffee, and read the paper. An hour or so later, Sean would get up, and John would make him breakfast. The rest of the morning was taken up with domestic chores, which might involve baking bread or strolling in the park with his son until lunch. Lennon would then have the afternoon to himself. At about 7:00 p.m. the boy would take a bath, followed by an hour of carefully monitored children's television. Sean remembers bedtime wrestling matches with his father, as well as a memorable nightly routine. "There was a little mobile of these planes over my bed and my ceiling was painted like a sky, so I thought the planes were flying. And then he'd say, 'Good night, Sean,' and he'd turn the lights on and off to his voice. I thought that was the greatest trick in the world!"

Sean recalls other pleasant memories of those days. "Dad would play guitar and I would sit on his lap. There's a tape of me just banging on a distorted electric guitar, sitting on his lap. He was very sharing with music. We'd sing constantly."

Lennon watched his son's food intake carefully, keeping him on a strict macrobiotic regimen. White sugar was unilaterally banned; John would order cakes made with honey for Sean. He also made sure his son exercised regularly, and took him to the nearby YMCA for swimming lessons. Lennon installed a jukebox in Sean's room, stacking it with R&B records and teaching the toddler to dance. As John once boasted, "He didn't come out of my belly, but by God I made his bones!" John's Aunt Mimi told the press, "John really seems much more settled and happy now than he used to be. When he phones he wants to talk about Sean and about when he was a little boy himself."

Although Lennon's "father knows best" attitude was admirable, he had a hard time staying the course with this sort of discipline. True to his nature, John quickly grew bored with baking bread and personally providing Sean's meals. He thus fell back on an excuse he would use time and again: "It was beginning to wear me out." Little by little, he ceded responsibility for Sean to Masako, the boy's nanny. He also vowed early on that the boy would never attend public school, pointing out that in many parts of the world children clung to their mothers until the age of two. John compared public school to a penitentiary, making kids conform to rules and regulations at an age when they are the most creative and expressive. As soon as Sean turned four, however, Lennon carted him off to nursery school as John wanted to get him out of the house for a while. He did, however, soon pull him out for the boy's own safety. At one point, the Lennons' bodyguard Doug MacDougall sighted a suspicious character following the child, and Yoko deemed further attendance too risky.

Strangely, Lennon once termed his relationship with Sean not really one of father and son but more of a brotherly relationship. Julian, too, has said pretty much the same.

Sean was also subjected to his father's well-known darker side. As Yoko herself stated, an enraged Lennon once kicked her in the stomach while pregnant during an explosive confrontation between them. After Sean's birth the abuse continued. Under pressure from lawsuits and mounting doubts about his career, John was insisting that Yoko vacation with him. Ono, distracted by business concerns, put off his request. One night, as the family assembled in the bedroom for their usual daily meditation, the simmering tension came to a head. As the three sat together in a triangle, Sean began fussing and crying. An irritated Lennon abruptly lost control and kicked the child. Yoko immediately swept up the screaming baby and fled to the nanny's room, screaming that her husband had gone berserk.

Similar problems persisted at feeding times. John admitted he lost his patience with his son on several occasions while giving him his bottle. Lennon would frighten the child and then beg forgiveness. On another occasion, while the family was at Montauk for a weekend, John admitted that things had gotten a little out of hand, remarking that he and his son had gone through a particularly turbulent day. A former Lennon friend and employee concurs that John, right up to the end of his life, indeed struck Sean a number of times.

These explosive episodes left a lasting impression on the young man. "I have some less than happy memories of him screaming at me, you know. He definitely had a violent temper. He would get very angry sometimes. And when he did, that soothing voice of his would become like a knife. Sometimes he would yell at me for no fucking reason, scream and shout, and I would cry hysterically."

In the early spring of 1976 Lennon received the unsettling news that James McCartney, Paul's father, had died. In the early days of the Beatles, Lennon enjoyed a real kinship with Paul's dad, sharing a dry, sarcastic humor with him. Although their relationship soured in later years due to the conservative McCartney's criticism of Lennon's overtly hippie lifestyle, John still harbored a soft spot for the old man and was upset by his passing. Paul's reaction was more muted. He continued to tour with Wings, and even chose not to attend his father's funeral. Paul's stepmother Angie later reported he also neglected to pay for the flowers he asked her to buy for his father's last rites.

Days after the elder McCartney's passing, Lennon's stepmother Pauline called with word that Fred Lennon was diagnosed with cancer of the stomach. John got on the phone to speak with Pauline and his father, but avoided the grim situation with cheery small talk.

"I read in the papers that you've finally got the baby you wanted," said Fred. "Guess what? I've got another little lad too, now. He's just two and a half."

"You cheeky old bugger," John replied. "Look, we'll get together just as soon as you're feeling better."

"It'll be great to meet you and Sean and catch up on your music, John. By the way, I loved *Imagine*."

A few hours later, a large bouquet was delivered to Fred's room with a card reading, "To Dad, get well soon. With much love from John, Yoko, and Sean."

It was Lennon's first conversation with his father in some five and a half years. Both father and son ignored this fact in the face of Fred's medical crisis. Lennon's lifelong resentment of his father is well documented. His father was pretty much a constant source of embarrassment to John. In an incident at the 1967 launch party for *Magical Mystery Tour*, Fred showed up drunk, dressed as a garbage collector in a suitably foul-smelling uniform he'd commandeered from a real-life garbage worker earlier that day. While staggering around the stage, the inebriated Fred misjudged the drop to the dance floor and took a long fall, landing flat on his face before his humiliated son and his guests.

Following a two-decade absence from his son's life, Fred intensified the ire of his famous son when he began talking to the tabloid press. He sought to defuse the tension between them during a meeting at the Scala Theater in April 1964. It was the first time they were face-to-face since the ill-fated launch party. A wary John, lying on a couch, asked his father, "What do you want then?"

His father replied, "I don't want anything. Certainly not to jump on the bandwagon, no matter what you've heard. I just want to make it clear there's no truth in the stories the papers are running about me. I felt I had to see you to get things straightened between us. Do you remember anything at all about the time we spent together when you were small?"

"Not really. Although I vaguely remember being in Blackpool with you. When would that have been?"

According to Fred's account of the meeting, John was happy to hear him out. They shared memories and agreed to "let bygones be bygones."

But Fred soon blundered again. He made a record titled *That's My Life*, and timed its release to coincide with the release date of John's *In My Life*, due in stores on December 31, 1965. An angry Brian Epstein promptly squashed the single. John was angry, too. Late one night when Fred called on him at Weybridge following the attempt to release the record, his son greeted him by snarling "Fuck you!" and summarily slammed the door in his face.

An entry in Fred's diary asserts that John wanted him to stay at his place in Kenwood, and later offered to pay his expenses for a flat in Kew Gardens, Surrey. Pete Shotton, for one, contradicts this claim, and accuses Lennon's father of being a rank opportunist. Furthering the tensions between father and son, Fred allegedly made a pass at Cynthia, prompting Lennon to escort his father out of his home. Later, when the bad feelings between them lessened, John purchased a £15,000 house for his troublesome dad, and provided a £30-per-week allowance.

Fred still couldn't leave well enough alone. He proposed to write an autobiography detailing his past with Julia and John. When John learned of his intentions, the relationship took a nasty turn. Fred and his young bride Pauline went to visit his son at Tittenhurst Park. It was John's thirtieth birthday, October 9, 1970, but it was hardly the loving reunion Fred anticipated. Pauline remembers, "The John we had known a couple of years ago was now unrecognizable. He sported a fiery red beard reminiscent of his mother's coloring, which gave him the appearance of a fierce and primitive warrior and made our birthday gift of aftershave laughably inappropriate. His jaw was clenched with grim determination, and behind his granny glasses the pupils of his eyes were contracted and staring. We had the impression he was heavily stoned, maybe even on heroin, which he admitted to sniffing occasionally at that time, when he was in real 'pain.'"

John went on the attack immediately: "I'm cutting off your money and kicking you out of the house. Get out of my life and off my fucking back!"

Before the shocked Fred had a chance to respond, his son began an explosive tirade: "Have you any idea what I've been through because of you? Day after day in therapy, screaming for my daddy, sobbing for you to come home. What did you care, away at sea all those years?

"Look at me! I'm bloody mad, *insane*! I'm due for an early death like Hendrix or Joplin, and it's all your goddamn fault. Do you know what it does to a child to be asked to choose between his parents? Do you know how it tears him apart, blows his bloody mind? You call yourself a father? You think that screwing some bird gives you the right to call yourself a father? You don't know the meaning of the word. You've treated me like shit, just like all the others. You've ripped me off, the whole fucking lot of you!"

Fred tried to calm his angry son. "Okay, John, I admit I was partly to blame and I do understand your feelings."

"How the hell can you possibly understand how I feel? How would you feel if you'd had nothing from your father all your life?"

Lennon caught sight of his tiny half-brother David, cowering behind his mother and frightened by the loud exchange.

"How the hell do you think he'd feel? Lock him away from his parents and ordinary human beings and see how he'll end up. He'll end up a raving lunatic just like me!"

As Fred moved to rise from the table, John lunged forward and grabbed his jacket, his face only inches from his father's. "As for your life story, you're never to write anything without my approval. And if you tell anyone what happened here today, I'll have you killed! Do you know what I'll do then? I'll have you cased up in a box and dumped in the middle of the ocean, twenty, fifty, or perhaps you would prefer a hundred-fathom deep?"

Pauline Lennon, watching the horrifying scene, later commented, "He spoke these words slowly and deliberately, as if he had been rehearsing them for a long time. And from the expression of malicious glee which lit up his face, it was as if he was actually taking part in the murder as he spoke."

Following the incident, Lennon stopped sending his father money, but later relented, giving him a meager £500 in exchange for his promise never to discuss their relationship with the press.

John also maintained the payments for his father's new three-story home in Brighton. When John descended the stairs to greet his father during that explosive visit, a grim-faced Yoko stood by his side. Perhaps she engineered the hostile exchange by fueling his anger toward his father. Ono almost certainly regarded Fred as a pest intent on bleeding his wealthy son. Or perhaps she saw him as an obstacle between the course she was setting for John and the family. Whatever her motivations, one thing was clear: she did not assume the role of peacemaker. John never saw his father again.

Upon Fred's death on April 1, 1976, John sent a lavish wreath and offered to pay for the cost of his cremation and funeral, but Pauline declined the offer. Fred had asked her to see that his son received a copy of his autobiography as well as a final letter after his death. She forwarded the memoirs to John at the Dakota along with the following letter, which Fred had written in 1971.

Dear John,
   By the time you read this I will already be dead, but I hope it will not be too late to fill in the gaps in your knowledge of your old man, who has caused you such distress throughout your life.

Despite your undoubted talents memories of your childhood appear to be non-existent, and so I hope reading my story will help you to establish what really happened in those early years. Of course, your only source of information has been your Aunt Mimi, who for reasons best known to herself refrained from telling you anything about me. Consequently, as in Hunter Davies' biography of the Beatles, it wasn't so much what was said about me, but rather, left unsaid, that caused you so much embarrassment and pain.

Since last we met on the occasion of your thirtieth birthday, I have been haunted by the image of you screaming for your daddy and it is my sincere hope that when you have read this, you will no longer bear me any malice. Perhaps the revelations in my life story may bring you a clearer picture of how fate and circumstance control so much of our lives and therefore must be considered in our judgment of one another.

Until we meet again, some time, some place,

Your father,
Freddie Lennon

John's favorite Aunt Elizabeth died shortly after Fred. Lennon had spent many happy school holidays in Edinburgh under the watchful eye of this good-natured woman, whom he knew as "Mater." She had opened her home to John, and provided an atmosphere of stability in his otherwise unsettled world. Some of Lennon's fondest memories stemmed from his time with her, and of playing with her son Stan* in the Scottish countryside.

John's grieving was interrupted when he flew to Los Angeles to help Ringo with his *Rotogravure* album. Upon his arrival he went into the studio to work on a song he had written for Starr, "Cookin' in the Kitchen of Love." He also played piano on the track. This mediocre effort would stand as John's final commercial recording for the next four years.

During this time there was increasing talk of a Beatles reunion, sparked by the California entrepreneur Bill Sargent's staggering $50 million offer for the group to perform a single concert on July 5th at Montreal's Olympia Park. Other offers soon followed. Promoter Stan Bernstein published an open letter in the *New York Times* urging the

---

*After the Beatles' first hit, John bought Stan a service station in Scotland which he happily runs to this day. In early 1997 he published in the *London Sunday Times* several private family letters John had written home during the mid-seventies.

Beatles to "rescue the world from famine, war and natural disasters." Part of it read: "Let the world smile for one day. Let us change the headlines from gloom and hopelessness to music and life, and a worldwide message of peace. You are among the very few who are in a position to make the dream of a better world come together in the hearts of millions in just one day."

Both George and John were irritated by the pressure. Harrison termed the *Times* letter "sick," and Lennon called the proposal "Jewish schmaltz, showbiz and tears, dropping on one knee like Al Jolson." When asked why he wouldn't reunite for a charitable cause, Lennon erupted, "I don't want anything to do with benefits. I have been benefited to death. I am not going to get locked into the business of saving the fucking world on stage!"

Upon his return to New York, Lennon found his wife unexpectedly indifferent to the controversy. The final hearing in John's immigration case was approaching, and though he'd won his deportation battle in 1975, his application for permanent residence was still undecided. There was a slim chance a judge could rule against his effort to become a U.S. citizen. From Yoko's point of view it wasn't really about John at all. In light of her growing role in the Lennon financial empire, Ono figured all eyes would be on her; therefore it was vital to portray herself as a savvy business dynamo. Frankly, Ono wanted to get her edgy husband out of her way so that she could concentrate on preparing for the all-important hearings. Lennon, with his usual complacency, was content to avoid the entire situation by visiting the family's shore retreat at Montauk.

On the home front the marriage was not going well at all. John was growing more estranged from Yoko. Where once the couple had shared common interests in art, music, and social causes, there was now a gulf of indifference between them. Having a child together had failed to bind them. Theirs was a marriage adrift. Lennon spoke of the claustrophobic tension in their home: "We get so on top of each other in the Dakota. It really isn't like a ten-room apartment, you know; it's more like three. Sean has his room, we have the bedroom, and then there's the kitchen. I can go up on the roof but there's so much fuckin' pollution and everything."

The Lennons were clashing with each other on a daily basis. John's temper erupted over little things, like who was first to see the mail, or his paranoia regarding what Yoko was telling Masako in Japanese. Their increasingly polarized relationship went from fireworks to icy silence. John remarked dourly, "We just sit around waiting for the next emergency to give us an excuse to talk to each other again. Then we pretend nothing's happened."

John Green noticed the growing tension. Lennon was experiencing wide mood swings from mischievous mirth to desolate depression. Favorite topics of conversation were no longer brought up and John rarely spoke of either composing or playing music.

Lennon spent the better part of the next two months banished to Montauk. These were peaceful days for the troubled musician. He passed the time in meditation, often on the limb of a favorite tree, or walking silently along the shore. Once again, he engaged in past-life regression via hypnosis. During one session he found himself taking a ride in a stagecoach. Another time he found himself back in the Middle Ages, romancing a young maiden.

While at Montauk Lennon introduced Sean to the ocean. Like his father and grandfather before him, the youngster took naturally to the water, much to John's delight. Sean was teething at this time, and his discomfort was a problem for his father. He was also rather precocious. By the age of nine months he was talking nonstop.

But as his time at Montauk passed, Lennon grew restless, morose, and lonely. He slept too much and ignored his diet. To divert himself, John played a memory game. He would repeat the events of the day, recalling them in his mind, and would even jot down the times he engaged in these exercises. His purpose was to gain insight into how the senses determine and shape experience; he concluded that experience was tinted by a subtle blend of perception and emotion.

Lennon's boredom, however, was broken by a visit from the Boyles. They joined him for long strolls along the shore, enjoyed a refreshing swim, and dined at a place called Grossman's.

By June 10th John was looking forward to Yoko's arrival. The pair walked along the beach with Sean, and enjoyed a nude swim at dawn. Their idyllic interlude, though, was short-lived. One night Yoko dreamed that Sean was thirsty, driving her out of bed to awaken Masako. The nanny confessed to feeding the baby fish, despite the Lennons' instructions to the contrary. That night no one got back to sleep.

John's great hope that he and Yoko might rekindle the passion in their marriage met with disappointment. She was too distracted by business to give him the attention he craved. Yoko returned to Manhattan soon after her arrival, pulled back to the city by problems with her legal team. She was also spending a lot of time consulting with Charlie Swan on a host of metaphysical matters. Ono returned to the Dakota on June 16th, a mere six days after her arrival at Montauk, claiming she had to settle a business dispute. John and Yoko's fairy-tale romance was dead. The facade was maintained only for the sake of appearance.

Soon after Yoko's departure a bizarre episode unfolded. On the night of June 19th, a frightening stranger broke into the Montauk retreat, waking the stunned occupants and sending Sean into hysterics. The following morning the man returned bearing a cryptic warning from someone calling himself "Juga Santana." A shaken Lennon feared the madman would return, and he was right. Six days later, the intruder came back, and John fled Montauk, taking Masako and Sean with him.

As the summer began, Lennon received some good news. The Morris Levy case was settled. The second trial, which began in January, dragged on for months. Lennon was summoned to several depositions. His attorney Jay Bergen categorized Levy's $42 million action as absurd and disorganized. His countersuit, in which Lennon was joined as a plaintiff by Capitol EMI, asked for reimbursement of lost income, as well as damages for harm done to John's professional reputation.

The proceedings got off to a contentious start. Levy's lawyer accused John of trying to play to the court by toning down his appearance. "Isn't it a fact, Mr. Lennon, that you cut your hair solely for the purposes of this trial?"

"Rubbish," Lennon responded. "I cut it every eighteen months!"

In fact however, John Green instructed John on this very point, telling him to get his hair cut and put on a conservative business suit. He complied with the former suggestion but rebelled at the latter, sporting a necktie with an odd spiderweb design by way of protest.

John was so exasperated by Levy's lawsuit that he even used "black magic" against his adversary: he placed Levy's name on a slip of parchment inside a raw cow tongue, wrapping it up and securing it with several long skewers. Each day he chanted a mantra for the purpose of encouraging his foe to "see the light." Clearly, John's penchant for magical thinking was rapidly taking over his troubled life.

The case turned on a crucial demonstration of evidence. When both versions of the album were played in court, it was apparent that Lennon's recording was of superior quality. The judge remarked, "I don't think there is any comparison. *Rock 'n' Roll* is much clearer. The voice was very poor and indistinct on *Roots*. It was almost hidden there. I could not tell it was John Lennon singing or anyone singing. It was simply a voice."

Following nearly a year of testimony and 2,200 pages of court documents, Lennon was awarded $109,700 for lost royalties and $45,000 for damage to his reputation. He would later remark, "All this trouble because I got bored after *Mind Games* and wanted to play some good old rock 'n' roll like when I was a kid." Judge Thomas Griesa stated, "I am convinced Lennon has a career whose balance is somewhat more delicate than other artists. Lennon has attempted a variety of ventures, both in popular and avant-garde music. Lennon's product tends to be somewhat more intellectual than that of other artists. What this means in my view is that Lennon's reputation and his standing are delicate matters and that unlawful interference with Lennon in the way that Levy and the *Roots* album accomplished must be taken seriously."

The finding established an important precedent: it helped elevate a rock musician to artistic status, and secured Lennon's ownership over the product he created. John had stood up for himself, providing a glimpse of his old fire. "They didn't think I'd show or that I'd fight. They thought I'd just settle, but I won't."

Lennon received even better news on July 27th. In a tiny hearing room at the offices of the Immigration and Naturalization Service, Ono's pit-bull preparation paid off. She brought an impressive array of celebrities to the hearing, including John Cage and Geraldo Rivera, to testify as character witnesses. Gloria Swanson, the actress-turned-anti-sugar crusader, spoke of Lennon's role in promoting healthy food habits. Norman Mailer praised his artistic contributions and commented sardonically: "He is one of the great artists of the Western world. I've always thought it was a terrible shame that we had to lose T. S. Eliot and Henry James to England, and only got Auden back."

When the judge asked the artist about his future plans, Lennon replied simply, "I hope to continue living here with my family and make music."

The judge announced his decision to applause in the courtroom: "I find Mr. Lennon statutorily eligible for permanent residence."

At the follow-up press conference Lennon waved his "blue" Green Card and exulted, "It's great to be legal again. I want to thank the Immigration Service for finally seeing the light of day. As usual, there is a great woman behind every idiot. I feel overwhelmed."

Asked why it was so important that he live in America, John replied, "I have a love for this country. If it were 2,000 years ago, we'd all want to live in Rome. This is Rome now!"

Immediately following the immigration battle things returned to normal. Yoko dispatched John to the family home on Long Island and turned her attention to the next fight: ousting financial adviser Michael Tannen, whose six-month tenure was merely a transition to ease Ono into full command of the Lennon empire. During this trip Julian came for a visit, but it was more of a trial than a pleasure for the beleaguered father. John also spent a few days in Boston visiting a friend.

Once the weather turned cold, Lennon returned to the Dakota, much to Yoko's dismay. Now that her husband was free to leave American soil and be assured of re-entry without problems, Ono sent him on a Far East trip that would keep him out of her way for the month of October. Yoko claimed it would rid John of his "bad karma" and end his string of misfortunes. She had discovered an Asian philosophy called katu-tugai, espoused by Manhattan restaurant owner Takashi Yoshikawa. The system combined numerology with cartography. It advanced the notion that traveling in a westerly direction ensured good luck. That dubious tenet, coupled with John's astrological chart, convinced Yoko that Hong Kong was the target city for John. Pete Shotton, however, disagreed with Yoko's plan. How could John "reset his cosmic clock," as Pete called it, by being banished to a faraway port? Shotton, for one, felt that it was Yoko Ono who was the source of her husband's so-called bad karma.

Yoko made things even harder on her neurotic, reclusive husband by insisting that he make the trip alone. That proposition left John paralyzed with fear. He hadn't done anything for himself since before Beatlemania. The reluctant world traveler and seasoned activist didn't even know how to check himself into a hotel or ring for room service. "The public doesn't understand the pain of being a freak," he lamented.

Getting off the plane in Hong Kong, Lennon might just as well have been stepping onto another planet. Hunkered down in his suite at the Mandarin Hotel, Lennon didn't dare venture out for some three days, instead taking solace in Scotch and Coke. He found a way to cope with his paranoia with yet another mind game. As he lay in the bathtub, he pictured himself peeling off his clothes, one piece at a time, envisioning each article as a disembodied personality. "I would actually lie there listening to the radio and wait till one of my other selves came up and took control. Then I would project, see it sitting in a chair or standing by the door and talking to me."

During this bizarre exercise Lennon placed his ghostly multiple personalities throughout the room like manikins dangling from hangers. The idea of the exercise was to cleanse them from his system so he might finally be rid of them. In doing so, Lennon was in such a state of mind that the slightest noise or shadow would terrify him. "I was exposing myself," he recalled, "and I was afraid that someone, that invisible, unknown someone, maybe my long-absent father, would come storming into the room and catch me and I would die of fright."

John eventually summoned the courage to test his theory. Leaving the hotel, he boarded the Star Ferry, which connected the island of Hong Kong with the mainland. A brief, early morning stroll in the mists of Kowloon, with the majestic Mount Victoria in view, reminded him of the times he spent in Scotland as a lad. In a moment of sheer exhilaration, John became convinced he had forever escaped the phantoms that haunted him all his life. He was once again the cheery John Lennon of his boyhood. "It was like a recognition," he said. "God, it's *me*! This feeling is from way, way back when. I know what the fuck I'm doing! I know who I am. It doesn't rely on any outside agency, adulation, nonadulation, achievement or nonachievement, hit record or no hit record. Or anything!"

But John's pleasant reverie came to an abrupt end. Feeling the press of the crowds, and struck by the realization that he was completely on his own, he panicked. He heard a cacophony of terrible voices in his head, and it filled him with terror. Thoroughly deflated, Lennon resigned himself to the fact that he would never kick his demons. He even went so far as to accept them as lifelong companions. "I went back for my suitcase and said to the rest of my ghosts, 'Okay, come on!' and we all went to Bangkok."

The Thai metropolis, a former playground for American military men trying to escape the brutalities of the Vietnam War, was Ono's most effective bait to lure Lennon to the East. The prospect of an open sexual market where anything was possible was far too tempting for Lennon to forgo. From his base at the landmark Oriental Hotel, overlooking the Chao Phraya River, John had easy access to the city's infamous red light district. Housed within was an unlimited selection of long-haired, hard-bodied adolescents, silent and submissive, holding up cards with their number, anxious to be selected.

Once Lennon picked two or three prostitutes, paying an absurdly low price for the opportunity, he would lead them to a room. These orgies would often include well-schooled Thai males as well. Lennon also indulged his senses in the cheap and readily available Chinese heroin and potent Thai marijuana.

Upon his return to New York, John found that his marriage had grown even more fractious. In November, Ono was preparing for the annual Apple meetings. John was under pressure from Yoko's advisers to attend the proceedings to increase her leverage. He refused. When pressed by those advisers, Lennon threw a tantrum, screaming that he was thoroughly sick of attending boring, mystifying business powwows with phony, backstabbing lawyers. Later, in 1977, Lennon admitted the real reason he refused to go: his irrational fear of Lee Eastman.

Yoko lost no sleep over John's refusal. She was quietly seething over advice that he accompany her to London. Her long hours of labor and dogged determination to rectify her lack of formal business education paid off. In light of John's abdication of any responsibility Yoko earned the right to run the business. To her closest associates, Ono expressed her opinion frankly, if brutally: "How can that oaf be so successful when I am so much more talented and educated?"

Yoko used her iron will, ability to intimidate, and sheer eccentricity to impose her will at Apple. An anonymous Lennon associate explained, "People [at Apple] could never fathom her constant references to astrology, numerology, and the tarot. It actually befuddled them. Or, conversely, made them mad. And it, therefore, gave her a great advantage. People didn't know how to react to her demands and went absolutely bonkers when she said her 'reader' told her this or that. As they subsequently lost control, she gained it. It was a very clever technique."

Clever enough to outfox even the cunning Allen Klein. After nearly four arduous years of negotiation, Ono's intervention finally helped to engineer a settlement of $5 million, a paltry fraction of the $35 million he originally demanded. The deal was officially signed on January 10th after an all-night negotiating session. Klein's comment following the settlement—that Yoko had driven the talks with "Kissinger-like negotiating brilliance"—may have been a face-saving stratagem. He later called her "the most conniving person I have ever met."

Later that year, Yoko met up with another Green, Samuel Adams, a flamboyant globe-trotting art dealer. She knew him briefly in the sixties, and their paths crossed again via their mutual friend John Green. Sam Green was another person cut from the Ono mold: the black sheep from a privileged family who socialized with people like Andy Warhol, and who was fascinated by the eccentric types the artist attracted. The son of illustrious professors, Green was an ingratiating personality who sought out the company of celebrity millionaires like Cecile Rothschild and Greta Garbo.

As for Lennon, he grudgingly accepted the new adviser, but his trust was not all-encompassing. That Christmas, the ambitious art dealer did his best to win John's friendship, with Christmas gifts of brown rice and caviar, high-quality blends of tobacco and coffee, and a cache of superior Bolivian cocaine.

Late in December, Ono decided it was time she paid a visit to her family in Tokyo. The trip had little to do with missing her family. Rather, she intended to flaunt her recent victory over Allen Klein, to show her parents their prodigal daughter had finally met their exacting expectations.

In later interviews Lennon spoke with pride about visiting his wife's homeland. In private and at the time, however, it was a very different matter. His extensive preparations for the trip included yet another strict diet regimen, Japanese history studies, and a six-week, eight-hour-a-day Berlitz language course. These efforts had less to do with his anticipation of the trip and more to do with John once again bending to Yoko's demands. When she told John about her plans for the trip, he protested that he did not want to go, and resented his wife for insisting.

Lennon confided to Green that the reason he took up Japanese had nothing to do with visits to the Orient. He wanted to find out what was going on at the Dakota behind his back, and he wanted to get closer to his comely young Asian language teacher. John further confessed that he understood more Japanese than he openly admitted.

In the end, Lennon had no choice but to accompany his wife and son. But his instinctive wariness about the trip would prove sound. The monumental journey to the Orient would wrap him in yet another layer of deep paranoia that would, in less than a year's time, almost totally consume him.

TUNNEL OF LOVE $\boxed{5}$
Born Again Beatle

1977

Lennon rang in the new year of 1977 by indulging in the deadly sin of gluttony. His revelry included a party at Shun Lee Dynasty thrown by Mick Jagger, with the Boyles and pop couple Carly Simon and James Taylor, whom John would later judge as tedious dimwits.

For her part, Carly Simon found the conversation stimulating. "It was the first chance I ever had to sit close to him, study his face, and have a good talk. At midnight everybody put on goofy hats and blew noisemakers. John had on this little pointed hat that brought all his features, including his nose, into a kind of pointed focus. I was pregnant with Ben, and John began to tell me the grim tale of Yoko's problematic delivery of Sean. It took twenty minutes to tell and all the while he wore that silly hat—it would have been difficult to take anyone else but John seriously." Following the birth of Ben, the Taylors' son, the Lennons sent his parents an engraved Tiffany porringer.

As he often would at gift-giving times, Lennon passed along the gifts he had received from Sam Green that Christmas to host Mick Jagger.

The week-long partying took its toll on Lennon when he embarked on a three-day cocaine binge. He joked that Sean was in charge of weaning him off the old Devil's dandruff. Horrified at finding himself five pounds overweight at 140 pounds, Lennon turned, once again, to an all-rice diet, and trimmed down to 135 pounds, an alarming weight for his 5'11" frame.

While involved in the final negotiations of the Klein settlement, Yoko was spending long periods of time away from the Dakota. John whiled away the hours in bed, drinking coffee and smoking marijuana. Occasionally, he would shop, or have a late-night meal at a 24-hour Japanese diner. During this time John was also seeing a lot of Ringo, who was in town for the ongoing Apple dissolution negotiations.

Having recently claimed victory in her business battle with Allen Klein, Yoko launched a massive public relations campaign that included a dialogue with Vice President-elect Walter Mondale, whom she reached through her contacts with the Japanese media. She also sought an invitation to the inauguration of newly elected President Jimmy Carter. Although she waited until just three days before the event to try to get a seat, she was successful—thanks to the maneuvering of Sam Green. Through his network of contacts Green managed to reach the producer, Robert Lipton. Once Lipton learned the Lennons were interested in attending, the necessary arrangements were quietly made.

In the days before the inauguration, Yoko and John traversed Manhattan searching out the perfect wardrobe for the event. She finally settled on a Bill Blass strapless gown and a pink Halston frock topped by a full-length fox wrap. Lennon then spent several thousand dollars on accessories for his wife.

The Lennons caught the very last flight out of New York to Washington for the Inaugural Ball, which was held at the John F. Kennedy Center for the Performing Arts. Because their arrival was delayed, John groused about having to forgo a nap at the Watergate Hotel, going straight to the event instead. After it was over, the Lennons went to the Lion D'Or, where they partied with Jack Nicholson, Warren Beatty, and John's old friend and foil Muhammad Ali. The relationship between John and Ali went way back to 1964, when the great fighter met the Beatles in Miami while they were on tour. As John climbed into the ring for some publicity shots, Ali needled Lennon, "Hey, you're not as stupid as you look!" John, unintimidated, shot back, "No, but you are."

The fact that he was at an important national event, however, didn't mean that John was going to deny himself. Plied with wine, cigarettes, and cocaine, Lennon enjoyed the festivities surrounding the inaugural, but later noted in his diary that he was on the verge of exhaustion.

Dressed in a dashing black cape, his hair swept back elegantly, Lennon made a dramatic entrance at the inaugural. But his introduction to President-elect Carter was a disappointment. "Hi, I'm John Lennon. You may remember me. I'm an ex-Beatle." Carter merely nodded politely and quickly moved on. Naturally, Lennon was hurt by the new president's mechanical reaction.

Lennon's excitement during the trip to Washington was followed by a deep winter funk, broken only occasionally by dinners with the Leroys, the Boyles, or Sam Green. In his diary John noted a chance meeting with author Peter Benchley, and being pleasantly surprised by a visit from Beatles producer George Martin.

With Yoko's birthday approaching, John began searching for a diamond. He had Green arrange for several fine stones to be delivered to the Dakota, and eventually settled on an exquisite light blue gem, which cost $11,000.

In February the Lennons spent a few days at George Macuinas's home in the Berkshire area of Massachusetts. Macuinas, Ono's dear friend from her days as a starving artist, was in poor health.

Despite enjoying himself in New England, John lamented in his diary about the unwise interlude when he indulged himself, pigging out on rich food and wine. The perils of food were never far from John's weight-obsessed mind. After he and Yoko left the farm, they celebrated Ono's forty-first birthday on February 18, 1977 with breakfast in nearby Stockbridge. Later that night, they dined with the Boyles at an Italian restaurant. John's diary also noted an irritating encounter with a waiter, who drove him to distraction talking about the Beatles.

While Ono was busy in meetings at Apple, or attending to personal matters that often kept her away from the Dakota for days at a time, Lennon quietly slipped into a dark hibernation. He spent entire days in bed, blaming his ill health on sugar, wine, tobacco, and marijuana, all of which he continually vowed to give up, though he lacked the willpower to do so. He noted in his diary that he had also returned to his habit of daily masturbation. On top of his incorrigible habits, John was engaged in a near-constant war of wills with Sean. Discomforted by a bout with the flu, Sean was disturbing his father's precious sleep. John was cranky enough to wonder whether his son's behavior was the result of illness or simply his own sour mood influencing the boy.

In another diary entry, the housebound musician acknowledged falling into a deep depression in February. Ironically, at the same time he was plagued by such severe self-doubt, Lennon was being courted with generous offers to perform, produce movies, and score sound tracks. Francis Ford Coppola was one of his suitors, but Charlie Swan warned him that the director was really only looking for financing. Filmmaker Frank Perry asked John to compose the music for a futuristic project called *Time and Again*, while *Let It Be* director Michael Lindsey Hogg invited John to score film about the rock scene. Unfortunately, Lennon was at a creative standstill, and had no choice but to decline. John had all but lost his creative drive and confessed he'd sunk so low he had even become terrified of composing. It frustrated the musician to refuse promising work, but he knew he just couldn't deliver.

In the meantime, while he was mired in such creative frustration, Yoko was busy planning a trip to South America. Well aware of her keen interest in matters related to the occult, Sam Green introduced her to a *bruja* known as Lena, a woman renowned for her skill as a witch in Cartagena (the notorious Colombian drug town, where Green maintained a villa).

Accompanied by Green, Ono left on March 1st for a visit of two weeks. Lena wielded significant political power in her country. She had a look straight out of Central Casting, complete with a clubfoot and several missing teeth. When Yoko met her, she immediately presented the woman with a list of wishes, telling her, "I think you should do something for my career and my husband's separately. Then perhaps do something for our career together, but certainly not his career with anyone else." Lena dutifully cast a few spells, concocted some potions, chanted, and even danced a little jig. She then pressed Yoko to sign a contract for her services, at a fee of $60,000. The gullible Mrs. Lennon was happy to oblige. (As Fred Seaman has often noted, "Yoko loves to be ripped off.")

During her absence the miserable Lennon was home alone. His frazzled nerves resulted in severe stomach distress, insomnia, and a notion to do something crazy. He tried to distract himself by spending time at a bookstore or by seeing Richard Ross, who by then decided to give up his restaurant due to his illness. George Macuinas also provided some company during Yoko's absence. Unfortunately, John became ill when he sniffed some tainted cocaine, which ravaged his already fragile system for several days.

In the middle of March, Ono arrived in New York by way of Alaska, a route she had traveled at the suggestion of her "directionalist." She told John that the family curse had been lifted, an assertion Lennon gleefully accepted as gospel. He returned to his macrobiotic diet, and practiced hypnosis and other dubious self-help remedies. Armed with various rituals brought back from Colombia, Yoko had him drinking goat's milk and meditating before an array of candles and lucky charms. She convinced him that he was thus protected from all evil forces. Protected by the magic of Charlie Swan and Lena, John and Yoko felt once more invincible.

As March turned to April, John was spending more time with Sean: a carriage ride through Central Park, a puppet show one day, a trip to the circus the next. Mick Jagger occasionally accompanied them on these outings. Julian was also speaking regularly by phone to John, who noted that he was excited by the idea of buying his older son a keyboard. Lennon was also visited by Hide Kase, a charming companion who kept him in high spirits. They often spent long nights trading stories.

At home Lennon cooked and baked, everything from fresh bread and apple pie to chestnut tempura. He returned to his daily Hatha yoga practice, and managed to refrain from marijuana and coffee, substituting the latter with a caffeine-free beverage called "Zen coffee." Determined to quit smoking, John tried a two-month program of cigarette holders that progressively cut back on nicotine intake. His efforts once again met with abject failure.

Lennon also left the Dakota to do some furniture shopping, visiting Cafe La Fortuna on the way. One morning John went out to purchase a bouquet for their nanny Masako. As he headed toward the florist, a stranger approached him and placed a blooming shrub in his arms. John was delighted by the incident and, in a diary entry, interpreted it as a sign that he had psychic powers.

On Easter Sunday John took Yoko and Sean to a local church service. Watching *The 700 Club* (evangelist Pat Robertson's television ministry) had recently inspired Lennon to re-explore Christianity.

While viewing the Sir Grade–produced *Easter Jesus* series on Robertson's network the previous Palm Sunday, Lennon was so moved that he fell on his knees in tears, declaring himself saved.

For the next four months John *believed*. Constantly reading and re-reading the Bible, he peppered his conversation with phrases like "Praise the Lord," "Thank you, Jesus," and "Jesus saves." He even attended church meetings and took Sean to a Christian theater performance at the Riverside Church. John also tried to convert friends like Neil Aspinall and Charlie Swan, and was keenly disappointed when the tarot reader refused to embrace his new beliefs.

John became convinced he was receiving divine communication from the Lord. He called *The 700 Club* prayer line on several occasions to seek help for his failing eyesight, troubled marriage, and various addictions. Lennon even recorded a tune that he never especially liked, "Talking with Jesus," and was further inspired to compose several other unrecorded Christian songs, including a musical version of the Lord's Prayer, called simply "Amen."

Like Paul the apostle after the miracle at Damascus, Lennon perceived the world through new eyes. He sympathetically observed some poor soul pounding on the door of a Manhattan church and demanding to know why, if it was actually God's house, it was locked. John prayed for forgiveness when he stepped on insects or snapped at the help. His new faith, however, did help him overcome his chronic agoraphobia. He and Sean took a ferry to Liberty Island and went to the zoo, where his son entertained fellow visitors by spontaneously joining a dance troupe during its public performance. John became convinced that Jesus was personally protecting Sean: the Lord kept him safe while he was in the swimming pool, and watched over the family's continuing health and prosperity. As John now saw it, Christ's benevolence extended to everything from Yoko's cooking to a sunny day for a picnic.

Not surprisingly, Lennon's conversion concerned Yoko. At first she refused to even discuss the subject. She worried that John's new faith would clash with her own ideas about spiritualism and thus threaten her iron hold over him. John was now condemning Yoko's interest in the occult and encouraging her to do the same. Her resistance to his efforts triggered several passionate arguments between them. John complained when Yoko refused to watch Pat Robertson, Billy Graham, or Jim and Tammy Faye Bakker on television, and speculated that satanic forces were preventing her from receiving the truth.

Of course, Ono knew her husband well. "If a monk tells him about his religion," she later commented, "John's going to become the most devout student of this monk. The next day another monk will come with a completely different theory, and he's going to be susceptible to him as well. John's always looking for a guru."

Realizing this, Ono reversed her strategy. Typically, John's "next big thing" flamed brilliantly before suddenly burning out. She let his infatuation run its course, and then slowly began to broach the subject, even encouraging discussion. Through extended conversations that sometimes lasted until dawn, careful to outwardly recognize many of his points, Ono gradually undermined his waning belief with her own clever counterpoints. Lennon's Christian conversion simply faded away in time: "The seed that falls on rocky terrain."

Even as he espoused his evangelical beliefs, John was practicing seemingly antithetical rituals: performing South American magical rites, reading his horoscope, celebrating Buddha's birthday, and complaining when Charlie Swan traveled to Washington, D.C. at a time when the former Beatle wanted to confer with him.

Moreover, Lennon wasn't always behaving in a strictly Christian manner. Unable to curb his violent temper, he would often erupt at Masako and lash out at Yoko. When friends Gloria Swanson and Bill Duffy, who stood by him during his immigration crisis, asked him to do a minor favor, lending his talents to a musical performance they were producing, he coldly turned them down.

His troubles too with Lee Eastman were escalating. With Allen Klein gone from the picture, the ambitious lawyer was more determined than ever to run Apple's affairs. He was throwing his weight around at Apple meetings and doing his best to influence the course of John and Paul's company, Maclen Music. With his father-in-law leaning on him, McCartney was calling Lennon almost daily. During one particularly tense day, in the course of a heated argument, John screamed at his former partner to go fuck himself.

Muhammad Ali was also calling, which added to Lennon's irritation and concerned Yoko. After her experiences with John's foray into Christianity, she was worried that he would find yet another a father figure in the charismatic boxing legend. Yoko refused to put

Ali's calls through, telling him that Lennon was tied up in the studio. (Around this time, Ono's interference was also something Julia Baird bitterly complained about.) Ali, not used to being ignored, dispatched curt telegrams to both Lennon and Ringo Starr, berating both. John was livid.

Lennon's short-term fascination with Christianity was also undercut by meeting a pair of missionaries from Norway. He joined them for tea and accompanied them on church picnics and birthday parties. The young men prayed on John's behalf for a cure for his addiction to nicotine. But the friendship rapidly deteriorated when Lennon questioned them on their literal biblical interpretations concerning the earth's creation and the Garden of Eden.

During one of these conversations, Yoko was present. Sensing an opening, she confronted the two with questions regarding the divinity of Jesus Christ, which was for Lennon a key issue as he had always felt that Jesus was not really the son of God. Their answers to Yoko's inquiry disappointed him. Lennon later complained that he'd never met a Christian who wasn't actually a sanctimonious hypocrite.

In late spring Lennon was preparing for yet another trip to Japan. The last time John had been to Tokyo was in March of 1971. His first meeting with the Onos was strained and awkward. He had done his best to impress them by drinking tea and sitting *seizan* style for hours at a time, but Yoko's parents remained uncomfortably cool toward him.

As departure time approached, Lennon dreaded the trip. Tense and anxious, he lashed out at Yoko over, among other things, the purchase of a new Rolls-Royce. Perhaps the real source of his anxiety could be traced to his assumption of the role of househusband, a factor that he felt contributed to the widening gulf between them. He accused Yoko of skipping off to corporate meetings to discuss big deals while John played baby-sitter all day.

John was also feeling very competitive toward his old partner Paul McCartney. Stung by Paul's success in acquiring the rights to Broadway musicals like *Annie*, and the huge profits they were bringing him, John even refused to attend a showing of the film *The Buddy Holly Story* because Paul owned the rights to Holly's music. "I wouldn't pay one dime I thought would go into that guy's pocket," he snarled. "Paul's just trying to buy up all the music in New York."

Yoko, meanwhile, was feeling some competitive impulses of her own. During the early months of 1977, Julian was phoning the Dakota on a regular basis, talking to his father for hours at a time. The return of Julian, even if it was merely telephonic, alarmed Ono. John had also been talking with his sisters Julia and Jacqui, as well as Aunt Mimi, Uncle Norman, and cousins Leila and David. Perhaps she feared that extensive contact with John's Liverpool relations might somehow undermine her hold over her fragile husband. All this contact with the past, coming as it did during the couple's continuing marital woes, made Yoko very uneasy. She finally questioned him about the wisdom of these overseas communications, which angered him immensely. Then when Cynthia began to call, Yoko really went to work. By targeting John's suspicion of Cynthia's motives, Ono managed to convince him that perhaps the Liverpool clan had ulterior motives after all. Her gambit worked. Not only was Cynthia cut off, but Julian's calls soon tapered off as well.

Mick and Bianca Jagger hosted a farewell party for the departing Lennons at Halston's. According to Lennon's diary, Ringo showed up looking bloated and unwell. John found the party tedious. He, Yoko, Ringo, and Starr's friend Nancy left before Bianca arrived. The four-some went to the Plaza, where they met Anthony Perkins and Marlon Brando. To John's dismay, Brando took the opportunity to suggest to John and Ringo that it was high time for a Beatles reunion.

At the end of May, the Lennons left New York for Japan. Since Yoko's fortune-tellers advised John to travel "directionally," she plotted a circuitous and tiring week-long journey via Alaska and Hong Kong. She herself left five days later. Despite the time and distance Lennon enjoyed the first leg of the trip to Anchorage, perhaps because of Sean's good mood. But the boy's spirits soon faded. The noise in the plane and the clouds of cigar smoke that filled the cabin upset the restless toddler. During one wearying leg of the long trip Sean's energy suddenly deserted him. Spent, he plopped down in his father's lap, directly into a plate of creamed chicken, and fell into a deep sleep.

Lennon checked into the Mandarin Hotel upon his arrival in Hong Kong. It was the same hotel he had stayed in the previous year. But unlike the frenzied, paranoid atmosphere that plagued the last visit, John felt relaxed and enjoyed his stay. Sean took an immediate interest in the Asian metropolis, and provided his father with delightful companionship as they strolled the bustling streets, sight-seeing and patronizing the exotic restaurants. The two awoke at dawn to watch the sunrise on the pier, after which they rode an aerial tram, and then boarded the Star Ferry to the mainland. Clutching his "Suzy Hong" doll, Sean toured the Tiger Balm Gardens with delight. Tethered securely to his dad by a harness, the handsome boy scrambled up the man-made rock formations, and posed for snapshots on statues of mythical Chinese figures.

A few days after their arrival John had a surprise visitor, David Bowie. Bowie had flown east to visit Iggy Pop in response to a dare from John. Like two sailors on leave, the pair dined on Peking duck, patronized a seedy topless dive called the Sea Palace, and took a swim in the South China Sea. Bowie left a message for Lennon afterwards, praising the food, criticizing the nudie show, and reminding John he had picked up the tab.

The blissful days ended abruptly with Yoko's arrival. The family went to Tokyo, where things took a turn for the worse when they couldn't check into the Okura Hotel, their first choice, and were forced to seek humbler accommodations at the Pukudaya Inn. At one point Yoko urged John to join her as she "borrowed" a pair of shoes from another guest to make her escape and avoid being spotted by the reporters camped out near the inn.

Unlike his wife, Lennon enjoyed the quiet hotel. The fact that an attractive young masseuse worked there did not escape his notice.

Every day John went to the local fish market and feasted on the rich variety of seafood on offer. His daily routine included baths, sometimes two a day, and an invigorating shiatsu massage. Even the arrival of his energetic young nieces did nothing to dim his mood. Reiko, Akako, and Takako, the children of Yoko's brother Kaye, were accompanied by their guardian, a woman Lennon referred to as "Grandma," who took to Sean immediately. The group moved to the inn, tramped along with John on sight-seeing excursions, dined out on his tab, and spent a great deal of their famous uncle's money.

Lennon's sense of well-being ended abruptly when the group moved to the Okura's Royal Suite. His arrival there was tense because Yoko had called a press conference without telling him. When John stubbornly refused to appear, Yoko panicked, and it was only through extensive pleading that she got him to make a statement. A thoroughly embarrassed John, put on the spot by Yoko's promise of a big exclusive, was forced to announce plans for his Broadway musical, a show which would never materialize. Ono's hopes for a grand homecoming backfired, and the Lennons lost significant prestige in the eyes of the savvy Japanese press.

The incident set a sour tone for the remainder of the visit. When Yoko phoned home to request an audience with her mother Isoko, and her ailing father Eisuke, convalescing from a stroke, her mother coolly informed her that they had made other plans for the summer and wouldn't be home until August. The substitute reception party of the "Japan-nieces," as John referred to them, would have to suffice.

The tensions of the visit frayed the nerves of the always hypersensitive Lennon. He reacted by locking himself in his hotel room, staring at the television, or listening to American radio while wolfing down Mars candy bars. His behavior was somewhat understandable. Longing for home, at times near tears, he didn't know the language, didn't understand the culture, and was frequently left to his own devices when Yoko went off by herself to look up relatives and old schoolmates. In addition, he resented having his young relatives dumped on him with the expectation that he would pay for all their incidentals.

Lennon's emotional distress finally shot to the surface when he shattered a glass one day in a restaurant.

John's unhappiness was intensified by several frightening nightmares. Lennon also battled frequent headaches and was beset by nausea and vomiting, which he blamed on the high sodium content of the food. He was also upset when Yoko announced she might be pregnant, though it proved to be a false alarm. Under the strain his weight fell to less than 130 pounds, causing him to look disturbingly thin.

John also felt hounded by the Japanese who gawked at him and by the paparazzi who pursued him. He complained that he felt like a tourist attraction, "part of a fucking parade." At one point the photographers provoked him to the point that he charged a group of them. In another incident, while shopping at an antique weaponry shop, Lennon attacked a photographer, slapping the camera from his hand.

Increasingly on the defensive, John began to lash out at the Japanese people, crudely parodying their speech and appearance. The worst incident occurred at an exclusive Tokyo restaurant. "You know, what they say about the Japanese is right. They do all look alike!" he bellowed to the stunned clientele. "What is the preferred term for you fuckers? 'Nip' or 'gook'?" A mortified Yoko worried that his outburst, should her parents learn of it, might give them an excuse to disinherit Sean.

The boy's sunny disposition darkened in response to his father's mood. John again laid the blame on the sodium in his food. He also asserted that Sean, formerly a strict vegetarian, now ate meat simply to spite him. The willful youngster responded by stubbornly refusing to eat anything but melon. He also took a nasty fall, slicing his lip "on purpose," according to Lennon. Nanny Masako's growing displeasure added to the atmosphere of tension surrounding the family. At various times during the trip she threatened to quit.

On several occasions, Sean's constant crankiness wore on John until he finally lashed out and struck the child, even kicking him in a restaurant. Following these outbursts, John tormented himself, praying that Sean would forgive him. Yoko, at her wit's end, finally encouraged John to take up cigarettes again, so desperate was she to calm his frayed nerves and restore some sense of peace to the family.

The tension again reached a crisis point when Sean, unhappy that his mother refused to sing him a lullaby, exploded in a temper tantrum lasting two hours. The outburst finally woke John up. Taking a hard look at himself, he decided to make a concerted effort to try and make things better for both Sean and Yoko. He rose early for a breakfast of tea and toast before taking a relaxing bath and massage. He located an organic restaurant that served food without salt or sugar, and adopted a diet of brown rice, vegetables, and fruit. Further, he determined he would get back to his music. John bought himself a custom-made guitar, on which he began to compose a tune called "Let It Flow," about rolling rivers and thundering heavens. He ventured out more often and found another restaurant, called Daigo, that met his dietary restrictions. He even traveled to Korea on a day trip.

John attended a Father's Day celebration with the Ono family, a formal fifteen-course Japanese dinner at the stylish Orchid Room. Yoko's father and grandfather took the occasion to present John with several fine robes once belonging to the family's priests. After the meal the entire group gathered for a formal portrait.

Upon reflection, Lennon came to the conclusion he'd been too restrictive with Sean and decided to give him a little more breathing room. Together they went shopping, and took daily swims and long walks during which John allowed him to frolic in the rain and muddy his clothes. He also enrolled Sean in judo class. The combination of recreation and discipline agreed with the boy, and his mood improved greatly. While they were having lunch one day, the boy spontaneously showered John with kisses for the first time in a long while. Several diary entries note that Sean was now asking for his father constantly.

Toward the end of July, Lennon rededicated himself to his marriage. Yoko, greatly relieved, finally made love with him after a long period of abstinence. The result was that his spirits immediately lifted. The couple spent some much-needed time alone, enjoying intimate dinners, dancing, antique hunting, and playing together at a piano Ono ordered. Mrs. Lennon also managed to put down the phone, ignoring telegrams from Allen Klein and Harold Seider, and refusing to acknowledge a potential crisis brewing at Apple. Yoko's astrological chart advised her to take no action, and in the end the impending power play turned out to be only a bluff.

During this idyll, the three Lennons played games in the penny arcade, visited the Tokyo Zoo, and took long, relaxing Japanese baths together. Lennon compared it to the ultimate LSD experience. Even his sometimes bizarre and disturbing dream life grew calmer, perhaps reflecting his new self-assurance. At the time he was working on a composition called "Real Family," a tribute to his renewed commitment to his marriage. The song suggested themes that would later be at the heart of the 1980 album *Double Fantasy*. The lyrics spoke of domestic bliss, putting down roots, and revering his family as a spiritual triangle. A contented John Lennon was expressing himself more gently, though less effectively: the new work admittedly lacked the cutting, haunting, insightful poetry that arose out of his deepest pain and had long defined his artistry.

With the arrival of August, the Lennons left the city by train for the 200-mile journey north to the mountain retreat of Karuizawa, the Onos' ancestral home. Although John was expecting a lavish, traditional estate, he found instead a disappointing Japanese version of a typical American split-level home, remarking that it reminded him of his late friend Ken Dewey's place in New Paltz, New York. Still, after the bustle of Tokyo, Lennon found the quiet, misty countryside very much to his liking.

Yoko's mother, though, had yet another unpleasant surprise waiting for the Lennons. Although John and Yoko had assumed they would be guests at the family home, Isoko told them the place was now in her son Kaye's hands, and that they would have to rent it from him. He charged them an exorbitant rate despite the money John spent on his children. Mrs. Ono herself had no intention of staying in a cabin in the woods, and booked an expensive hotel room, which she charged to John's credit card.

Although he was paying for both Kaye's place and his mother-in-law's suite, John spent most of his time at the Mampei Hotel, a Westernized inn with an impressive public garden complete with several intricate pagodas. To his dismay, Lennon found he could not elude the press. He was followed day and night as he shopped and dined. As a result, he and Yoko battled over eating out in public, John preferring the privacy of the hotel. One morning John and Sean were having breakfast at the Mampei when photographers spotted them. Ever protective of his son, John angrily left, spending the rest of the day locked in his room, smoking marijuana and sulking.

Although he constantly worried about his son, John continued to take his anger out on the boy, often raging at him with little provocation. One night he screamed at Masako for having put Sean to sleep before he had a chance to reconcile with the child. Yoko finally stepped in and smoothed things over by spending more time at the house, preparing lavish meals and otherwise trying to soothe her neurotic husband.

As the novelty of being in Japan was wearing thin, John found an outlet to relieve his moodiness: bicycling. With Sean perched on a child seat on the handlebars, father and son peddled around the resort town, even in the rain. On a typical outing they would go to a nearby lake with a picturesque waterfall. Sean would delight in the natural wonder, dipping playfully into the water. Sometimes John would rent a small boat and row peacefully across the lake.

One morning after a hearty breakfast he dropped Sean off with the nanny at a playground, and then joined his mother-in-law for lunch at the hotel. Afternoons were often spent riding to favorite spots, like a Buddhist temple at the top of a mountain, or a nearby volcano whose ashes covered the ruins of an ancient city. On one of these trips John came across a rabbit hutch bearing a Japanese bunny and a Russian Blue cat, a sight Sean found mesmerizing.

Lennon enjoyed frequent dinners out with the Ono family, once even sampling turtle soup. John often joined his relatives in singing traditional songs and dancing. Sometimes Yoko, an expert cook, prepared dinner at home, reluctantly inviting her mother. One evening Mrs. Ono almost ruined the meal by pointing out to John that the seafood he was eating had been scaled while still alive. In the evenings John would curl up in bed, devouring books like *The Boys from Brazil*, *The Bell Jar*, or the *Memoirs of Marion Davies Hearst*.

At one point in the trip Lennon was in such a positive frame of mind that he shoveled out a refuse trench with Nishi Saimaru, a photographer he had enlisted to take photographs of the family during the trip.*

Not forgetting his other son, Lennon dropped a postcard to Julian in rural Wales. John expressed the usual having-a-great-time, wish-you-were-here sentiments and welcomed his firstborn to ring him if he could take time out from his busy summer schedule. Yoko, too, wished him a good holiday. John signed off by sending his love to the boy, something he always found difficult to vocalize.

In August the family's peace was shattered when Masako reported to Mrs. Ono that John and Yoko had made a very unflattering remark about Isoko. She immediately confronted her daughter, igniting a nasty blowup. Before Mrs. Ono stormed out, she threatened to disinherit Yoko. John blamed his mother-in-law's anger on envy of her daughter. He also felt she was trying to undermine the Lennons' marriage. In the aftermath of the explosive incident Yoko rebuked Masako harshly. The nanny, forced to apologize, did so reluctantly.

Only days later, Lennon learned that Elvis Presley had died. Publicly, John appeared unsympathetic, stating, "I never wanted to be a forty-year-old who virtually died singing his golden oldies in a tatty jumpsuit in Vegas. Don't try and sell 'em on the myths of these people. *Elvis is dead*. It's very unhealthy to live through *anybody*." Pri-

---

*Nishi's wonderful photographs of the Lennons were later published in Japan. So rare was the elegantly designed paperback that when it was first imported to the States copies were going for well over $100 among collectors. A less expensive U.S. edition was later released.

vately, he grieved, sending a huge bouquet of white gardenias to Presley's Graceland grave site. Presley's passing wore on John for weeks afterward, leaving him in a foul mood. In response to his sadness and the uneasiness caused by the fight with Isoko, Lennon went on a cocaine binge, which soon made him more irritable than ever.

Lennon's diaries reflect that he suddenly felt lonely and defeated once again. He noted his unhappiness even as he was outfitting Sean in tennis whites for a match with the child of the CEO of Coca-Cola. Dressed in an immaculate linen suit, Lennon feigned at playing the rich man on holiday, later making the afternoon rounds with Yoko for tea or picnics with her former classmates. Afterwards, he reported he suffered head-crushing hangovers from drinking heroic amounts of sake during these encounters.

Lennon's vivid dreams grew darker still. In one nightmare Lennon—caught in a melee with Paul McCartney and George Harrison—knifed a young lady. While Paul managed to escape, John was hauled off to a Victorian-style asylum, where he was certain he'd be drugged senseless.

Lennon's mood soon deteriorated to the point that he would no longer accompany Ono on her family get-togethers. Instead he became a virtual hermit, retreating to his room, sleeping his days away, mindlessly standing at the window watching the rain. Once Yoko found him staring off into space groaning that there was no place he could go where he didn't feel abandoned and isolated—a bitter legacy from his troubled youth, when he was at the mercy of the often needlessly cruel Mimi.

His friends too were no help. In the *London Observer*, Mick Jagger gave an interview that drove a wedge between the two men. "I like John very much, but he's hiding behind Sean"; "*Yoko has him all locked up*"; "Come on John, get out of there!" In the wake of his sadness and Jagger's attack, a sullen and disheartened Lennon phoned psychic Swan and reported, "I'm a dead man, Charlie. Yoko killed me, this place killed me, the damned Japan-nieces killed me!"

Ono, fearing her husband was nearing a serious breakdown, realized she must take quick action. A suggestion that they produce an erotic Japanese film piqued John's interest for a moment, but what he really needed was a male friend to spend time with. Yoko called on

Sam Green, who was happy to enjoy Yoko's hospitality at the luxurious Tawarya Inn. Green also saw the trip as an opportunity to do some business with the wealthy Japanese, who seemed to love everything American.

Admittedly Green's arrival did lift John's mood, and even Sean seemed to enjoy his company. The trio toured the resort town together, taking in the sights. They patronized the sushi bar across the street from the Mampei, plus a number of restaurants. Lennon even abandoned his usual strict macrobiotic regimen for a hamburger.

Green's visit soon came to an end. John turned once again to cocaine to get him through the day. He kept company with a stray kitten he rescued, nursing it to health, and even occasionally taking it to bed with him.

Yoko, noting John's continued loneliness, summoned Elliot Mintz. The Lennons first met Mintz in 1972 when he interviewed Ono for BBC radio. Mintz, however, fit Ono's ideal of the delicate, elfin "yesmen" she preferred in her inner circle of loyal confidants. (Mintz's acceptance in the Lennon circle was not absolute: May Pang disliked Mintz, whom she derided as obsessive and boastful of his access to the reclusive Lennon.) As for John, his "friendship" with Mintz was superficial at best. Often, when he was drunk, he would maliciously refer to Mintz as a "fucking Jew bastard."

But John was desperate for a familiar face. In fact he was so enthusiastic about Elliot's impending arrival he decided to give him a traditional Japanese welcome.

John and Yoko, both adorned in native costumes, made a stunning welcoming party. Lennon had freshly washed his long locks in a special Japanese herbal bath which made them shine. He looked like a noble samurai warrior in a spectacular antique kimono. According to a duly impressed Mintz, his friend was the picture of exuberance and well-being.

Energized by the arrival of his companion, Lennon spent that first overcast afternoon with Mintz at the Mampei, treating him to a meal, before taking him to the Onos' Karuizawa retreat in the woods. When they arrived at the family home, Lennon sat down at the piano and they all enjoyed an old-fashioned sing-along, running through classics like "As Time Goes By." John and Sean entertained the gathering with a brief song-and-dance routine.

Even Japan's rainy season couldn't dampen Lennon's renewed spirit. As a surprise a friend delivered some art materials and John set to work. He spent hours sketching his trademark doodles, including several that would later form the 1990 collection *Japan Through John Lennon's Eyes*, published posthumously. John was overjoyed to return to his artwork after so long an absence.

Mintz was there to help John free a couple of stray kittens trapped inside a wall at the hotel. Following that episode, John desired to travel, and so made a long excursion to the ancient city of Kyoto. According to Mintz, Lennon delighted in the beautiful city's Buddhist temples and Shinto shrines. The ex-Beatle, seemingly reverent, would even bow his head and fold his hands in apparent prayer. Elliot noted that Yoko, evidently less engrossed in these Eastern rites, grew restless with such displays.

Once again, Yoko turned her attention to the family business. She justified her actions after consulting with a psychic from Rome, who told her that the year would be productive and busy right up to 1978. The same psychic predicted that John's next productive phase would not begin until 1980, but that it would last for some two years.

In September the Lennons and Mintz headed back to Tokyo. This time Ono made sure the family was lodged in the spacious Presidential Suite at the Okura, a massive residence with ten private quarters and a living room so immense it served as a soccer field for John and Sean. The youngster also occupied himself by riding a motorized children's racing car down the hotel's long corridors.

According to Mintz, John, Sean, and he sang together regularly. John would pick up a guitar, and the three of them would spend hours each day singing golden oldies. Ono would always request her favorite tune, the schmaltzy "The Way We Were."

Still, not all was sweetness and light. Mintz observed that the often bad-tempered John was growing ever more unhappy over the early Tokyo autumn. John wistfully confided to Elliot that all he wanted was to be back in his comfortable bed, surrounded by his Scott amplifiers and his favorite reading material. During the course of this particular conversation Lennon took up his acoustic guitar and strummed the opening chords of "Jealous Guy." Just then an older Japanese couple strolled in, apparently unaware they were in John's private suite. The pair were not at all impressed by the entertainment. "They had a cigarette or two," says Mintz, "and I guess, because no waiter arrived, they finally looked at John, exchanged some words, and got up and left, obviously very displeased. That was John Lennon's last public performance. It wasn't the Madison Square Garden show with Elton John in 1974; it was in the Hotel Okura in Tokyo in 1977 for a select audience of three."

In October the family returned to New York, but not before a last, seemingly pointless, press conference during which a sheepish Lennon had little to say, remarking: "We've basically decided without a great decision to be with our baby as much as we can until we feel we can take the time off to indulge ourselves creating things outside the family. Maybe when he's three, four, or five, then we'll think about creating something else other than the child."

Before leaving Japan, John took his curt, humorless mother-in-law around Tokyo, struggling to impress her with his rudimentary Japanese. He showered her with presents, and even, as he put it, "hugged her once or twice." Surprisingly, Yoko was not pleased by his efforts. The way she saw it, John's display only further served to elevate her mother's status while knocking his own wife down to second best. Not to mention that her inheritance was on the line.

Late in the family's stay, Ono's younger sister Setsuko approached John for a loan. She was always favored more than Yoko because she caused no problems for her parents. She married a diplomat and entered the family banking business. John did lend her some money, noting that in the future the transaction would provide leverage with her mother when financial matters like the family will were at issue.

Yoko departed before John, taking the direct route home. She instructed him to fly a grueling 26-hour commute that took him from Hong Kong to Singapore, and from there to Dubai, then Frankfurt, and finally, New York. Lennon resigned himself to his wife's odd directional philosophy, noting in his diary that it took an equally bizarre mind-set to accept it.

While John and Elliot were staying over in Frankfurt, a humorous episode occurred. When told by the hotel that there were no vacancies, Mintz convinced Lennon to use his status as a celebrity. When he asked for two rooms, the clerk eyed him and said, "Where's Paul?" Lennon pointed to Elliot, "That's him over there!" The clerk brightened, and two rooms were immediately secured. While Mintz had a lovely suite with a sauna, Lennon was put up in a virtual broom closet! John peeked in at his companion's luxury accommodations and huffed, "What's all this?" Mintz quipped, "Well, I guess the clerk liked the fact that I wrote 'Yesterday.'"

Although the family returned to New York in time for John and Sean's birthdays, neither felt like celebrating. Sean was running a temperature, and unhappy with his substitute nanny. As for John, he was plagued by the endless Apple struggles, the overwhelming tax burdens, and the constant parade of sundry bottom-feeders ever begging for a handout. The Lennon solution was to wash it all from his system by returning to his liquid diet, along with lots of yoga and meditation, punctuated by the occasional use of cocaine. John's latest spiritual diversion was a fascination with Islam. He adopted the Muslim tradition of fasting, glorifying Allah, and constantly thanking him for his many mercies. As usual, his conversion lasted only a few frantic, over-the-top days.

When their accountant totaled the expenses of the extravagant four-month trip, the Lennons found that they had spent a staggering $700,000. Their shock was heightened when they learned that Yoko had misread the tax law, and they wouldn't be able to write off the extended excursion as a business expense. Financially strapped, they were forced to donate John's vintage, hand-painted, psychedelic Rolls-Royce from the sixties to the Smithsonian, which earned the family a $250,000 tax credit.*

In early November, Yoko received a call from her daughter Kyoko. After a brief greeting Tony got on the phone with a proposition: a visit from Kyoko in exchange for Yoko's signature on an important document for which he needed her approval. John was excited by the idea, elated by the thought of the entire family reuniting—John, Yoko, Sean, Julian, and Kyoko. A week later Kyoko called again, and John was able to chat with her. When Cox's brother Larry came to the Dakota bearing the contract, Lennon was thrilled that things were at last moving forward. To John it looked as though Yoko would finally get to see her daughter. The visit was scheduled for just before Christmas.

---

*The extravagant car was later sold to a Canadian businessman who put it on tour at state fairs throughout North America.

▲ Together in Spain, April 1971—the last tender bloom of love. From here on, John and Yoko's great love was pretty much a public charade designed to help prop up their often flickering careers. (19)

▲ The Lennons at the Cannes Film Festival in the balmy summer of 1971. (20)

▼ John at the unhappy height of his well-known heroin addiction. (21)

▲ Meeting the press at the Everson Museum, John was there to promote Yoko's fairly meaningless *This Is Not Here* exhibition of conceptual art. (22)

◀ John arriving in Syracuse, New York. (23)

▼ The Lennons sit for yet another staged photo op at the Everson Museum of Art, Syracuse, October 9, 1971. The occasion was John's thirty-first birthday. (24)

John at one of his final public appearances to promote the often abstract tenets of his peculiar ove and peace philosophy. (25)

◀ April 6, 1972: At the Record Plant for work on the enigmatic *Mind Games*, a deeply flawed effort that never really caught on with the fans and is today almost completely forgotten. (26)

▲ May Pang, Harry Nilsson, and John making trouble at the Troubadour, Los Angeles, March 3, 1974. (27, 28)

▼ Hanging out at the Troubadour. *Left to right*: John, Canadian songbird Anne Murray, Harry Nilsson, Alice Cooper, and former Monkee Mickey Dolenz. Here was an out-of-control John at his most lost and alone. (29)

▶ John and May relaxing in Florida, during one of Julian's sporadic trips to visit his troubled dad. To her credit May always encouraged the tenuous relationship between father and son. (30)

▲ A rare John and Yoko button touting their bid to fight their impending deportation. (31)

◀ Running the gauntlet of reporters during the extended hearings relating to John's complex immigration matters. (32)

▼ Putting on a brave face in light of John's pressing legal woes. New York, 1975. (33)

▲ Doctor Winston O'Boogie making the
scene at the Grammys, March 1, 1975. (34)

▲ Backstage at the Grammys. *Left to right*:
John, Yoko, singer/songwriter Dave Loggins,
and crooner Andy Williams. (35)

▼ The Lennons face the camera yet again with close friends they have never met. (36)

▲ Outside the Dakota. (37)

▲ Arriving at the Inaugural Ball for Democratic President Jimmy Carter with "Sweet Baby" James Taylor in tow. John and James shared a long, uneasy acquaintance dating back to the Beatles' final days together in swinging London. (38)

Joking with fans in Philadelphia, 1975. John could, of course, be infinitely charming when he was in the mood. (39)

▶ A rare example of some of the 26 pounds of FBI documents relating to the turbulent life and times of John Lennon. Just why the Bureau considered John worthy of such sustained attention is anybody's guess. (40)

FBI

Date: 7/27/72

Transmit the following in _____
                                    (Type in plaintext or code)

Via ____ AIRTEL _____
                                    (Priority)

TO: ACTING DIRECTOR, FBI)(100-469910)
FROM: SAC, NEW YORK (100-175319) (P)
SUBJECT: JOHN WINSTON LENNON
           SM - REVACT
           (OO: NY)
           MIREP

           ReNYairtel, dated 5/25/72, and Miami airtel, dated 6/5/72,

           Attached are 5 copies for the Bureau, and five copies for Miami, of an LHM dated and captioned as above.

           Miami should note that LENNON is reportedly a "heavy user of narcotics" known as "downers". This information should be emphasized to local Law Enforcement Agencies covering MIREP, with regards to subject being arrested if at all possible on possession of narcotics charge.

           Local INS has very loose case in NY for deporting subject on narcotics charge involving 1968 arrest in England.

           INS has stressed to Bureau that if LENNON were to be arrested in US for possession of narcotics he would become more likely to be immediately deportable.

    2 - Bureau (Encls. 5) (RM)
    2 - Miami (Encls. 7) (RM)
    1 - New York

ALL INFORMATION CONTAINED HEREIN IS UNCLASSIFIED EXCEPT WHERE SHOWN OTHERWISE

SEE REVERSE SIDE FOR ADD. DISSEMINATION

▲ On stage at the *Salute to Sir Lew Grade* television special, June 13, 1975. This was a gig Lennon never really wanted to do because he despised the cigar-puffing, big-talking Grade. (41)

To pass the time while he awaited Kyoko's arrival, Lennon spent his days filing his mountain of cassettes and watching television. When Yoko hired a contractor to begin remodeling the kitchen, John retreated to the bedroom, where he watched movies like *Close Encounters of the Third Kind*. He also dined out with the recently married Boyles, who were contemplating a move to the Dakota's seventh floor. John was greatly troubled by the news that Richard Ross had suffered a recurrence of his Hodgkin's disease. Lennon spent a considerable time with his ailing friend, who was by then separated from his wife. Not always a paragon of empathy, at one point John grew impatient and charged that Ross simply didn't possess the desire to recover.

John felt it was his parental responsibility to see that Sean left for nursery school each day well-fed and happy. The experience of having to leave his father every morning was a difficult adjustment for the boy. The two-year-old insisted on sleeping with his parents and clung to his father, which made John very edgy. Yoko tried to calm her husband by explaining that his restlessness was fated until the beginning of the new year, but John saw things differently. He felt he was doing more than his share, and that it was his support which allowed Yoko the domestic stability she needed to meet her growing business duties.

During this time Lennon was smoking a great deal of marijuana. He often complained of feeling drugged, even after a full night's sleep. Furthermore, he feared he might be damaging his health. John wondered whether it was his karma to keep repeating the same mistakes: he felt powerless to find a new direction. Various mental exercises to focus himself failed. He consulted with Charlie Swan, who interpreted this personal impasse as being dictated by the moon, an explanation John readily accepted. In the Lennons' world, it seems, responsibility did not rest with them. The blame could always be placed elsewhere.

Lennon was also being bombarded with pressure to restart his stalled career. Old musical colleagues were calling: Jesse Ed Davis and Jim Keltner were among the number. Apparently ready to let bygones be bygones, even Phil Spector reached out to John. Terry Doran, the former managing director of Apple Publishing and George Harrison's close friend and aide, was another old acquaintance who approached John.

Lennon, however, remained unmoved and immovable, categorizing these appeals as "self-serving messengers panting at the door." John, perhaps too cynical, refused to acknowledge that he needed to be pushed. He thus continued to flounder.

But when it came to satisfying his relentless sexual desire, Lennon was always able to summon abundant energy. As ill as Richard Ross was, John saw his friend's misfortune as an opportunity to resume his relationship with May. The stricken Ross agreed to act as an intermediary, getting May's number for John and providing the pair with an opportunity to meet. For May the opportunity was precious and fleeting. Following these brief encounters, she would not see John again for another full year.

Then something happened that rocked the Lennons' world. Late one November night Yoko received a call from a male who called himself Rivera and coldly informed her that a vital message would be delivered to the family on the final day of the month. The letter arrived as promised, a harrowing demand for $100,000. According to the note, if Lennon didn't pay, the extortionist would kidnap both Sean and Yoko, with murder an ever-present option. The letter warned against calling the police or FBI. Lennon was given only nine days to raise the money. He consulted Charlie Swan, and the two discussed several grisly scenarios, informed by past interactions with unhinged people like members of the Manson cult, who at one time sent John terrifying blood-stained letters.

Lennon bravely defied the letter and notified the FBI, which promptly sent over two of its finest agents, whom John immediately liked. His admiration for one of the men was heightened when he learned that the agent adopted a baby from Korea.

The bureau took the threat very seriously, placing undercover agents outside the Dakota who posed as workmen from New York's electric company, Con Edison. A tap was also put on John's telephones.

As the Lennons nervously awaited further contact, a second call came in, this time with specific instructions. "Leave the cash in a package at the downstairs desk. Don't try anything stupid, like having me followed. Remember, I can get to you anytime."

The FBI instructed Lennon to place the money in a newspaper and leave it at the appointed spot. With armed men guarding all the entrances and other strategic locations, the FBI stationed two agents with John and played a nerve-racking waiting game throughout the day. The FBI did pursue one suspicious character, but lost him. Charlie Swan decided that John should leave the city, but he refused to bail out on the family when the going got rough.

Two days later Rivera phoned just after midnight, driving an exhausted Lennon out of bed. Stumbling to the kitchen, his heart racing, he tried in vain to contact the FBI. Fumbling with the telephone he dropped the receiver and his glasses. He finally got through to the agency, but they were unable to trace the call because the recording device had not been set up correctly. The incident spurred the fury of the mysterious caller. Because the switchboard hadn't put him directly through to Lennon, the madman threatened to bomb the Dakota. Angrily reminding the anxious John that *he* was in charge, the ruthless Rivera left Lennon no choice but to sit tight and await further instructions.

As the days wore on, John received a number of calls from a party who would ring and then immediately hang up. Tension was heightened by the fact that Sean was sick, coming down with an earache, complicated by a mysterious fever and, of all things, dysentery. After a short period of improvement the boy took a sharp turn for the worse and was rushed to Lenox Hill Hospital where X rays and blood work revealed the presence of a badly infected mastoid. The infection left the boy in critical condition. Lennon was barely holding up, existing on coffee and orange juice and losing weight rapidly. Covering all the spiritual bases, John chanted Islamic prayers as he placed a statue of the Virgin Mary and a picture of Krishna near Sean's bed. The youngster's condition slowly began to improve, much to the relief of his anguished father.

The extortionist was later identified as a Latino in his forties who lived in Queens and was loosely connected to the Puerto Rican Liberation Front, a noted terrorist group.

In December things finally began to settle down. Yoko returned to her Apple business, while John ticked off the days until New Year's Eve, when, he resolved, he would quit smoking for good. After nursing his favorite cat, Gertrude, back to health following a viral infection, he resumed his daily yoga, although he was unable to endure the four-hour session Lena the witch had suggested.

In his diary Lennon remarked that he enjoyed a pleasant day of holiday shopping. After brunching with Yoko at Leo's, they saw *Annie Hall*, followed by tea at the Plaza. John was now speaking by phone with his cousin Leila on a daily basis. She'd become involved with a

Russian immigrant living in the States. John consulted with Swan about preparing a reading for her. Swan's forecast for the romance, however, was not good. He was right. The relationship didn't pan out.

John tried to cheer his heartbroken cousin in several letters, quoting Woody Allen's famous line that there are two states in which we live: "miserable and horrible." He then assured her that fate would surely intervene and the man of her dreams would seek her out if only she would be open to it. John further counseled Leila to keep seeking divine guidance as her prayers would ultimately be answered.

In the final week before Christmas, John was anxiously awaiting Kyoko's arrival. He baked several loaves of bread and planned to give the girl two kittens for Christmas. But his hopes were dashed when Tony failed to show with his daughter at the appointed hour. Lennon stormed around the Dakota, slandering Cox in the vilest terms, but to no avail. John would never see the child again.

Sean's homecoming from the hospital was much-needed good news. As soon as Sean was healthy enough, John took him to Central Park. Lennon, the agoraphobe, also braved the public to attend Sean's puppeteer program at school, though he made a quick exit as soon as the show ended.

The crisis in his life had John, yet again, determined to quit his bad habits. Noting that the character traits he found so irritating in his son were elements of his own makeup, John looked toward his son as a reflection of himself. He vowed to himself that he would use this insight to improve himself, but it was a vow he could not keep.

Just before the new year the extortionist contacted the family again, warning John to watch out for January 15th. Shaken by the threat, Lennon took his anger out on the household staff, screaming at them and slamming a glass to the floor.

New York, John's adopted home, where he once boasted he could walk without fear, was now a city wherein he felt haunted, betrayed, and threatened. His utopian existence, the world he sang about in "Imagine," was poised on the brink of destruction.

From this point on, Lennon would always be looking over his shoulder.

PAPER SOUL 6

Genius Of Pain

1978

Lennon's preoccupation with his Liverpool family underscored a profound homesickness that had slowly crept over him the past two years. John frequently called his half-sisters Jacqui and Julia, eager to discuss his roots and their troubled mother. "He *needed* to talk about Mummy," recalls Julia, "anything and everything we could bring to mind. Jacqui and I were the only two people in the world who could share his feelings about her in quite the same way, and that's why he had to find us."

"It's such a bloody shame she isn't around," John lamented bitterly to his sisters. "It still haunts me. There isn't a day she doesn't cross my mind at least once. I *hate* her being fucking dead!"

Lennon also proved himself a prolific letter writer with not only his nuclear family, but also the extended clan of aunties, uncles, and cousins. A post holiday letter to a cousin spoke about his spectacular view of Central Park in the snow as he unwound following the hectic holidays. John noted his celebration was a bit odd, since he quipped he was hardly a Christian, more like a Zen Buddhist.

John reminisced about past Christmases at the Cottage, Leila's home near the Smith family dairy, where Julia and Jacqui had gone to live following the death of their mother. He fondly recalled hanging paper chains on the tree, while an old record player played "The Good Ship Lollipop." He and his cousins watched the shadows creep across the ceiling during sleepovers. He also recalled his kindly Uncle Norman falling asleep by the fire.

Lennon was obsessed with collecting mementos of his Liverpool youth, requesting old family photos from his sisters and cousins, and badgering Mimi to ship over her Mendips china, cutlery, Toby jugs, even an old grandfather clock belonging to his Uncle George. Anything John's relatives could send comforted him, reminding him of his faraway home and extended family.

Renewing old ties also brought its share of frustration. A happy 1978 New Year phone call to Mimi went quickly downhill. She complained about John's Christmas gift—a purse—intimating her multimillionaire nephew could have afforded much better. His naughty holiday greeting card repulsed her. In turn, her barbs hurt Lennon, although he should have expected her reaction to the card. As always, he allowed her to push his buttons, and complained bitterly that he could never meet her impossible standards. John took deep satisfaction in her unhappiness, opining that she'd made her bed, and that now she was all alone with little to show for her life. Underlying Lennon's typical sound and fury was a hurt little boy desperately seeking approval.

During the first week of January, Julian flew in for a visit. John looked forward to the visit, rising at dawn to bake bread for his son's arrival. The gum-chewing kid he had last seen eighteen months ago, bopping around Disney World, was now a moody fourteen-year-old. Julian was at an age where he greatly resented his father's absence. He also realized he had the power to use John's parental guilt to his advantage. John tried to re-establish their bond by forgoing material gifts and spending more time with his son. The well-intentioned idea backfired. Julian, whose peer status was then defined by his possessions, pointed out that far more was expected from the son of John Lennon. He also put his dad on the spot by asking him if his new attitude was merely a ploy. Lennon was no match for his wily son. He soon caved in and presented the boy with mountains of gifts, but Julian wasn't done. He furthered his father's insecurities by fawning over John's assistant Nishi Saimaru with a display of filial attention designed to make his father jealous. The savvy teen hung around with the photographer, spending days away from the Dakota to help out on photographic shoots. Charlie Swan tried to console John by saying it was Julian's way of getting his father's goat. Lennon was doubly disappointed because the boy all but ignored Yoko, barely even acknowledging her presence.

John plunged himself into the puerile competition, foolishly trying to outdo the attention Nishi showed Julian. He took his son tobogganing, followed by a meal at La Pomme and a trip to Spanish Harlem to buy him a backpack. They also spent four hours walking around Greenwich Village in the frigid cold, and were caught unawares on Fifth Avenue by a camera crew working for an evening news program. A wary Lennon was grateful he and Julian went unnoticed because of their woolen face masks.

By the middle of January, John bid farewell to his son. After Julian left, John found himself sketching a portrait of the boy. Although it began as a likeness of Julian, John was surprised to discover that it was rapidly evolving into a picture of himself. While working on the sketch, Lennon was struck by a painful reality: he had neglected Julian in the same careless way his own father overlooked him. "I completely screwed things up," he once confessed to his sister Julia.

When Julian returned home to North Wales, he phoned to tell his father that he, Cynthia, and her new husband were planning a trip to Ireland or perhaps California. A jealous John insisted that Cynthia and her spouse, kindly architect John Twist, couldn't possibly make a go of it in Los Angeles. He quite rightly predicted that they would settle for a visit to Ireland.

John was heading into a long winter of boredom punctuated by the usual demons: too much food, too much Thai stick, too much wine, and his constant battles with influenza. John tried to cheer himself by socializing with the Boyles, but by this time they decided that being John's neighbor wasn't really a very good idea, and thus were relocating to Manhattan's East Side. Even from that distance they got on John's nerves. Their preference for cheap restaurants, as well as Lorraine's unpalatable attempts at cooking, were two more sources of irritation for the hypercritical Lennon. He was further disheartened to hear that his old friend George Macuinas was rapidly losing his battle with cancer.

Things were no better at home for the beleaguered ex-Beatle. Sean, now well into the "terrible twos," was irritable: a pampered boy-prince whose every wish was his father's command. Fearing Sean was coming down with chicken pox, Lennon was convinced the boy's poor health was the result of his diet. Sean's health thus became another item in John's long laundry list of obsessions.

In addition, the Lennon household continued to be rattled by extortionist threats. The villain finally made good on his promise to contact John, paralyzing him with fear. The FBI began to doubt that he was the same Hispanic male they had first identified. The Bureau now suspected he might be an Italian from Nassau County. To his horror, John discovered that the suspect was slipping in and out of the Dakota, his visits facilitated by the gullible doorman.

A few days later, the would-be kidnapper mailed yet another extortionist letter, keeping John on his toes by saying he'd be in touch on February 2nd.

This time the FBI stepped up its efforts. Agents hunkered down in the building's cavernous basement. During the ordeal John got to know one of the agents, a man named Mike, whom he wryly suggested was a clone of his old IRS nemesis Sol Markes. On one occasion a lovely Puerto Rican girl accompanied the agent. John spent the afternoon quietly sketching her.

All appropriate precautions were taken. A bodyguard named Steve was assigned to Sean and accompanied him everywhere, from visiting the park to attending school.

Sean Lennon later recalled the terrible tension surrounding that time. According to him, there were both pros and cons about his tight security. In the early years it wasn't easy to make friends when a pair of beefy, gun-toting protectors tailed him to class, to the gym, even to the bathroom. However, one day while in the park Sean was playing ball with his guards when a few of his schoolmates took notice. Before long, they got a spirited game going and suddenly being Sean Lennon with his fun-loving bodyguards was supremely cool.

Lennon seriously considered sending Sean to Florida as a safety measure. The extortionist sent John yet another letter, wherein he spoke knowledgeably about the layout of the Dakota, further upsetting the tense father. The news that designer Calvin Klein's young daughter had recently been kidnapped only intensified the household's fears.

Lennon tried to divert himself by searching for a summer place on Long Island. He had several prime properties in mind. The first was set on a lake surrounded by trees, and came with both a pool and a boat slip. Lennon loved it on sight, particularly impressed by how easy it would be to secure the grounds, but he really had his heart set on an oceanside property. A few days later Yoko went by herself to check out an estate with some forty rooms, but it too was ruled out. A week later Lennon took an early morning trip to yet another property, this one with ties to the Du Pont family. The 10,000-square-foot mansion, set on four beautiful acres, impressed him immediately. He was taken by its charming, nineteenth-century atmosphere. The huge house, perched on a slight hill overlooking a bay, held genuine appeal for Lennon. The bay reminded him of a body of water he recalled from his boyhood in Liverpool. A couple of weeks later, he was shown yet another mansion on 128 acres selling for $400,000, but Lennon deemed the property too expensive.

One real estate agent who worked with the Lennons around this time reported that Ono would practically barge into these million-dollar homes without even waiting for an invitation. If the premises had a piano, Lennon would sometimes sit down and play. The agent found John warm and without pretensions, but considered Yoko cold and affected.

For a time John and Yoko were seriously considering a waterfront place in Bellport, Tony Cox's home base. Tony's brother Larry later speculated that the Lennons may have planned to buy the property and put it in Tony's name, to lure him out of hiding in an attempt to get Kyoko back. But when Ono found that there was a ghetto nearby, the idea died. Among Yoko's considerations was the threat of nuclear war. She told Charlie Swan that she wanted real estate in a safe haven that afforded the best opportunity to survive ground zero and the fallout that would follow. He suggested that she should move to Oregon.

In the end John, apprehensive about his precarious financial situation, backed off from making any decision. Ono was engaged in a long-term plan to ensure the family's security. To that end, she sent a large sum of money by courier to Lena the witch in return for some protective magic, which Lennon admitted to friends he considered a con. She then called on Sam Green, who introduced her to his accountant. Yoko and the CPA came up with a surprisingly successful strategy: a corporation called Dreamstreet Farms, which provided investment opportunities in various dairy farms across the Northeast.

What convinced Ono to become involved was that their initial invest-ment would permit them a fourfold amount in tax deductions. Even John had to admit it seemed an excellent tax shelter.

Later that winter, the family traveled north to investigate a farm in Delaware County. It must have been a unique sight: a pair of smart black limousines snaking elegantly through rural Catskill country, one car transporting John, Yoko, and Sam Green, the other bearing Sean and his nanny. Valley View Farm turned out to be a fifty-year-old homestead with peeling paint set on 316 rolling acres. Lennon quickly warmed to the role of gentleman farmer. He had fond mem-ories of his Uncle George's dairy, and so he put down $2.7 million for not only Valley View, but three other properties throughout Delaware County. Altogether the Lennons purchased four farms, including over 2,000 acres of land and 132 head of prize Holsteins.

An elated Ono filled John's head with ambitious plans. Besides the obvious milk sales, she envisioned worm production, selling bottled water from the farms' natural springs, as well as producing organic beef. She even drew up plans for an exclusive vacation retreat. If all else failed, the investment would still increase in value due to its prox-imity to the tourist-rich Catskill region.

But before the ink had even dried on the contracts, Dreamstreet Farms proved a bust. A rash of arson fires destroyed two of the prop-erties just months after the purchase. The investment was saved from complete disaster by the Holstein herd, which proved to be truly prize-winning stock. Yoko later sold one beautiful bovine at the New York State Fair in Syracuse in 1980 for an unprecedented $265,000. At that time the entire herd was valued at an astounding $60 million.*

The Lennons continued to diversify their investments. They began buying apartments in the Dakota in 1977, until they had accumulated seven of its finest. They also began to seriously invest in art. While the centerpiece of several valuable paintings was a Renoir, the bulk of their investment was poured into ancient Egyptian artifacts. Relics included a skull, an infant's breastplate, and a seven-foot lion statue. Ono suspected these artifacts possessed magical powers. (Her fa-vorite mythological figure was the Egyptian goddess Isis.) The

---

*Lennon later referenced this event in a humorous aside at the end of the song "Dear Yoko," from *Double Fantasy*, released in 1980.

Lennons also purchased a 3,000-year-old Persian mummy from a Swiss vault for their "Pyramid Room" in the Dakota. The four-and-a-half-foot-long, gold-embossed sarcophagus, decorated with anti-quated lettering, while a sound investment, personally disappointed Ono. Her obsession with the ancient merchant's mummified wife was based on an assumption that the mummy's features resembled her own. This fueled Yoko's notion that she was a reincarnation of the mummified woman. Ono was reportedly immensely disappointed when she discovered that the artifact bore absolutely no resemblance to her.

As Yoko's forty-fourth birthday approached, John turned his atten-tion to finding her the perfect gift. He decided to create a silk-screen portrait of his wife. To that end he spent several weeks, slipping away at night to Andy Warhol's workshop, the Factory at 860 Broadway. With screen printer Rupert Smith helping him, John began the process of carefully layering each color. It was tedious work. As the work progressed, Lennon worried it wouldn't match his vision.

The day before Yoko's birthday, she and John had a pleasant lunch at the Spring Street Bar with Rupert Smith before stopping by the Factory, where Liza Minnelli was sitting for her portrait. The Lennons had known the eccentric Warhol for years, each having at-tended the other's parties and exhibitions. Andy had often cruised the East Village for young men in Lennon's limo. According to Sam Bolton, an assistant at the Factory, Warhol wasn't exactly fond of Mrs. Lennon because he felt she took life far too seriously. Bolton men-tioned another factor that figured in Warhol's critical assessment of Mrs. Lennon: "Yoko drove him crazy because she always got him to do things for her." In 1972 Ono pressured Andy to attend her *This Is Not Here* exhibition, as it was also Lennon's birthday. Warhol mis-chievously agreed, but only if Ono would divulge the size of her hus-band's penis. A few years later, because of his fondness for Sean, Warhol volunteered to do the boy's portrait free of charge, an under-taking for which he usually charged $25,000. Much to Andy's dismay, Yoko made it an annual tradition.

According to his close friend Paul Morrisey, Andy wasn't that taken with Lennon either: "Frankly, Warhol thought Lennon was a pest, a leech. And worse, a professional grouch—just an uninteresting, nasty person. A real smart ass."

A February 17, 1978 entry in Warhol's diary reads: "John Lennon came by and that was exciting. He's lost weight. Rupert's working on some art thing with him. He refused Catherine Guinness an autograph in a restaurant the other week, but Paul McCartney's picture was in the paper the other day, and when she asked him again, he drew a mustache on Paul and signed it."*

At exactly 12 a.m. on February 18th, John presented Yoko with his surprise, reducing her to tears. But it proved a day of minor disappointments. A sky-writing message was delayed due to heavy snowfall, and her extravagant birthday cake was not delivered on time. Moreover, John's plan to shower her with gardenias failed, as no florist had them in stock. Kay Leroy came to the rescue just in time with a fabulous cake, and the aerial birthday greeting flew over Central Park the next morning.

Lennon still wasn't entirely pleased with his gift for Yoko. Intent on reworking the face, he later returned to the studio where he encountered a man who fascinated him with tales of his adventures while living with an African tribe. Finally satisfied with his efforts, Lennon put the finishing touches in the studio's hands. When he brought her to see the now completed silk screen, a critical Ono pointed out that it had been botched. Lennon, crestfallen, spent the next 24 hours despondent, despite the Factory's promise to repair the problems with the work.

Tragedy struck Lennon in February when his beloved cat, a young Russian Blue named Gertrude, relapsed with a stubborn bug that left her with a runny eye. Further tests found her calcium-deficient, causing John to note in his diary that Asian felines obviously weren't as strong as their street-living counterparts. As February drew to a close, a definitive diagnosis was reached. Gertie had a serious virus contagious to humans, which might put Sean in danger. Not only would she have to be put to sleep but Lennon's other cat, Alice, would have to be placed in quarantine for ninety days.

A heartbroken Lennon took the feline to be euthanized, a devastating experience for the lifelong cat lover. He would later tell May

*Catherine Guinness (of the Guinness brewery family), who worked with Warhol on *Interview* magazine, had asked Lennon for an autograph in Ballast's. John initially turned her down because he had read that actor Robert Redford didn't give autographs.

Pang that he held the cat in his arms and wept as the vet put the animal to sleep.

Allen Klein, meanwhile, was still trying to ingratiate himself with his former client. He made a pest of himself, phoning, writing, trying to make dinner plans, but Lennon always turned him down. When they did finally get together, John had a little surprise in store for the notorious agent. Over drinks he told Klein he had received an unexpected windfall from Yoko's family and was therefore was no longer interested in settling any claims with him. Lennon, who enjoyed delivering that piece of news, later noted that the sweetness of the moment was dulled by his being forced to spend the rest of the meal listening to Klein's vapid conversation.

As the drab New York winter moved slowly into March, Lennon once again slid into his old ways, provoked in part by an astrology reading that predicted a difficult month. Retreating to his agoraphobic state, John hunkered down, locking himself in the Dakota and reading *The Lazy Man's Guide to Enlightenment*. He ventured outside only to walk down Broadway for the morning paper, accompanied by Sean, or to join the frumpy Boyles for an occasional dinner.

Lennon was also growing more resentful of the intrusions of people like photographer Bob Gruen, Terry Doran, and even the stricken George Macuinas. The terminally ill Richard Ross was also testing his patience. Old friend Spike Milligan, speaking to John from England, urged him to get back to work. Lennon, however, was unmoved.

John was talking almost every night with Aunt Mimi, another exercise he found taxing. She was in a perpetual state of indignation over tabloid stories about her famous nephew, which she took as gospel. Unfortunately, Mimi passed along several unflattering quotes she attributed to John to the media, leading to inevitable misunderstandings. John had to quickly exercise some damage control. He wrote Leila, assuring his cousin that the whole mess was the usual tabloid game and therefore much ado about nothing.

Meanwhile, the lonely Mimi was planning to relocate from her bungalow in Bournemouth, purchased for her by John in 1965, to Chester on the Welsh border. She claimed the move was for economic reasons, but Lennon felt it was simply a ploy to try and pique his conscience.

Financial problems remained a major concern. Apparently the Lennons were given bad advice regarding their farm tax shelter. It turned out they weren't entitled to anywhere near the deductions they expected. The miscalculation brought them a tax bill of $800,000, which hung over their heads like a sword. Yoko went to work on a solution immediately, conferring with her army of accountants and psychics. Oddly, they suggested that a two-year exile in Japan would ease the burden. Things got to the point that John feared he might have to sell some of their Dakota properties.

A break in Lennon's funk came with the couple's ninth wedding anniversary on March 20th. Determined to spend the day together, John and Yoko saw the Hal Ashby film *Coming Home*. John's response was vintage Lennon: he enjoyed the picture but felt there was too much Stones music at the expense of his own. After the film the pair ate a late lunch at La Pomme, and then had afternoon tea at the Plaza, where they ran into journalist Carl Bernstein. Later still, they picked up a small gift for Sean, and ended the satisfying day with a big meal at Ballato's. John noted that despite the inevitable indigestion and headache, he truly had a good time, his first in months.

Paul and Linda McCartney arrived in town two days later, and joined the Lennons for an evening out. They took in the Louis Malle film *Pretty Baby*, which John loved, praising both the movie and its young star Brooke Shields. The McCartneys then took the Lennons to a Chinese restaurant they favored, where John's appetite was spoiled when he observed the waiter eating from customers' plates in full view of the restaurant's clientele.

Following the McCartneys' departure on Good Friday, Lennon was stricken with a bad case of influenza. For the next eight days a miserable John kept to his bed, sleeping fitfully, but plagued by high fever, congestion, and severe back pain. He felt so poorly he feared he wouldn't survive, and blamed his sluggish immune system on years of drug and alcohol binges. Despite his discomfort, sex, as ever, was still very much on his mind. He had a dream wherein Yoko was cheating on him, and in response he dreamed up his own retaliatory indiscretion, a bizarre episode in which he found himself oozing blood. He confessed that his thoughts were again turning toward infidelity, and sought temporary release in ritual masturbation.

The threat of kidnapping continued to hang over the Dakota as the extortionist was still calling. Yoko decided she'd had enough of being a victim and would pick up the phone leaving the sociopath hanging on the line; at other times she would boldly engage him in conversation, refusing to succumb to fear. With John, however, it was a different story. On one occasion the man called after midnight. Lennon picked up the phone but was too petrified to confront him.

One March 31st another call came in and Lennon quickly slammed down the receiver, screaming "screw you!" He ranted that if it wasn't for Sean and Yoko, he wouldn't care, and that the lunatic might as well do him in. Later, after his temper cooled, he admitted it was a foolish and self-serving gambit.

Three days after that call, Lennon, out for a stroll, was followed by a young woman on a motorcycle whom he called "Boo." She trailed him until he finally paused to chat with her. She chattered on for nearly half an hour about James Taylor, Carly Simon, and the Grateful Dead, a conversation that left him bored and uneasy. This time she followed him all the way to the Dakota. Lennon then confronted her sternly, ordering her to leave and not bother him again. Boo was nonplussed. Her response was to mail him a copy of a novel she admired.

It wasn't until after Easter that John managed to finally ward off the flu. He took Sean and Yoko to the circus, where they were interviewed by a local television reporter. Although John's weight was down to just 133 pounds, he felt well enough to stroll around town, accompanying Sean to the skating rink or to the barber shop. Lennon was intent on teaching his son to swim, so he enrolled the boy in a toddlers' class at the YMCA. Every morning at 10:00 a.m., father and son headed for the pool. Sean took to the water like a young seal, delighting John with his natural aquatic skills. These were happy days with Sean basking in his father's good mood. John always had an affinity for the water. He found it a reliable tonic, releasing his tensions and toning his body.

During this interlude Lennon went on yet another fast, which included substituting decaffeinated coffee for his regular brew. Escaping into literature, John explored the life of Saint Germain, the sixth-century bishop of Paris known for his heroic compassion for the city's destitute. He also took long walks; during one he met Mitch Miller and Sammy Cahn conversing on a street corner. Another day he thought he spotted May Pang walking down Madison Avenue. It turned out to be a false sighting, but he was convinced the lunar phase of the month was responsible for bringing her image to mind.

The same night, he and Yoko made love for the first time in nearly two months, an experience John found comforting.

Toward the end of April several small incidents upset his always fragile equilibrium. A visit to the eye doctor revealed that his vision has seriously deteriorated, causing him to lament the effects of aging. Early one morning the sound of breaking glass shattered Lennon's sleep. He rushed to the kitchen to find the floor covered in shards, a mishap caused by a domestic worker. Cleaning up the mess took more than an hour, after which the groggy ex-Beatle found solace in a mug of steaming almond milk.

Sean, meanwhile, was involved in his own problems. Engaged in a war of wills with Masako, he threw a dish at her one day, a tennis racquet the next. A concerned Lennon confined him to his room for a twenty-minute time-out after the racquet incident, and Sean emerged remorseful and eager to please. Julian, meanwhile, was giving his dad the silent treatment, refusing to phone for weeks. Although John understood this behavior as yet another form of teenage rebellion, Julian's attitude hurt him, leaving the composer in a grim mood.

Ringo was also pestering John to guest star on his upcoming CBS television special, but he flatly refused. The program floundered badly in the ratings, much to Ringo's disappointment, though John felt it turned out better than he thought it would. The show coincided with the rush release of Starr's solo album *Bad Boy*, a recording so weak one *Rolling Stone* critic wrote that it "wasn't even passable cocktail music."

While Ringo was promoting the album, he stopped by to visit John, who felt Starr had aged considerably since he'd last seen him. Lennon speculated that his old bandmate was at the same crossroads he had faced during his Lost Weekend in Los Angeles. Hillary Gerrard, a longtime Starr employee, confirmed that the ex-Beatles drummer was going through difficult times and erupting into frequent fits of temper. Unknown to Lennon, Ringo was also suffering serious health problems that dated back to his childhood. A collapse in March 1979 sent Starr to the hospital, where he underwent emergency surgery to remove over five feet of intestines. He nearly died on the operating table.

Lennon also learned that ex-wife Cynthia was writing her memoirs. Expecting the worst, John vented his rage on Terry Doran, whom he blamed for encouraging the project.

John was also concerned about how deeply his involvement in the IRS investigation of Allen Klein would go. The government agency was examining a charge that Klein had not reported income on some unmarked Apple Records. Lennon, burdened with his own extensive tax problems, and still recovering from his Kafkaesque ordeal at the hands of the IRS, was very nervous about being dragged into the fray. The first week of May he and Yoko met with IRS agents at the Plaza. The paranoid pair provoked the disdain of the agents when the Lennons recorded the proceedings. After wading through the details, the IRS decided the Lennons didn't know enough to be subpoenaed in the case, leaving John astonished but relieved. Trying desperately to rally old friends, Klein had the gall to invite John and Yoko to a party. A Klein associate, trying to drum up sympathy for the beleaguered agent, pleaded with John that the poor soul deserved a break, a proposition Lennon found amusing.

Plans for a lengthy tropical vacation brightened Lennon's mood considerably. The itinerary included Bermuda, two months in Hawaii, a stay in the Antilles, four months in the Caymans, three months in exotic Bali, and finally another trip to Tokyo. Despite Lennon's claim that "no one controls me," it was clearly Ono—along with Charlie Swan and "directional" guru Yoshikawa—who put the trip together. John was as excited as a schoolboy with the prospect of such a sojourn, lobbying Yoko to incorporate a side trip to Tahiti. He also suggested stopping off in Britain, but Yoko met that idea with a stony silence. The last thing she wanted was her husband getting closer to his relatives, thus she put him off, telling him, "England isn't going anywhere."

Once plans were finalized for the Caribbean getaway, Lennon set to work buying luggage, selecting clothes at Saks, and poring over photos of their island destinations. On the eve of the departure, though, some minor problems arose. Masako was having a last-minute holdup with her visa, and Sean needed to go to the dentist to fill a pair of decayed teeth (caused by John's habit of putting him to bed with a bottle). Sean was also acting up, perhaps made anxious by the unknown and extended nature of the trip. To soothe him, John drew a storyboard to explain and illustrate the family's plans.

Charlie Swan injected a note of tension into the atmosphere, planting the idea in John's head that "the cards" were predicting hard times between him and Yoko. Lennon interpreted his forecast to mean the usual bedroom problems. He had been considering pursuing an extramarital fling on the islands, but he was conflicted: John prayed he wouldn't give in to his desires, as deep down as he truly loved his difficult wife.

Rather than flying to the Caribbean in their private jet, the Lennons, concerned over media attention, opted for a commercial flight. Despite several minor problems (too much luggage and John's perpetual anxiety regarding border crossings), the trip went well. He soon felt at home in the tropical haven. The staff greeted them with a delicious home-baked dessert and tropical fruits, and John took a dip in the beautiful ocean waters only a few feet from his front door.

The first week Lennon relaxed, enjoying a swim at dawn, reading in the shade of the palm trees, and listening to Ravi Shankar. He reserved the late afternoon for meditation. He read novels such as Gore Vidal's *Myra Breckenridge*, as well as the work of Leon Uris. Lennon became a great fan of the popular author, reading virtually everything Uris wrote. He was especially taken with the epic tale *Exodus*, as he connected the Israeli experience to the Irish one.

In this idyllic and isolated island world, even Yoko and Masako were having a good time. In his diary John proudly noted Sean's first erection, while Yoko snapped a fuzzy photo of the momentous occasion. New York seemed not only far away, but a distant memory. Lennon, now truly enjoying himself, began talking about leaving Manhattan for good and living out their days "in paradise."

Unfortunately, it didn't take long for things to sour. The Jamaican help began to piss off the mercurial musician. One maid tried his patience with her incessant chatter, while Watson, the maintenance man, was less than reliable in his efforts to assist the family. Lennon asked him to provide fresh fish for a seafood meal, and Watson agreed to go fishing for him over the weekend. John was unhappy when he never showed with the catch, and unconvinced by Watson's weak excuse that he was unable to track John down.

A problem soon arose concerning the family's housing. The Shaws, the Lennons' landlords, told them that part of the estate had been closed due to a faulty cooling unit. To John's dismay, the Shaws' in-laws showed up one night to stay at the house, and opened the locked apartment, which had a fully functional air-conditioning system. To make matters even more vexing, the air-conditioning suddenly broke down in the Lennons' rental unit.

The situation deteriorated further when John lost his glasses, leaving the myopic former Beatle without spectacles for the first time in nearly thirty years. Reading became an adventure, though he slowly grew accustomed to reading without glasses. And he had soured on Leon Uris. After deeming *Trinity* a literary masterpiece that left him in tears, John abruptly changed his mind and decided he'd grown tired of the author's fictional account of the religious struggles of Northern Ireland.

To make matters worse, Ono and Lennon began bickering over their stay in the tropics. Never one for sun (in the upper classes of Japan a tan was considered a sign of low birth), a restless Yoko began to find fault with the climate, pointing out, among other things, how the rich salt atmosphere was, in fact, very bad for them. Lennon, countering her complaints, reminded her how stale and suffocating New York had become.

Tiring of the rental home, the Lennons planned to relocate to the local Holiday Inn. But, despite the fact that Sean was taken with the hotel's pool, a quick tour of the place convinced both John and Yoko that they weren't yet prepared to go slumming, so they reluctantly returned to their former housing.

Then a pressing matter arose. The Lennons' tenuous foothold at Apple was imperiled by the determined infighting of the stockholders. The battle halted the release of the corporation's annual dividend at the first of the year; these were funds the Lennons were relying on. As he waded through numerous depositions and taped testimony, John was convinced that Lee Eastman was provoking the conflict, to compel the financially beleaguered couple to accede to terms more favorable to the McCartney faction in the dispute.

In response, John hatched his own plan. He hoped to use possibly incriminating information regarding McCartney's tax records to bring Eastman to heel, a tactic enthusiastically endorsed by ally George Harrison. Lennon, pleased at the prospect of finally getting the better of Eastman, was keenly disappointed when strategy and sense deemed he couldn't immediately show his hand.

But a critical negotiation didn't go as planned. By this time the other Apple factions had learned how to deal with Yoko, and a proposed gambit to turn the tide in the Lennons' favor failed. Their Apple foes called their bluff, and the news left Lennon so distraught he vented his rage on an already stressed-out Yoko. She was so overwhelmed by the pressure she began vomiting. John admitted he was ashamed of his behavior, and sadly concluded that both sides were simply money hungry. He hoped divine intervention would guide all parties through the morass.

Lennon was still determined to make the best of his vacation. Eager to get out on the water, he accepted a sailing invitation from a pair of British accountants he met at a nearby club. They provoked John's curiosity with harrowing tales of their marginal navigational skills. Although he branded the duo as bigoted, he was not above joining them for a breakneck race on the Caribbean waters, where he nearly fell out of the boat.

As a holiday weekend drew near, New Yorkers descended on the island for a quick getaway. Comedian John Belushi was staying at the hotel, and reggae king Bob Marley was soon to follow. Sean, meanwhile, was smitten with a four-year-old Manhattan girl whose father John labeled a humorless, Madison Avenue Jewish professional, married to a hippie (though admittedly seductive) woman. Despite his battle with a sun-induced headache, John enjoyed himself, and the results of the extended weekend weren't as bad as he feared.

After consultation with psychic Patrick Walker, Ono decided it was finally time to leave the island. The Lennons headed for Japan by way of San Francisco, with the stopover in Tahiti that John had been pushing for. Yoko, preoccupied with directional matters, suggested they might need to circumnavigate the globe twice, each in a different direction.

Leaving the Caribbean in a torrential rain, Lennon ditched his cache of marijuana before boarding the jet, and was also forced to abandon several suitcases. A brief layover in San Francisco was just the tonic he needed. The family cruised the hills of the beautiful city and later explored Sausalito. The Lennons were guests of Mrs. Hong, the widow of the acupuncturist who assisted them in the trying process of conceiving Sean. John regretted that the acupuncturist had seen only a snapshot of the boy. He treated the widow and her teenage daughters to an extravagant noonday meal, as well as a ferry ride to Alcatraz Island.

Following an exhausting flight on a commercial jet (where John complained that coach passengers were able to recline, while those in first class were not), the family arrived at Tokyo's Narita Airport and checked into their suite at the Okura Hotel. Things got off to a less than auspicious start. First, John's luggage, with all his formal wear, remained behind in California. After that, he gorged himself on his first full-course meal since leaving New York. A quick trip to the toilet to purge himself of the meal, however, assuaged any fears he might have had concerning any undue weight gain.

John spent his first days settling in, working the jet lag from his system with steam baths and shiatsu massages. A sightless masseur said Lennon's blood pressure was too low, accounting for his fatigue, and also opined that his sluggish digestion was due to a congenital weakness in his system.

Sean was clearly enjoying the trip to Japan, sight-seeing at local temples with Masako. The Lennons also enrolled him in school.

John had just begun to unwind when an earthquake rocked the hotel. He remained calm, even brushing his hair and joking he had to look presentable should he perish. Yoko, by contrast, panicked, dropping to the floor and imploring the heavens for divine aid. She then grabbed John and Sean, dragging them from the room to the safety of lower ground. Lennon insisted that they move slowly and sensibly to the basement, where they huddled together, waiting out the tremors. The aftershocks came three days later, but the damage was limited. Throughout the family's long summer stay, several small seismic disturbances plagued the Japanese metropolis.

It was a tremor of a different kind that next jolted Lennon. Cynthia moved ahead with her book *A Twist of Lennon*, and serialization was set to run in London's *News of the World* on June 15th. For days John and Yoko made frantic phone calls to the paper and tried desperately to halt publication of the excerpt. Lennon claimed that the paper did not make an effort on their behalf because its middle-class staff despised the couple. He claimed their spokesman actually relished relaying the word that nothing could be done to stop the piece. The Lennons eventually gave up their attempts, acknowledging that they were, frankly, on very shaky legal ground.

Labeling the book a seamy retaliatory tactic, John also charged that Cynthia had turned Julian against him. In reality, the book was devoid of any real malice. The fact was the long-suffering Cynthia acquitted herself with her usual grace and dignity. She even stated that Yoko and John were made for each other. This unexpected show of decorum was something Lennon couldn't reasonably attack. Perhaps the fury he exhibited was spurred by his own deep feelings of guilt.

The Japanese trip was not without problems. Increasingly, little things were continually upsetting the sensitive Lennon. He complained incessantly about the hotel pool's frigid water, his lukewarm tea, or a meal falling short of the usual standards, despite the restaurant's best efforts to tailor the menu to his stringent requirements. Sunstroke, constipation, and insomnia also plagued him. And he was at constant odds with Masako, outraged when she allowed Sean to ride a kiddie car with a loose chain that, he felt, could have injured the boy.

Another incident that rattled John occurred as he and Yoko were getting into a hotel elevator. According to Lennon, two Arabs were ogling his wife. The lack of sexual intimacy in his marriage was also never far from his mind. John arranged an intimate dinner at La Belle for a discussion of the couple's struggles in the bedroom, but his efforts did not bear any fruit.

Thankfully, tensions cooled by Father's Day. John was delighted to receive a greeting card and floral bouquet from Yoko. He spent a pleasant day swimming with Sean and strumming his used Yamaha guitar, a purchase he made after consulting with Swan. Later that day, John got some much-needed rest before embarking on a shopping expedition to Tokyo's famous Ginza District, where he purchased clothing, cassettes, a stuffed animal for Sean, and several extravagant wigs for Yoko. After a few weeks had passed, Ono pointed out to her husband that he neglected to note Paul McCartney's June 18th birthday. John suspected some subconscious significance to his oversight, perhaps because his old partner still invaded his dreams regularly.

For the next few weeks Lennon was reasonably content to play the typical Western tourist. He began his days by swimming at least twenty lengths of the pool, and then helped Sean with his schoolwork. Sometimes John followed the swim with a relaxing lounge in the sauna and a massage. The often agoraphobic ex-Beatle even enjoyed an outing at Tokyo's answer to Coney Island. Sean squealed with delight on the rides; John enjoyed the extensive floral gardens, picnic areas, and the petting zoo of barnyard animals.

While Yoko spent much of her time conducting business on the phone, Lennon found his own diversions. One favorite was shopping in Tokyo's underground mall, where he enjoyed using his new Japanese credit card. He made the rounds of the city's finer restaurants, discovering an American diner that served Kobe beef, clams, and a wicked baked pudding that quickly became a staple. One evening, dressed in casual attire, he walked into the elegant Maxim's de Paris, where an officious maitre d' held out a selection of required neckties. Lennon promptly asked if the restaurant served anything else. His quick gibe got him the best table in the house. John also spent time in the Kinonkumya bookstore, noting in his diary that during his Tokyo stay he'd been a prodigious reader. His days usually ended with a walk in the park with Sean, followed by a nightly bath together.

As July began, Lennon and Ono boarded Tokyo's honeymoon train for a few quiet days in the mountains. Leaning his head out of the window, admiring the meadows carpeted in purple laurel, and inhaling the clean crisp air, John enjoyed the chance to get out of the city. The couple lodged at a luxury hotel that reminded him of the Mampei Hotel in Karuizawa. While there, he indulged in a soak in the hot springs and an expensive manicure. He also telephoned Elliot Mintz, who described running into Elton John at Mr. Chow's in New York. Mintz also mentioned that he had spoken with May Pang, and remarked that she looked fabulous and was doing very well.

The next day Lennon became irritated at a disruption in his travel plans caused by a session with the *I Ching*. The forecast warned of impending danger and counseled against making any unnecessary journeys. Since the unusually hot weather made travel difficult, John cooled off with Sean in the hotel's indoor pool.

Shipping Sean and Masako back to Tokyo, John and Yoko moved on to picturesque Lake Kawaguchi in the shadow of the majestic Mount Fuji. Lennon was right at home in the spacious hotel with its 150 luxury rooms and clear view of the mountain. The next morning, following breakfast, he hurried off to the lake to row in quiet, blissful solitude. His enjoyment, however, was short lived. A trio of local Japanese in motorboats buzzed his craft, clipping the side and filling him with terror.

The incident set a grim tone for the remainder of his stay. He returned to Tokyo by car, and blamed his cranky mood on excessive caffeine. John hoped a trip to a local Chinese botanical garden might lift his spirits.

Back at the hotel, letters from both Ringo and Mick Jagger awaited him, full of information about their various projects. Mick wrote about his latest release, *Some Girls*. In his letter Ringo remarked that he had been dropped from his record label and so was pursuing a film career. John also learned that sales of Bob Dylan's gospel-flavored album were poor, but his world tour was getting rave reviews. Lennon glumly noted that he was preoccupied with househusband duties, while Jagger, Starr, and Dylan were sustaining largely successful careers. When Robbie Robertson of The Band called, Lennon chose not to answer. Although his efforts at parenthood were admirable, John still felt the stubborn tug of personal ambition. But his shattered confidence, his fear of failure, and an ego beaten into submission by Yoko left him creatively silenced.

Elliot Mintz also relayed the news that Robert Stigwood's production of *Sgt. Pepper's Lonely Hearts Club Band* was set to premiere in New York. The film, which featured Peter Frampton and the Bee Gees, would become a commercial disaster despite its expensive budget and heavy promotion. John was disturbed by Yoko's hunch that Lee Eastman had worked secretly on Paul's behalf on a financial arrangement that was separate from the other Beatles' shares. John dispatched a good-luck telegram to Stigwood, signing it John, Yoko, and Brian, the last name being a pointed reference to Eastman's top aide.

In another diary entry, Lennon reported that his old preoccupation with erotica was again invading his dreams, from a tryst with Pattie Boyd to an episode of passive oral sex with George Harrison! These nocturnal apparitions were so provocative that his movements roused Yoko's suspicions, and he awoke to a barrage of rapid-fire questions. Lennon's thoughts constantly wandered to extramarital sex, but Ono was vigilant. Desperate, he fantasized about his next overseas excursion, and was determined to find a mistress. Yoko cut off those thoughts by telling him that any trip he might plan they would be making together.

John, severely tempted by a young masseuse named Reiko, arranged midnight massages during which he allowed himself to become aroused. Their sensual encounters involved Reiko making bold advances, and then offering sexual services that were unclear to John due to the language barrier. Yoko, sensing a game was afoot, informed him coldly that in Japanese marriages, the wife *allows* a husband to take a mistress *after* the age of forty. A red-faced Lennon responded that males were universally alike and he'd be content to wait. It was an assertion he secretly doubted.

Toward the end of July, after Ono secured a suite at the Okura and began searching for a private residence, doubts about the wisdom of a long-term stay in Japan began invading John's thoughts. The cramped spaces of the tiny houses he was seeing unsettled him. He hated the idea of an extended stay and desperately wanted to return to New York. He even considered working again if it meant he could alleviate his tax burden and return to America.

As usual John opted to do nothing. Instead of confronting his wife and discussing other alternatives, Lennon retreated to a hotel room and sulked. He took out his unhappiness on Sean, snapping at him, and once childishly refusing to tuck him into bed. He balked at paying a visit to Yoko's family home, and sought an escape in sleep. Even books no longer diverted him, and he stopped reading. During this agoraphobic spell John left his room only to eat at the hotel's sushi bar, or to take Sean to his swimming lessons. Lennon also found himself brooding morbidly over his longing for England and his Liverpool family.

After a month of trying to bring him out of this funk, Yoko saw she had little hope of making the self-imposed tax exile work. She had seen John heading toward a breakdown before, and it was an experience she did not want to endure again, especially in such a public place as a hotel. In early September the family packed up and returned to Manhattan, though without Masako. The nanny's health was poor and despite taking time off, her condition had not improved. She had also tired of Yoko's dictatorial manner, and so chose to remain in Japan rather than return to America with the family.

For Sean it was a harsh loss. Masako, like Aunt Mimi, represented a deeply maternal, if iron-willed influence. And unlike Yoko, the nanny was there no matter what was happening in the household or with business. Lennon, worried about Sean's reaction to losing Masako, drew up more cartoon panels to ease his son through the difficult mourning period.

Although he was once again back home, Lennon's frame of mind had not improved. Mimi's correspondence, with its perpetual criticisms, rankled him. She found fault with nearly every aspect of his life, from his music to his wardrobe. In one letter she charged that wealth and fame had changed him, and not for the better.

He responded in a lengthy, explosive letter dated September 10th, comparing his aunt to the clueless parents in the song "She's Leaving Home." She could not handle the truth, he told her, even when it was presented in a harmless, joking manner. Her behavior conjured up bad memories of his youth, when she screamed and flung things at him.

John further slammed Mimi for her outdated Victorian attitudes and for being influenced by her catty neighbors who apparently looked down their nose at those in John's circle. He charged her with hypocrisy, inferring she and her friends loved to keep up on the latest celebrity dish, but closed their minds to anything productive they might have to offer.

Despite her constant undermining, John managed to make something of himself, he told Mimi, and challenged her to speculate what he would have amounted to had he heeded her counsel. Bitterly hurt by her attitude, John lashed out that she was right on target: yes, he did believe in his own worth and was proud to stand up for himself. If he didn't, who else would?

He also addressed Mimi's potshots at what she termed those "meaningless, shameful women" who had taken advantage of him, no doubt pointed directly at Yoko. John countered that she'd never found a shred of decency in any of his friends and that she belittled everything about him ever since he broke free from her influence during his teens. He concluded that he was a perfectly wonderful nephew and surely the only one to endure her constant verbal slings.

Yoko was concerned enough about his state of mind that she contemplated yet another "directional" voyage to ward off bad luck. Well aware that he had been considering another affair, she was apparently willing to send him off alone and risk certain infidelity. Later that month, Lennon flew to Hawaii to shake off his gloom. But Hawaii, like Los Angeles, held temptations he was unable to ignore. The first person he encountered was his pal Jesse Ed Davis. When a surprised Davis asked what brought John to the Pacific, he quipped, "I'm running away from Yoko!"

According to Jessie, Lennon didn't waste any time getting high. The pair took a cab to the nearest dealer and scored some Polynesian heroin. Tucked safely away in Lennon's suite at the Sheraton, they pulled out the powder and, as Davis would later recount, cooked it up in a spoon and injected it. Davis asserted that John was no novice: "He knew just what to do. He didn't even need a tourniquet. John told me he had been shooting smack since back in the Beatle days." As they followed the injections with tumblers of screwdrivers and watched reruns of *Star Trek*, John abruptly decided he wanted to jam. The two packed their guitars and headed to John Barleycorn, a popular Waikiki Beach bar. Davis claimed that there John Lennon played his final public performance, an extended set that included Chuck Berry's "Roll Over Beethoven" and Buddy Holly's "Peggy Sue."

After a couple of weeks of relaxing on the beach and indulging in alcohol and drugs, John caught a flight back to New York in early October. He was just in time to celebrate his birthday with Sean on October 9th. The party was held at the Tavern on the Green.

Hawaii had drained more than fortified John, so he locked himself into his pristine, white-bricked, white-carpeted Dakota bedroom. Lying on the bed, he chain-smoked Gitane cigarettes and stared blankly at his giant television, while the muted phone at his side was lit by calls he never took. As he reflected at the time, "I watch the shadows on the wall. I watch the park change through my window. I spend most of my time here."

Mick Jagger, living only a block away on Central Park West, was one of the artist's frustrated friends who tried in vain to bring him out of his funk. "On one or two occasions I visited someone in the Dakota," Jagger recounted later. "I'd leave him a note saying, 'I live next door. I know you don't want to see anyone, but if you do, please call.' Sadly, he never did."

Paul McCartney accused his once close friend of copping out, saying that John had accomplished everything but "being himself."

"What the hell does that mean?" Lennon retaliated. "Paul didn't know what I was doing. He was as curious as everyone else.* It's ten years since I really communicated with him. I know as much about him as he does about me, which is zilch."

Bearing a guitar later in the year, Paul and Linda arrived unannounced at the Dakota. "Do you mind calling before you come round from now on?" Lennon chided. "This isn't Liverpool, you know. In New York you just don't drop in on people without any warning."

"Sorry, man," McCartney responded meekly, more than a little taken aback. "We only wanted to stop by and say hello."

"Yeah, I know, man, but I've had a particularly fuckin' long day today with Sean. It's bloody hard work looking after a kid his age, you know."

"Well, so . . . we'll shove off then. See ya."

John shut the door without comment, not knowing it was the last time he would ever see his old partner.

May Pang was shocked when she saw John one morning in early December. Out of the blue she received a call from him demanding to see her. He arrived at her door like an apparition: ashen-faced, thin, and under enough stress that he was hyperventilating. Once he calmed himself, Lennon said he was thrilled to see her. Sounding like a husband who's just returned from a long business trip, he professed his love for her. Then he proceeded to babble about how happy he was. He referred to Yoko as his manager and implied that his career was thriving. "I never stopped wanting to make music," he told her. He promised to call her before he left, but May would never see him again. For Lennon, December was a month of many endings.

Back at the Dakota, John was less optimistic than he had feigned to Pang. He sat in a dark room with the curtains drawn and listlessly smoked joint after joint. He told Swan the real Lennon was no longer really required. They were running enough replicas around via the stageshow Beatlemania that improved on the real thing. He might as well be dead and buried. But if Lennon the artist resigned from the world, Lennon the corporate business entity still had full-time demands that required all the energy of the beleaguered Yoko. Tired of

*John reflected this attitude in the ballad "Watching the Wheels," from *Double Fantasy* in 1980.

hunting John down when she needed his signature, she lobbied him for power of attorney. Surprisingly, Charlie Swan, usually an immovable Ono ally, advised John not to sign the paper that would surrender his last vestige of control over the business. Lennon did so anyway, giving her the power to forever rule the corporate entity that bore his famous name.

With all of the Yoko-authorized, posthumous commercialization of John's name, image, and songs, Lennon might as well have signed over his soul.

CONSPIRACY OF SILENCE $\boxed{7}$
Love, Lies, And Death

1979

At just thirty-eight years of age, John Lennon was already an old man haunted by his past and frightened by the future. Forty, a benchmark, though still nearly two years away, had become a fixation he did not know whether to embrace or to flee. He lamented to Cousin Leila that if the old adage about life beginning at forty held true, he was counting on a little more peace of mind in his later years.

Yoko's cadre of mystics had forecast John's resurgence, targeting the year 1980, as though he was in a state of suspended animation. But the prospect petrified him as much as it intrigued him. After all, John would be forced out of hiding to face the public and under the gun to produce the old Lennon magic. Also daunting was having to confront another existential dilemma: what was he searching for that he hadn't already attained?

The troubled musician explored these conflicts regarding the second half of his life in the way he knew best—by writing a song (whose title remains unrecorded by history). The lyrics, stark and cynical, revealed a fatalistic attitude and depicted his first forty years as an abject failure. The few positive aspects of himself—the desire to atone for past mistakes, the will to look to a brighter tomorrow—were juxtaposed against broader, deeper images of personal stagnation, hopelessness, and the specter of his own death. John employed a brilliant metaphor that likened him to a British soldier in the American Revolution, an image which elegantly encapsulated both his longing for home and the isolation he felt in his adopted land. The song's final verse, bleak and poignant, harkened back to his childhood, with its author crying out for the parents who thoughtlessly abandoned him so many years ago.

The new composition provided the kind of piercing insight and riveting honesty missing since his Plastic Ono days. Lennon was openly exposing himself and his many faults, stating flatly, "This is me, take it or leave it!" Unfortunately, this blistering, truth-or-dare musical manifesto never appeared on his final two albums.

The song underscored the artist's recognition of what he saw as his growing loss of control over his own life. At home, he felt overrun by intruders: from the servants who cleaned the apartment after holiday festivities to the repairmen trooping through the Dakota, John's fragile life was disrupted. These interlopers included a plumber who came to fix a leaky ceiling, a talkative piano tuner, and an antique restorer. The never-ending stream of invaders wreaked havoc on John's increasingly fragile state of mind. Around this time Helen Seaman entered the Lennons' life as Sean's new nanny. Helen and her upscale husband Norman had known Yoko since the early sixties when Norman, a respected concert promoter, produced several of her avantgarde "recitals." Following her arrival, yet another Seaman, the couple's clever bookish nephew Fred, began to frequent the Dakota. He would become John's personal assistant in February, a move that would ultimately play out in a controversial drama of crime and betrayal. At least as far as Ono was concerned.

Topping the list of Lennon's resentments was the latest cook, Mrs. Lee, a taciturn Korean who clashed almost immediately with her famous boss. The prospect of working for a world-renowned ex-Beatle didn't awe her in the least. Ono merely ignored his complaints that Lee was a terrible cook who "didn't know her place." John grumbled it was simply a case of "Asian solidarity."

Lennon especially resented the fact that these myriad strangers disrupted his sacred daily routine and commandeered the kitchen, his turf, to watch television for hours at a time with the volume blaring. He was forced to endure this torment even on weekends. Yet, rather than lay down the law in his own home, Lennon characteristically retreated to his bedroom.

John also felt utterly helpless regarding his two sons. Julian was expected for a post-Christmas visit the first week of January, but the inclement weather delayed his arrival. Lennon was secretly grateful for the postponement, claiming he wouldn't be good company anyway with the IRS bearing down on him again. In truth, he dreaded dealing with the awkwardness he felt around his firstborn. Unfortunately, young Julian would forever remain a stranger to his conflicted father.

On the other hand, Sean, no longer a toddler, was growing increasingly aware of the chaos around him, and was lashing out in response. Without the dependable and familiar Masako at his side, he was escorted to school by either the forbidding Mrs. Lee or the fussy Helen Seaman. Sean was also sensing the turmoil that swirled outside the Dakota. His father had been clashing recently with photographers determined to shoot exclusive photographs of the boy. As a result of the tension, the three-year-old began to fabricate excuses to stay home, feigning sickness so convincingly that John worried he might actually have kidney problems. Sean soon began to resist going to school and eventually flatly refused to leave the Dakota. One morning a violent tug-of-war erupted between Sean and Helen, who was trying to coerce the youngster from the apartment for school. When the determined Mrs. Lee stuck her nose into the conflict, John exploded, a response that sent Sean screaming in terror. The boy was mirroring his father's insecurities and fears more with each passing day.

That evening, after finally getting the rattled youngster to sleep, an infuriated John dashed off a nasty note to Yoko about the impudent, out-of-bounds staff, and in his rage trashed the apartment while filling the air with a stream of profane invective. Lennon gained a measure of satisfaction soon after when Yoko and Mrs. Lee had their inevitable clash. Arguing with Ono over the proper way to wash Sean's hair, the fiery Lee lost control and assaulted her, breaking a small bone in Yoko's hand. She was dismissed from the Lennons' employ in a Tokyo minute.

In the wake of this latest wave of hysteria, John sank further into a dangerously depressive state. A concerned Yoko dispatched Swan to the White Room to play amateur therapist. Lennon lamented his plight, confessing that he had sold out to the public, and complaining bitterly that fame had become a trap. It didn't take a professional to recognize that this irrational tirade was a desperate attempt to assert some measure of control over his life. John agreed with Swan's assessment that his eruptions were examples of displaced anger.

A period of tenuous calm pervaded the Dakota toward the end of January. Reflecting his father's mood, Sean was uncharacteristically listless and morose. Lennon, who often turned to television to help solve problems, watched a child psychology program on PBS. The show portrayed permissive parents as well-intentioned blunderers who undermined their children's development, and showcased a more reasoned and disciplined approach to child rearing. Even though John couldn't refute the show's premise, he honestly didn't know if he was up to the challenge of being the kind of concentrated parent the program recommended.

Lennon had all the textbook signs of being immersed in a profound clinical depression: periods of insomnia offset by excessive sleep; see-sawing weight loss and gain; lack of interest in usual activities, or pleasures; feelings of worthlessness, self-reproach, or excessive guilt. "A depressed person may be slowed down, lack energy, and have fewer ideas," states psychiatrist Demitri Papolos in his book *Overcoming Depression*. "Decisions are next to impossible to make, and everyday tasks become intimidating. A person may experience persistent feelings of sadness and emptiness, and become tearful for no apparent reason, or become irritable and hostile."

Another symptom of John's mounting troubles was his continuing reliance on drugs and alcohol. Yoko, desperate to keep him on an even keel, seemed more concerned with securing the needed drug for her spouse than weaning him off it. Several advisers from the family's inner circle suggested that Lennon needed clinical attention, but Ono resisted their advice. "What if the doctor wanted John committed or something? I couldn't risk that. They couldn't give him better care than he gets right here. I make sure he gets everything he asks for, drink, cigarettes, grass, anything. He wouldn't get that in a hospital."

Although it was obvious Lennon was seriously troubled, no one dared to challenge Yoko. The reason was clear: their jobs could be jeopardized. If John's condition went public, it could hurt the bank accounts of those who had a vested interest in his fortunes by undermining the Lennon myth. Of course, nobody stood to lose more than Yoko herself. Her tenuous hold on the empire was dependent on her ability to influence John, to keep him calm and submissive in order to deal freely with her opponents at Apple. Yet, she was vulnerable to attack by her adversaries within Apple. "I can't risk exposing him to anyone important right now," Ono privately told friends. "Apple lives on rumors, and they could start saying John has had a breakdown or something; that would be just the encouragement they need to attack me. I just can't have that."

For his part, John's reliance on Yoko was profound: "Without Yoko I couldn't cope with life. I really need her and could not survive without her. She is the answer to everything. Being with her makes me whole. I don't want to be without her. Our relationship is in part teacher-pupil. Few people understand that. She's the teacher, and I'm the pupil. I'm the famous one, the one who's supposed to know everything, but she's my teacher. She taught me everything."

A worried Ono admitted that she may have often misused her power in their relationship, and that their role reversals had ultimately been detrimental to John, conceding she "might have hurt him." Despite Mrs. Lennon's iron-knickers personality the fact was she did care deeply about her husband. If not always as a wife, then perhaps a mother, a reality just fine with the emotionally immature ex-Beatle.

But Yoko too was certainly a victim of John's dilemma. She bore the twin burdens of keeping the Lennon ship afloat and maintaining John in one piece utterly by herself. Trying to juggle too many deals and demands in the business arena, stressed by John's erratic moodiness, she was haunted by the always lurking threats of kidnapping and violence.

An increasingly somber mood descended upon Apartment #72. An insomniac Yoko would retreat to her bedroom and collapse in a heavy induced slumber until almost noon, leaving John to fend for himself, as well as to supervise the household staff, a task for which he was ill-equipped. When she wasn't in bed, Lennon observed, Yoko usually looked like a walking corpse.

Lennon himself was fighting just to get through the grim winter days, and managed to sleep only with the aid of various narcotics. Perfect strangers were eager to indulge his weakness. One day he went downtown to have a neck chain belonging to Sean repaired, and the jeweler offered him a sniff of heroin.

Both John and Yoko realized that they had to venture outside the Dakota. A puppet show in the Village provided one opportunity, and made for a relaxed afternoon. But the next day they didn't fare as well. When the Lennons forced themselves to eat a disappointing dinner, followed by a forgettable movie, they were in low spirits.

Things became worse later when a couple of young thugs on a street in lower Manhattan menaced them. Afterwards, the agitated couple ended up sniping at one another all night.

As January rolled on, an exotic adventure, engineered by Yoko, promised freedom from their lethargy. Sam Green learned from one of his colleagues about a clandestine archeological dig being conducted in Egypt to unearth an ancient temple. The project, however, needed funding to complete the excavation. When Green relayed this news to Yoko, she could barely wire the money to Cairo fast enough, and began planning a visit to the site. Lennon, too, excited by the prospect of an intercontinental hunt for artifacts, couldn't wait to get on the plane.

John wrote excitedly to Leila that he was departing the following day for Cairo, stopping in Geneva for a week to take care of some business. He asked if any of her friends or relatives lived in Egypt and made a pun about wanting to exhume a few of her dad's kin. He promised to write her all about the trip.

His gloom momentarily lifted, John plunged enthusiastically into his sketchbook, drawing romantic Egyptian deserts dotted with camels and Bedouins. He purchased the proper wardrobe, got himself a new passport photo, and even changed his hairstyle. At the same time Yoko and Sam Green were finalizing the details of a complicated plan to sidestep the Egyptian authorities. Because Egypt's ancient national treasures were under assault by international art poachers, its governmental authorities instituted safeguards to protect these sacred gravesites, and even resorted to aerial searches to catch would-be raiders. John, eavesdropping from the next room on Yoko and Sam's conversation, was thrilled to hear that accompanying them would be a cache of potent marijuana.

The Lennons left New York on January 23rd, stopping in Geneva, where they checked into an elegant hotel. The couple took the opportunity to stroll casually around the city, and later enjoyed a nice meal with an old acquaintance. Lying in their bed that night, they had their first intimate conversation in a long while. John commiserated with Yoko regarding her concern for Kyoko, knowing that Tony was somewhere underground in Europe with her. Away from the pressures of home, Lennon felt so relaxed that he even added a melody to an old composition, "Tennessee," which would later become "Watching the Wheels."

The next day, while the couple was rushing to make their flight to Cairo, Yoko got into a dispute with the hotel concierge over her attempt to purchase a pair of diamond watches with an inadequate deposit. Just as all seemed lost, he recognized John. For once the harried musician was grateful for his celebrity.

Arriving in Cairo, the Lennons checked into the Nile Hilton. John took a nap before venturing into the city to purchase a wardrobe for the excavation. He ran into Thomas Hoving, former director of New York's Metropolitan Museum of Art, who was in Cairo on his own expedition for art. An enraptured John spent his first night exploring one of the seven wonders of the ancient world, the great Cheops Pyramid, built by Pharaoh Khufu, founder of the Fourth Dynasty, around 2680 B.C. Afterwards, he took in the nightly Giza light-show extravaganza, a gaudy commercial tourist attraction he enjoyed thoroughly.

The next day Lennon awoke energized and refreshed. An ardent history buff, he enthusiastically toured the pyramid at Saqqara, which he found even more fascinating than the Cheops site. As he explored the underground chambers, he ran his hands across the hieroglyphics and marveled at the intricacy of the ancient artwork on the stone walls. Coming upon an open sarcophagus, Lennon was unable to resist the temptation and recklessly tore off a scrap of material as a souvenir. Only later did he wonder if his blasphemous action had incurred the mummy's curse; he was worried enough to call an emergency meeting with one of Yoko's mystics.

While Lennon was exploring various sites, Ono was finalizing details for the proposed visit to the illicit excavation. The more intent she became, the more Green feared her presence might cause problems. An internationally known celebrity couple wasn't likely to go unnoticed by the Cairo authorities. Green used Thomas Hoving as a means to discourage Yoko's plans. He concocted a story that the renowned art director had gotten word of their scheme for obtaining artifacts and stood prepared to alert the authorities himself unless all parties left Egypt immediately. Marlene Weiner, Yoko's psychic du jour, confirmed the imagined threat, telling her that a certain assertive six-footer they'd meet in Cairo should be avoided. It wasn't clear if Green encouraged her to make this statement, but he did recruit Charlie Swan to dissuade Yoko. She was concerned enough to abandon the plan. Surprisingly, John wasn't all that disappointed by the abrupt turn of events. He had already had his fill of Egypt and was more than anxious to go home.

The next morning, before the return flight, Lennon stopped for coffee at the Ibis Cafe. Spotting Hoving at a table, John suspected he was keeping tabs on him. Back at the Hilton, while packing, Lennon, in a surly mood, sat on Sam Green's attaché case and refused to get up. The normally congenial art dealer blew up, setting the tone for an abysmal flight back to the States. The trip home proved arduous, complete with a horrible stopover in Rome and a tedious detour through Boston. During the flight the embarrassing *Sgt. Pepper's Lonely Hearts Club Band* was the featured film.

Once the Lennons arrived home, a period of relative calm ensued. A now bearded John would flop around the Dakota in T-shirt and jeans, his hair done in a topknot, channel surfing television or his latest kick—collecting gadgets via mail order. One particular favorite was a roto-stripping drill used to strip paint from wood surfaces. The problem was, John didn't have any paint he wanted to peel off, so he went bopping around the apartment applying the tool to walls and cabinets, gouging out pieces of beautiful hard wood like a beaver. A kid with a new toy, Lennon discovered that the thing operated just like the commercial promised and he was thoroughly delighted.

After the couple shipped Sean off on a short trip to Pennsylvania with Helen Seaman, they began yet another round of house hunting. Lennon was attracted to a stately historic mansion on Long Island's south shore with plenty of charm. He was confident that an astrological reading would render a favorable forecast, but the deal never came to fruition. The Lennons didn't restrict their search to Long Island, making similar trips to Connecticut, Maine, Pennsylvania, and finally Virginia, where they bought two Jefferson-era estates.

The separation from his parents seemed to do Sean a world of good. He went off to school eagerly and stayed the entire day. He proved himself a capable athlete, and his confidence grew. Lennon was working with him on his basketball skills, and felt proud when Sean made half a dozen baskets in a schoolyard game, easily outplaying his fellow students.

During this time Lorraine and Peter Boyle were arranging to leave Manhattan for an extended stay in Europe. Ever since the couple moved from the Dakota, they eased themselves out of John's life. Despite the fact that he complained about them, the concrete distance their trip would create hurt him. He saw their departure as further evidence that he had no "real" friends.

On the musical front Lennon found Bob Dylan's conversion to Christianity amusing, conveniently forgetting his own intense "Born Again" phase and his fleeting allegiance to *The 700 Club*. He took particular satisfaction too in the disintegration of Mick Jagger's marriage. He felt that Jagger was getting his just deserts after the barbed comments the Rolling Stone had made about John's role as a househusband. The news that James Taylor was back on heroin also drew a smug response from Lennon, who unfairly blamed Taylor's relapse on Carly Simon. Once again, it didn't seem to occur to Lennon, so quick to hurl stones from his own glass house, to take an unsparing, candid look at himself.

By this time another key figure entered the Lennons' inner circle. Sam Havadtoy was a bright, 28-year-old Hungarian, born near Transylvania and raised in Budapest. He had moved to America to capitalize on his talent for interior design, and met the Lennons in the fall of 1978 while working at an antique store on Lexington Avenue. He sold Yoko a beautiful white Egyptian desk for her sprawling Studio One office. Tall, slim, and fresh-faced, the decorator was living with gallery assistant Luciano Sparacino. Because Havadtoy fit right into her conception of the ideal assistant, Ono took to him immediately. As they discussed ideas for decorating the office, the charming designer was already insinuating himself into her good graces.

John consulted with Havadtoy for a gift for Yoko's upcoming birthday. Lennon was leaning toward a custom-made garden clock. Over this period the two struck up a casual friendship. They often met for lunch at La Fortuna or visited a shop called the Map Room. Little did John know he was befriending the man who would later replace him in Yoko's life before he was even cold in the ground.

Ono's birthday celebration, unlike the disaster of the previous year, proved a great success. Elliot Mintz contributed a humorous taped rendition of "Stardust," while Kay Leroy surprised everyone by arriving with nine cakes in honor of Yoko's master number. The big hit of the day was Sam Green's gift from Paris: an erotic video titled

Lesbian Wedding. Ono reportedly enjoyed it fully. Although the hypersensitive John was eventually driven back to the safety of his room by the children present, who were running round the apartment and playing in the kitchen, the day ended pleasantly with a dinner with the Seamans at La Fortuna.

About a week later, Lennon received an unexpected visit from bassist Klaus Voorman and his partner Cynthia. The former German art student, a friend of John from the earliest Beatle days, was looking for work. He hoped to land a spot in Ringo's band and lobbied John to that end. John, however, ignored his old friend's request for help, and curtly advised him to return to Germany to become a record producer. That night Lennon was far more interested in the rare prospect of a night of passionate lovemaking with his wife, inspired by yet another erotic video.

Although Voorman left, two weeks later he was back knocking on John's door, asking for a place to stay for the night. John waved him off to the Seamans' new place, Apartment #4 on the second floor, and then washed his hands of the matter. He didn't even bother to see Voorman again before the bassist left town.

In early February, John, always interested in matters of family, began to research the roots of the Lennon clan. He contacted the British Society of Genealogy for help. He particularly wanted to find out how members of his family had died, his interest perhaps sparked by the continued decline of Richard Ross. Convinced his friend's life was near its end, he devised a secret password so that Ross could contact him from beyond. It was something Lennon and McCartney had also spoken about when they were younger. Paul once noted in a radio interview after John's death that, though he and John worked out a word to alert each other from "the other side," to date he has never heard from his former partner.

Around the same time, Mimi sent her nephew his school badge from Quarry Bank Grammar. Shortly after the badge arrived in New York, Lennon dreamed his aunt traveled to Manhattan to live at the Dakota, and that morning he awakened to a strange sadness. A few days later, Mimi rang to inform John she'd taken a nasty fall on a patch of ice, the same day as his dream.

Not long before, John wrote to Cousin Leila, giving his best to the family. He sounded less than convincing when he spoke of getting together with his Liverpool family. Almost cryptically, he voiced fears about returning home, realizing it would probably be a final farewell to Mimi. After all, he admitted, he lacked all backbone when it came to saying good-bye.

Shortly after John sent the letter, there occurred a total lunar eclipse that had a disturbing effect on him. Intuiting that this might be the last event of its kind he would ever witness, Lennon composed a bizarre memo to Sean "from the afterworld." John's greeting declared his earthly passing, and proclaimed his great love for his son.*

As spring approached, Yoko, her fear over the possibility of a kidnapping heightened, pulled Sean out of school. It proved an unwise decision. Sean had just grown accustomed to the daily separation from his father, and even looked forward to school. Attending school full-time was also instilling in him some much-needed discipline. With his routine abruptly altered, the boy reacted by developing one fever after another, bed-wetting, and always clinging to John. To make matters worse, Sean's friend Nishi Saimuru was leaving the States to return to Japan, where he was getting married. After a farewell party for the photographer Sean got violently ill, vomiting all over the apartment.

Who could blame the child for his erratic behavior? His father, barricaded behind closed doors every day, saw few people and was usually high from various substances, which made Lennon swing radically from snappy impatience to bouts of uncontrolled weeping. Sean's mother, on the other hand, was either agitated or physically distant, spending more and more time consulting with Charlie Swan in her downstairs office. She barely gave her son more than a perfunctory wave good-bye before heading off in the morning. This cold distancing was the very behavior she had so resented in her own mother. As Fred Seaman observed, Sean, like any child his age, required full and loving attention from his mom. When he didn't get his way, he would throw a rip-roaring tantrum and no one was permitted to interfere. Woe to anyone who got in the path of the pint-sized tornado; Sean would simply tear right through them.

---

*There were many similar telling events near the end of John's life. Most puzzling perhaps were his lyrics to the *Double Fantasy* classic "Losing You," in which several sounds reminiscent of gunshots and a pitiful moan are heard, followed by Lennon singing, "So what the hell am I supposed to do? Just put a Band-Aid on it? And stop the bleeding now. Stop the bleeding now. I'm losing you!"

The couple's tenth wedding anniversary did nothing to defuse the tension. Lennon began the morning in a foul mood after snorting some tainted heroin. He was in no state of mind to be receptive to Yoko's sentimental anniversary poem that referred to him as the ruler of their little kingdom, a reference he interpreted as mockery. And when Yoko presented him with an expensive pearl-and-diamond ring he exploded. He would tell her later that she never got him what he really wanted. After the morning's uproar John retreated to his room and collapsed into a narcotic-induced slumber punctuated by a round of sexual self-gratification.

Ono, again faced with the prospect of her husband nearing the brink of collapse, decided that a visit to Palm Beach would be the perfect cure. Lennon, despite his professed love for warmer climates, always despised the family's vacations in the stuffy, old-money town. This time he felt like he was being forced to go, recognizing the trip as yet another desperate attempt by Yoko to get her vampire out of his coffin and into the light of day.

The Lennons flew south on March 23rd to rendezvous with a group that included Ono's three nieces and Julian. Yoko tried to postpone Julian's arrival by five days, but he refused her request and arrived as scheduled. Also accompanying the Lennons on the trip was Fred Seaman, who drove the family's new Mercedes-Benz station wagon, packed with John's clothes and guitars, down from New York. The extravagant Mediterranean villa, which loomed over South Ocean Boulevard, boasted two pools and a private beach. Its 22 rooms were anchored by a magnificent ballroom, lit by the sun through breathtaking 20-foot Palladian windows.

John's trip, however, began on a sour note. The *New York Post* ran an article on March 31, 1979, picked up off the wire by the *Palm Beach Daily News*, that accused the couple of turning from animal rights activists into greedy exploiters for wearing fur. The story was based upon reports of a Christmas shopping spree at Bergdorf Goodman Furriers, where the Lennons purchased over twenty coats at a cost of nearly $300,000. To make matters worse, the piece came on the heels of an earlier exposé that claimed the previously vegetarian pair was seen eating several meat dishes at New York's Serendipity Restaurant. The bad press irked him, but the reporting was certainly accurate.

As always, John's relationship with Julian showed the strain caused by the emotional father's distance. In an intimate conversation with

Fred Seaman, John confessed that his son was a complete stranger to him. Lennon sheepishly admitted that he didn't even know if his son was heterosexual.

On April 1st, John rented a deluxe cabin cruiser to celebrate his son's sixteenth birthday. It began well, with Julian sporting a pair of fangs and clowning with his father. "Dad made me laugh a lot," Julian once reflected. "He was a real comedian. He had a real sarcastic sense of humor. He could really make a fool out of people. I have to watch it a little bit because I caught that habit from him." The teen also enjoyed playing pirate on a nearby island with Seaman and the other children before returning to the boat, where John scheduled a surprise party.

But just as father and son were sharing a rare intimate conversation at the bow, they were spotted by a passing launch filled with giggling schoolgirls who screamed, "John, we love you!" Instead of deflecting this minor intrusion with a smile and a neighborly wave, his irrational instinct to run for cover set in, and with that the birthday outing ended abruptly. Lennon later charged that Seaman somehow alerted the girls to his presence.

The remainder of Julian's stay was a futile attempt for John to re-connect with his son. Father and son, unable to bridge their long-standing chasm, sat stoically side by side at meals or around the pool. Even bike riding and a trip to a nearby magic shop did little to loosen things up. Only when they played guitar together did the ice finally begin to thaw. "Dad and I jammed together a couple of times, but it was never anything serious," Julian remembered. "I was too young. We hardly even talked about it."

The bottled-up disappointments erupted the day before Julian was to leave. The angry teenager exploded, and John responded by snarling back at him. He was impatient for his son to leave, and sup-posed that Julian, whom he wrongly suspected came only for the gifts, felt the same. He failed to see that poor Julian was just a boy, trou-bled and confused, who needed a father, not a legend, for guidance and discipline. As Julian himself astutely observed, "Actually, he was much more an uncle to me than a father."

Surprisingly, it was at Yoko's prodding that John finally mended fences with the boy before his departure. For Julian's sake it would be important. When he boarded the BOAC flight back home to Britain, it was the last time he would ever see his father.

One positive note, however, came from Lennon's spring break. He completed the final verse of a song that would appear on *Double Fantasy*, his touching lullaby to Sean, "Beautiful Boy." At that time the working title was "Darling Boy," and Lennon was very pleased with the effort. While in the studio John listened to McCartney's latest Wings release. And although he conceded that Paul's catchy single "Goodnight Tonight" could become a chart topper, he denounced the subsequent album *Back to the Egg* as McCartney at his self-indulgent worst.

As Swan noted, "Paul was a constant reminder to John that his old partner was doing well, while he was sitting home sucking his thumb. John sneered at Paul's success. He said it was overtly commercial and it goaded him." (Perhaps tellingly, the melodies of both "Watching the Wheels" and "Beautiful Boy" were largely written during his time with May Pang.)

Back in New York, during the second week of April, Ono attempted to reach a settlement at Apple acceptable to all parties. This round of talks also involved George Harrison, who came to the table with a proposal of his own. He was beginning to mistrust Denis O'Brien, his longtime manager and partner in Handmade Films. Years later, Harrison sued O'Brien for some $25 million, charging the manager with stealing from him for years.

Yoko had come up with what John felt was a brilliant solution, one that pleased even Paul, who was willing to bypass Eastman at one point. But the flare-up between Harrison and O'Brien threatened the deal. John unwisely tried to mediate the dispute but succeeded only in alienating George. The tentative progress toward the long-sought settlement was derailed. An agreement was eventually hammered out, but not until the autumn of 1979.

Lennon, still very worried about Sean, read endless child psychology books, especially taken with the concept of parent effectiveness training and trying to find the right path for Sean. The boy recently abandoned his bedroom for his parents', and was so overwrought that John worried it would take months to get him back on track. After some deep soul-searching, Lennon rejected the experts' advice and trusted his own instincts, praying his son wasn't yet ruined for life. John began with simple father-and-son outings: taking long strolls, visiting the Statue of Liberty, and enjoying long, happy carriage rides through Central Park. He even had a trampoline installed in the boy's playroom on which they both romped and laughed. Best of all for Sean was the jukebox Lennon received when he first reunited with Yoko. Lennon stacked the machine with fifties classics, like "Bee-Bop-a-Lula" and "Hound Dog," to which Sean would sing along. "He can dance like nothing on earth," John once proudly boasted. "He has perfect pitch in key."

Sean finally felt secure enough to leave the house with Helen or his bodyguard Steve. There was the inevitable backsliding, like the time the boy returned home from an outing at Jones Beach and hurled a sharp shell at his father. John summarily lost his temper, and a terrific shouting match ensued.

John's thoughts were also turning back to Alexa Grace, the lovely illustrator. Ever since their platonic interlude in 1975, the young woman had never been far from his mind. She had become John's unattainable object of desire. A year earlier she contacted Lennon, a move that Charlie Swan read as a gold-digging ploy, and that Ono characterized as an attempt to exchange sex for money. Both were dead wrong. During the winter, having lost Alexa's address, the lovelorn John scoured the East Village on a brutally cold day, trying to find her apartment.

Lennon's current sexual restlessness was growing so obvious that even psychic Marlene Weiner noticed, warning Yoko that her husband was poised for a fall. For the next six weeks John struggled with his emotions. Whenever his thoughts turned to Grace, he'd fantasize about being a young man frolicking with her. Twice he phoned, but lost his nerve, hanging up before she answered. John knew he was only courting disaster, sensing that any potential relationship would devastate his already fragile marriage.

A desperate Lennon, trying to banish Alexa from his thoughts, turned to pornographic videos supplied to him by a friend. After initially finding them a release, he quickly grew bored.

As in the past, Lennon readily gave into temptation and finally mustered up the courage to meet with Alexa. A mid-May visit lasted for three hours, leaving him deeply conflicted: he felt both euphoric and disillusioned. They were both role playing—he, the unattached artist, and she, the coquettish young muse. With the memory of his Lost Weekend and its aftermath still fresh in his mind, John was ultimately unwilling to gamble his marriage for a few random moments of bliss.

In his absence a bombshell hit the Lennon household when Yoko received a surprise visit from the Internal Revenue Service, calling to inform the Lennons that they owed the government $1,000,000. Overwrought with guilt, John silently prayed for absolution, and proclaimed his undying love for his beleaguered spouse.

But Alexa continued to invade his thoughts, and over the rest of the year the pair exchanged letters, cards, and an occasional phone call. His lovesick distraction was making Ono suspicious and edgy, adding to the strain on their relationship. Ironically, it was in this troubled atmosphere that Yoko composed their notorious "Love Letter," an extended statement that ran in major newspapers on May 27, 1979. A mawkish and absurdly simplistic treatise, the open letter/advertisement was clearly designed to perpetuate the John-and-Yoko myth— "our silence is a silence of love"—under the guise of updating the public on their latest activities. The letter spoke of a "spring cleaning of our minds," and goals achieved through magic and wishing. "Sean is beautiful. The plants are growing. The cats are purring. The town is shining, sun, rain, or snow. We live in a beautiful universe." In light of the actual circumstances of the marriage, the letter was at best nothing more than wishful thinking. The public had no idea that the Lennons were all but leading totally separate lives in their deeply alienated relationship.

As June loomed, Lennon became convinced it was to be a painful and emotionally wrenching summer. Still longing for Grace, the emotionally vulnerable artist found easy temptation in a young masseuse named Kimi. John fostered no illusions of a great romance. She was simply a vehicle to satisfy his enormous libido. As the weeks wore on, it became clear to John that Kimi came armed with an agenda. She would coyly play the seductress, and then coldly break appointments. She'd be intentionally cruel, and then sweetly repentant, which sent the fragile Lennon tumbling off-guard. One time Ringo came by to take part in the Apple discussions and stumbled upon John and the masseuse in a compromising position. Although Lennon, slightly embarrassed, thought nothing much of it, Kimi filed the incident away for later use.

In the midst of the Lennons' marital chaos, Ono, incredibly, was intent on becoming pregnant. Her advisers forecast that she and John would have two more children. Realistically, Ono had already passed her forty-sixth birthday and had a long history of miscarriages. The chances of her becoming pregnant and carrying a child to term were remote. And given that she and John rarely made love, perhaps she was counting on a miracle. In any case, Yoko's attitude illustrated her fanatical belief in soothsayers, a faith that often flew in the face of even the most basic common sense.

The gullible Lennon believed, too. Suddenly, he exuded a renewed faith in the family unit, as if he had just discovered the meaning of life. Ono showered him with diamonds for Father's Day, this time telling him that if he turned them down, she would present them to her sister as a homecoming gift. (Setsuko had by now moved to Washington, D.C. and had taken a job at the World Bank.) This time, unlike his churlish response of the previous year, Lennon was thrilled.

But after a delightful Father's Day boat trip along the Hudson, John's bubble burst: he came home to find an article in *New York* magazine that delved into the Lennons' reclusive Dakota lifestyle in excruciating detail. He was convinced an insider must have informed the journalist, and accused Kay Leroy, an assertion she hotly denied. Another temporary employee confessed, claiming he was duped into spilling the private details.

Following this crisis, Yoko's mother Isoko visited. Lennon escorted her to La Fortuna and the Russian Tea Room, where they met Angela Lansbury, who was then starring in *Sweeney Todd*. They also ran into Andy Warhol and Rupert Smith. In an unusually benevolent mood, Yoko suggested her mother stay for a while, offering her one of their other apartments. Lennon, alarmed by the prospect of a lengthy visit, breathed a sigh of relief when it was determined there was no suitable space to host the visiting matriarch. (The only possibly available apartment was being used to store John's impressive collection of treasured guitars.)

For John, a terrible blow that summer was the horrific death of his favorite cat, Alice. For several weeks she had been acting strangely, becoming increasingly clumsy and deviating from her usually gentle nature. In late June, frightened by repairmen, Alice plunged through a window to her death. Lennon recently had several dreams, which he later viewed as omens, in which Alice was searching for him in a public building.

Although he went right out and bought a pair of finely bred Persian kittens to replace Alice, Lennon was devastated, and spent several days weeping inconsolably in his bedroom.

Ono managed to draw him away to Virginia to check on renovations to their farm. John had a miserable trip by train, and pronounced the accommodations foul. On the way home, some kid snatched his hat at Penn Station. The episode left the perennially paranoid Lennon badly shaken. To make matters worse, their car didn't show up, leaving him vulnerable, and triggering an agoraphobic attack. When he finally arrived home, Lennon erupted violently, reducing the apartment to a shambles.

Adding to his turmoil, John heard that Julian called and declined an invitation to join the family on their annual trip to Japan, but asked for money. Julian's decision not to accompany his father hit John hard. Yoko burned a candle for a healing of the rift between them—a disingenuous gesture of dubious efficacy.

The Lennons left New York for Tokyo on July 23rd for a month-long vacation. John was eager to visit Japan, anxious, as always, to get away from America for a while. Childishly, it never occurred to him that every time he arrived in a foreign land he was soon anxious to return home. After checking into the Okura, John slept soundly. Determined to enjoy himself this time, he gathered together his Japanese family the following day for an afternoon at the movies and the by-now traditional shopping spree via the gold-plated Lennon credit card. John was so up he didn't even mind when the shops played several Beatles classics.

Relieved to have temporarily escaped his woes, he spoke rapturously of his extended family, proclaiming his Japanese hosts the gentlest, most open-hearted people on earth. He watched with pride as Sean competed in a Sumo wrestling match and walked away with a medal. John relaxed at a seasonal celebration, even getting on his feet to dance. This time he didn't mind going to the Ono retreat at Karuizawa. While there he managed to compose two more songs, "Face It"* and "Sleep Alone,"† companion pieces to "Beautiful Boy."

---

*Later known as "I Don't Wanna Face It," from the *Milk and Honey* album.
†Unreleased to date.

One of Yoko's cousins had a telling insight regarding Lennon as she observed him during the visit. She contended that his shifting appearance, bearded and pony-tailed one day, clean shaven with his hair hanging freely the next, was part of a complex game he was playing. John seemed to change his attitude as well as his appearance with with uncanny ease. Ono's cousin theorized that, in hunting for a fresh persona, he was hoping to shake off the multitude of demons that clung to the old one.

In early September the Lennons returned to New York. Almost immediately, the phone started ringing with journalists from around the globe wanting to know: What did he think of the impending reunion of the Beatles? Would he finally step on stage with McCartney and bury the hatchet? When and where would the reunion take place? The papers were filled with rumors fueled by an article in the *New York Post*. Concert promoter Sid Bernstein was pressing relentlessly for the Beatles to take the stage and rescue mankind, and promised to raise a fantastically unrealistic half a billion dollars for the cause.

The concert backers' intended goal was to aid the Southeast Asian boat people trying to flee Vietnam. Moreover, the United Nations had gotten into the act, tapping Secretary General Kurt Waldheim* as the flag bearer for the Beatles' bid to save the refugees. Lennon was blitzed with telegrams, phone calls, and letters from UN officials and celebrities from every arena, including Muhammad Ali and Leonard Bernstein, all pushing for the big benefit. Joan Baez soon became a nuisance with persistent calls and telegrams pleading for the Beatles' return.

The rising wave of hysteria brought Timothy Leary, Jerry Rubin, civil rights attorney William Kunstler, and even Dr. Joyce Brothers into the public dialogue. John condemned their input as misguided and inane. Even ex-Apple employee Peter Brown entered the fray, suggesting to Waldheim that all four Beatles might do the concert provided they were invited to appear solo. The pair composed a letter to that end, and sent it to each member of the group. Yoko responded to Brown's efforts by scolding him: "Peter, you're naive. You don't understand the subtleties of this international situation, especially when you're dealing with the Orient." Ono had one of the great-

---

*Waldheim was later accused of having been associated with various Nazi atrocities.

est stakes in the outcome. If John were to step on stage with the Beatles, the repercussions could have had devastating consequences on Yoko's tenuous hold over the shaky Lennon empire, from diminishing her personal influence over John to thwarting her efforts to resolve the therefore delicate Apple debacle. She could not, and would not, allow the reunion to happen. According to Brown, Ono "blocked the whole thing. She wouldn't even let me speak to John." Lennon, though, applauded her efforts, seeing his wife's actions as a heroic attempt to shield him from the entire unpleasant matter.

Not surprisingly, the story refused to die over the next four months. The *Washington Post* reported that John agreed to begin personal talks with Waldheim. One source claimed the secretary general contacted McCartney and requested that he use his influence to persuade the other three to play the benefit. In fact Paul did call John to discuss the issue. When Yoko answered the phone, Paul did his best to convince John—through his wife—to at least consider doing the show. John may have even briefly toyed with the idea. A postcard he wrote to a friend at this time reads: "Looks like the boys and I will be playing for those downtrodden sailing enthusiasts, the Boat People." But in the end only McCartney and Wings appeared. The Concert for Kampuchea, a bargain-basement Concert for Bangladesh, held at London's Hammersmith Odeon in late December, was less than a rousing success.

As time went on, the public spin pitted the other three Beatles' initial interest against John's immediate refusal. One paper wrote that "Lennon had broken off talks with the UN because he was 'angry and hurt' he was not asked to do the show before the media informed him of it." John was convinced that, by making him the heavy, the press was merely trying to draw him out and corner him into relenting. John complained of not being able to concentrate on composing, as the media circus dredged up all the horror of the Beatles' breakup a decade earlier. This extracurricular distraction discouraged John from returning to the studio to record, even though the music was flowing from him once again.

Oddly, only gossip columnist Rona Barrett rushed to Lennon's defense, saying it was far too late to resurrect the Beatles. According to her, the reunion might have come off back in 1976 had not Lee Eastman single-handedly killed it. (At that time, a reunion would have undermined his position in the Apple negotiations and upset his plans for McCartney's solo career.) Upon learning of this backstage maneuvering, Lennon compared managers Klein and Eastman to dictators.

The suspicious Ono also believed that the United Nations conspired with government agencies to try to gather damaging evidence against the couple, so she had the Dakota swept for surveillance devices. A jittery Lennon pointed to an obese character who was continually watching them from the street, identifying him as a possible government operative. But the man turned out to be Paul Goresh (later dubbed "Fat Dave" by John in his diaries), a pesky photographer who lurked outside the Dakota hoping to shoot candid photos of its celebrated residents and their visitors. One time the wily Goresh even posed as a video repairman, getting all the way to Lennon's bedroom, before he was shown out of the building.

It was in this frame of mind that John vented his frustrations in his September 6th audio diary. With the Beatles' fiasco weighing on him he struck back with a stinging volley against his fellow artists, starting with Bob Dylan. He'd just heard Dylan's latest record "You've Got to Serve Somebody" and with typical sarcasm chided Bob's sincerity about his conversion to Born Again Christianity. He attacked everything: the song's woeful lyrics, Jerry Wexler's lukewarm backing track, even Dylan's insipid vocals.

The old road warriors of rock and roll—Dylan, Jagger and especially McCartney—had sunk into hopeless mediocrity, according to Lennon. Just a few short years ago. Back then, when these rock chieftains put out their latest material, it was like throwing down a gauntlet, which triggered in John an acute sense of urgency to meet their challenge. But now he didn't even bother to check out their records, although he had to admit part of him could never completely disavow himself from his musical contemporaries. But his reaction to their newest work—that it was nothing but garbage—did bring a kind of sadistic satisfaction. The way John saw it, by his self-imposed exile, he was getting the final laugh.

But where Paul McCartney was concerned, Lennon was anything but disinterested. He doggedly tracked his former partner's every move and never missed an opportunity to belittle him. He accused Paul of misrepresenting the Beatles' breakup on the news magazine

20/20, and wondered how the public could even be fooled by him. His constant criticism of both Paul and Linda was, of course, indicative of his deep feelings for the couple. He conceded that Paul got to him more than he cared to admit. Watching the McCartney television special *Wings over America* had him briefly entertaining thoughts of actually getting back up on stage.

The rivalry also led John to reconsider his idea about composing a Broadway musical. Tentatively entitled *The Real Ballad of John and Yoko*, the project had been on the shelf for some time. Yoko conceived it as a way to turn a quick profit, noting that Lee Eastman had made a hefty profit for Paul by investing in musicals. She saw the work as "a day in the life of John and Yoko." The couple would star in it, and use their own furniture and prerecorded music to keep costs down. Yoko was even prepared to write all the material if John could not come up with any.

But it was clear that Lennon wasn't about to become the next Andrew Lloyd Webber. Fred Seaman later found the preliminary script and quickly discerned that it was hardly Tony Award-winning material. He described it as a cutthroat dialogue fired at Lennon's many naysayers, along with plenty of potshots at the other Beatles. "Beyond that," stated Fred, "it was merely a rambling discourse on life with Yoko."

Other pressures too were brewing that autumn as several presidential hopefuls were courting Lennon. With the election only a year away, the candidates were all looking for vital support. Now that he had fought and won his own battle of independence against the incumbent Republican administration regarding his Green Card, John was high on the list of Democrats seeking celebrity endorsements. Even though he had been out of the limelight for the past few years, the Lennon name was still magic. John, however, despised being pulled into the political undertow. He felt he was being exploited by Ted Kennedy, who courted his support through Sam Green, whom the senator invited out to the family compound in Hyannis. The only record of the visit was revealed many years later when Robert Kennedy's widow, Ethel, remembered John stopping by her home to meet the family. But it was Jerry Brown, the maverick governor of California, who most vigorously sought John's support. Elliot Mintz appointed himself as liaison between the candidate and Lennon. After John told him that he had absolutely no interest, the ambitious Mintz

enlisted the band Chicago, a top act in the 1970s, and went to work or-
ganizing a big promotional concert to support the California governor.

John later condemned both Elliot and Sam Green in his diary as
opportunists and turncoats. Ono, who always demanded absolute loy-
alty from those in her circle, warned her husband that the two were
untrustworthy. Lennon was especially harsh in his appraisal of Mintz,
labeling him nothing but a sycophant, and predicting he would come
crawling back as soon as all the excitement faded.

The lone bright spot in an otherwise gloomy fall was the annual
October 9th birthday party for John and Sean at Tavern on the
Green. Although he had been dreading the event, John actually
enjoyed himself, gorging on meat pie and fruit custard while guests
donned personalized T-shirts and sang in the sunlit atrium. The
39-year-old Lennon, sporting yellow shades and a bushy beard,
delighted in his unique gift from Yoko: life-sized soft dolls of himself and Sean.

But as the days grew shorter and an autumn chill descended upon
Manhattan, Lennon fell once again into a dark hole of desperation.
He was shooting heroin with alarming regularity, whether to ease the
pain of a sore tooth or simply ward off boredom. John also noted that
Tony Sanchez's newly just released rock exposé, *Up and Down with
the Rolling Stones*, portrayed the Lennons as absolute addicts. John's
existence throughout October and November consisted of lounging
in bed, smoking pot, and masturbating, so steeped was he in misery.
At one point he grew ill. Headaches and dizzy spells led to blackouts,
which Swan blamed on Lennon's daily vitamin regimen. A week later,
he was vomiting explosively and his legs could barely support his
weight. John attributed the problem to excessive drug intake and,
once again, fruitlessly promised to quit.

The substance abuse, however, wasn't limited to John, who grew
concerned that Yoko was heavily indulging herself. Alarmed, John
begged her to stop, but couldn't very well preach what he himself
didn't practice. Seaman, too, noted an obvious decline in Ono's appearance: "Her face was haggard, her eyes glassy around pinned
pupils, and she began to spend much of her time in the bathroom,
making loud snorting noises, frequently followed by frightful retch-
ing. At first I thought Yoko was ill, but then I realized she was simply strung out on smack." The fact that both John and Yoko had re-

lapsed made it virtually impossible for them to kick their habits. Someone would turn up with some quality cocaine, and the pair would invariably succumb to temptation, even as an exasperated John secretly prayed for divine intervention.

Sean continued to be a barometer for the increasingly dysfunctional life in Apartment #72. Up at all hours, he was cranky and belligerent, once defiantly viewing a television program his father had forbidden him to watch. Frequent explosions of temper marked Sean's relationship with his new nanny, Uda San, who reminded John of Aunt Mimi. To make matters worse, Sean was insisting on sleeping in his parents' bed every night. Once, an exasperated Lennon refused to allow him into their bed. In retaliation, the boy stood by the bed and tugged at his father's mouth. Tired and prickly, John slapped the child, only to reproach himself bitterly afterwards.

One evening Lennon, examining a life that seemed worthless and directionless, confessed in his audio diary that he had been looking out the window and contemplating whether to leap. But even suicide, it semed, would have required more passion than Lennon had at his disposal.

Around this time Ono decided to draw up John's will, which she encouraged him to sign. Perhaps she feared her husband might be headed toward suicide, and sought to get his signature on the all-important document before it was too late. Certainly she, more than anyone, knew how perilously close Lennon had come to a complete collapse over the past few years.

Along with his morbid ruminations, John also spent a great deal of time obsessing about his health and general welfare. He admitted to friends that the couple's preoccupation with property hunting represented a pressing need to escape their problems.

Lennon's longing for the U.K., too, was tellingly acute, as he hoped to uncover a little corner of the British Isles fifty miles outside Manhattan. At this point, however, he'd be willing to forgo the Scottish Highlands and the sea for a tree and a bit of grass.

Lennon once again put his thoughts on tape while waiting to go on another real estate expedition. In a reflective mood he reminisced about his childhood visits to the Edinburgh Festival, a spectacular showcase of the world's premier marching bands. He remembered when the lights went dim and one bagpipe player remained in a single spotlight. That melancholy, touching moment never failed to move the emotional little boy.

John spoke of taking Sean to the festival in two years' time, thinking the boy would then be the right age. Scotland was always liberating for John, similar to his experience in Japan. (Lennon, it appeared, had a very selective memory.) The idea of going abroad was especially appealing, he said, giving a person license to toss out the usual rules of behavior. You could let loose in another country; in fact, he said, many people did. John reasoned that some vacationers went over the top because they simply couldn't handle all that freedom!

John's search for an idyllic hideaway finally ended when he purchased a sprawling property on Long Island's north shore, in Cold Spring Harbor. Nicknamed Canon Hill, the wooden three-story Tudor house boasted a gorgeous oceanside view and plenty of privacy. Over Thanksgiving, John and family, accompanied by Fred Seaman, decided to spend their first night in the manor house. Although John regretted breaking his yearly tradition of watching the annual Macy's Parade from his balcony at the Dakota, he was eager to get away.

Lennon loved the rambling retreat, praising its well-worn character. On one of the first evenings there, he settled down to watch an ABC television special *Birth of the Beatles* produced by Dick Clark, and was highly amused by its fantasized version of history.

Seaman's account of the extended weekend contrasted dramatically from John's recollections. Fred spoke of everyone wandering aimlessly in the empty house, with a bored and restless John about to go out of his mind. The traditional turkey dinner on November 27th fell flat. "John could usually keep a table of people going for as long as he liked," Fred remembered, "but this time his wit failed him. Eventually, he too fell silent, absentmindedly poking his fork into 'dead bird' as he called it."

Lennon did perk up a day or so later when he called on his assistant one night, offering Seaman a joint and launching into a lengthy discourse on Kundalini yoga. One particular aspect of the discipline was on John's mind. He explained to a somewhat confused Fred that, by abstaining from ejaculation during sex, a certain fluid which gathers at the base of the spine begins to ascend the spinal column. The longer one remains celibate, he said, the more the fluid rises upward, until it reaches the brain, leading to the state of perfect insight. Fred wondered to himself if Yoko sold this to John simply as a ploy to avoid sexual relations with her libido-driven husband.

Even as he entered his fortieth year, Lennon's powerful sex drive showed no signs of abating. When he wasn't thinking about the joys of the flesh, he sought out erotic images on television, in porno magazines, and even in voyeurism, staring at women as they walked down Central Park West. He discussed his frustration with his unrelenting sex drive in his audio journal. He recalled an elderly gentleman reflecting on his erotic daydreams. With each passing year the guy kept waiting for these libidinous thoughts to abate, and when he got into his forties, he was certain they would tail off. But these fantasies continued to rage into his sixties and beyond, even when senility set in, when of course he couldn't act on them. John found the whole matter disillusioning since he had thought aging would somehow quell his appetite. Only death, he quipped, would put out the fire.

Meanwhile, the situation with masseuse Kimi was spiraling out of control. Her games with John, from taunt-and-tease to bait-and-switch, seemed designed to drive a wedge between him and Yoko. Finally, she played her trump card, threatening to inform Yoko of the true nature of their relationship.

It relieved him to finally clear the air. Yoko had long suspected something, but she gave Kimi the cold shoulder and kept John on edge with the fear he'd be discovered. One time Ono even told her husband she had dreamed he was making it with the masseuse. When he relayed this to Kimi, she used her mother's illness as an excuse to disappear for a time while the heated feelings cooled, but she came back. Marnie Hair, a Dakota resident and close friend of Yoko, feels that Kimi, like May Pang, was simply Yoko's vessel to see to her husband's physical desires while keeping an eye on him. When Lennon journeyed to Cold Spring Harbor, Kimi would often follow in a second car, spending time at the house "looking after John."

Charlie Swan later told a London tabloid that John had dropped many hints to his wife that he found the masseuse highly attractive, and an obliging Yoko took the lead from there. Ultimately, Swan revealed, Kimi was dismissed because Yoko caught on to the power games she was playing.

That December, the Lennons donated holiday food baskets to the poor and sent a $1,000 check to help outfit New York's Police Department with bullet-proof vests. Elliot Mintz was, as John predicted, doing his best to crawl back into the family's good graces. His campaign began with phone calls, during which he flattered John and played on his sympathy, reminding him of their long history together. He sent John some audio tapes, as well as an early Christmas present, and before long he was back in New York on the Lennons' doorstep. It poignantly illustrates the depth's of John's loneliness that a man whom he had reviled as an opportunist and a sycophant was one of his closest friends. Even as he lamented missing their conversations, John was privately excoriating Mintz as both a fake and a threat.

The holidays also brought greetings from England, although family members admitted having a hard time getting past Yoko. Lennon's sister Julia remembers having to submit to Ono's interrogation. Furthermore, Yoko would frequently listen in on another line. Once, while engaged in a deeply personal conversation with Julia, and sensing his wife's presence on the line, Lennon barked, "Get off the phone, you fuckin' Nip!"

John's fellow Liverpool pal Pete Shotton recalls similar problems when he tried to reach him. It took John a long time to get to the phone, and even then, Pete got the distinct impression his friend was distracted by something. Then Shotton overheard Yoko cackling about something in the background followed by John's muffled voice over the receiver. "Look, Yoko," Peter heard John bark, "he's fucking coming over and that's that!" Shotton arrived to find both Lennons on edge and John looking worn and tired.

More disturbing to John were the ongoing trials with Julian. The sullen teen continued to vex his father with his on-again, off-again plans to visit over Christmas. At first Julian said maybe, as long as they didn't go to Florida. Then it was a flat no, using school exams and a new girlfriend as an excuse. At the last minute he called saying he would come to New York only if he could bring a friend, but Yoko turned him down. As usual, John didn't challenge her. Julian retaliated by sending his father a tabloid article about rock stars' sons, which focused on both him and Ringo's son Zak Starkey, and went into detail about the trials of being the offspring of a Beatle.

Behind the gambit was filial resentment based on the fact that John never made the effort to visit Julian in Wales. "Just being with him and having fun was the most important gift he gave to me," Julian said a few years after his father's death. "I went to see him whenever I could, but he never came to see me. That is where I felt left out."

Lennon, upset by Julian's attitude, sought solace in several sessions of self-hypnosis, as well as the use of potent narcotics. When his drug intake concerned him yet again, John's way of tackling the issue was to have a deprivation tank installed at Canon Hill. The tank was an oversized wooden chest filled with a saline solution, warmed to a bathlike temperature. John would close himself in the darkened container and lie back, hoping the craving for drugs would pass. They didn't.

Meanwhile Christmas greetings were pouring in from all points: Nigel Walley (formerly of the Quarrymen), Pete Shotton, and David Bowie were only a few who sent the Lennons holiday cards. John also heard from his old friend from Liverpool, Ivan Vaughan, who was suffering from Parkinson's disease. Although he cracked that Ivan was no mental giant, John kindly sent his old friend a parcel of books. In a burst of holiday spirit John phoned Elton John, Keith Richards, and even Paul Simon and Muhammad Ali.

One night John tuned in to Tom Snyder's late-night talk show, which had as its guests Paul and Linda McCartney. John, amused and intrigued, noted that Linda was in a particularly ornery mood. But he admitted that Paul, whom he termed superficial, appeared to be flourishing. After the show John heard from McCartney, who phoned the Dakota to talk about music.

As soon as he retired to his bedroom that night, John pulled out several old Beatles records and even played some McCartney tunes, including "Obla-di Obla-da" and "Eleanor Rigby." Despite his often volatile feelings toward McCartney, theirs was the kind of deep connection for which John continuously yearned. It was a void no one else would ever fill. Yet Lennon never put his stubborn pride aside to repair the once-treasured friendship.

Among the Christmas cards flooding into the Dakota, there arrived a letter purporting to be from Francie Schwartz, McCartney's former girlfriend from the Apple days in London. The writer, who explored her liaison with Paul in her book *Body Count*, for some reason felt the urge to make a confession to Lennon: she wrote in the letter that she had borne McCartney's child. She went on to assert that Paul had never been told about the child, ten years old by this time.

But in a recent correspondence with this author, Ms. Schwartz hotly denied either bearing a child or authoring the letter, saying simply: "I've never had any children." All we know for sure is that John recorded otherwise in his diary.

Following Christmas, John heard of an earthquake in Edinburgh, and was deeply concerned that Aunt Mimi had been caught in the fray. Relief came a week later when she called to report that she was unharmed.

Between Christmas and New Year, John worked on his latest idea, "Club Dakota," his private in-house nightclub. Picking a suitable spot in one of the apartments, Lennon moved his prized Wurlitzer jukebox, plus a Yamaha piano Elton John had given him, into the space. He furnished the room in art-deco style and flamingo colors, complete with a vintage cigarette machine. A few days before New Year's, he planned special opening night festivities, shooting Mintz's photo and recording him, even though it appeared that Elliot had once again overstayed his welcome.

New Year's Eve marked the official opening of Club Dakota, in the tradition of an exclusive British men's club. Its members were but three: John, Yoko, and Elliot. Lennon was dressed in white T-shirt and tails, adorned by his Liverpool school tie. At midnight, the blaring Wurlitzer, shooting a rainbow of neon colors about the walls, played *Auld Lang Syne*, and the Lennons, in a rare show of affection, danced in celebration. The trio toasted one another as a brilliant fireworks display flashed over Central Park. According to Mintz, John never looked more content.

Within a month, however, the club was history, John quickly losing interest. Perhaps he, Mintz, and Ono were not the three musketeers Elliot portrays. Behind Mintz's back, Lennon continued to snipe that he found him personally insufferable and intellectually challenged, and that his overbearing presence had become stifling. In any case, John's version of the New Year's Eve was much different. According to Lennon's account, Mintz had been sent off tactfully, and it was Sean, Yoko, John, and a bodyguard who had seen the light show in Central Park that marked the turn of the year.

In the first hushed hours of the new decade, Lennon looked toward the future and hoped he would somehow grow more comfortable in his skin. Two dreams informed his mood as he stood on the brink of the eighties. The first John caught inside a mirror, grinning at his own reflection. He then walked out of the glass into clarity, wide-awake; he was certain that the dream had been visionary. The second was a chilling nightmare in which he saw his own obituary. It read that he himself had been charged with his own homicide, which occurred at the Dakota. John, both the accused perpetrator and the victim, kept insisting to those who would listen that he wasn't guilty.

Despite these two odd dreams, Lennon felt hopeful that he could put his unique and powerful mark on music history once again. But the tragic truth was that he was moving inexorably toward a dark fate from which there was no escape.

STUPID BLOODY $\boxed{8}$
TUESDAY MAN
The Assassination Of John Lennon

1980

The year 1980 began with a flurry of controversy surrounding the McCartneys. On January 16th Lennon awoke to the news that his old mate was stewing in a Tokyo jail. Paul had been detained at Narita International Airport for possession of 219 grams of marijuana, found in a small carry-on bag while he was going through Japanese customs to play a sold-out tour with Wings. John's first reaction was one of schoolboy delight that his old rival was being sent to the headmaster's office. He joked that McCartney was probably on a suicide watch, in case he drove himself mad singing "Yesterday." He also suggested that Paul subconsciously wanted to be caught, to show the world, and particularly the British, that he's still a bit of a bad boy.

But there was much more to the incident. Paul telephoned the Dakota only the day before, and remarked that Linda had some "dynamite weed." They wanted to stop by and share their good fortune. Paul also revealed that he and his wife would be staying at the Okura Hotel, in the Presidential Suite. The Lennons took the news quietly, but inside John was livid. He later raved that the family's "hotel karma" would be ruined. Yoko, for her part, wasn't about to tolerate the invasion of her sacred turf. While Charlie Swan dutifully cast a dark spell over the McCartneys, Ono reportedly also went to work. Many insist she called a relative who worked for Japanese customs and alerted him that the McCartneys were carrying contraband. In 1981 Swan confided to a friend that he felt Yoko set the whole thing in motion by telling Japanese immigration authorities that McCartney didn't think much of their people. Sam Green later backed up the charge, revealing that Yoko's cousin headed Japan customs. All it took was one phone call from Ono to nab McCartney. Ironically, never aware of his good wife's alleged impropriety, John believed the bust was someone's idea of a sick joke. It had to be a setup, he confided to Charlie Swan. No way would Paul be so foolish as to try to smuggle in contraband to Japan. It would be nothing for customs agents, John surmised, to plant pot on anyone they wanted. The mighty McCartney gets hauled over for inspection and it's suddenly worldwide news.

Upon further reflection, Lennon worried that Paul's Japanese jailers might be mistreating his ex-partner. He expressed relief when Paul was released nine days later. "I feel like I've been keeping vigil for him. Not that I care, you understand."

Soon after the incident, the Lennons traveled to Palm Beach. That February, two strange incidents occurred, the first as John was shopping at an alternative bookstore. He came upon an old photo of an elderly white-haired man. When John asked the clerk who it was, he told Lennon the man was the renowned Hungarian mystic Beinsa Duono. A stunned Lennon informed the clerk that someone years back predicted he would resemble the mystic in his later years.

The second episode related to Yoko's forty-seventh birthday. During a stay in Florida, John hit upon the idea to surprise his wife by showering their El Solano mansion with no less than 1,000 gardenias, at a cost of $3,000. But the surprise soon turned sour as she awoke to the overwhelming perfume of the exotic blooms. When one of the staff, out of John's hearing, asked her what was wrong, she replied that, to the Japanese, gardenias were a symbol of death.

Several weeks after the pair arrived back in New York from that trip, they decided to spend some time at Canon Hill. Yoko ordered John to undergo a ten-day silence. Among the rules laid down were the edicts that television viewing must be done without sound, that an hour had to be spent rowing alone in the harbor each day, and finally, that John must find a "tree friend" with whom to commune. Although she told Sean that the exercise was a kind of fast for the mind, it was simply John submitting to another autocratic game of "Yoko Says."

Despite the Ono-imposed austerities, John still had sailing on his mind. He made an arrangement with Tyler Coneys, proprietor of

Coneys Marine (near the Canon Hill retreat), for a five-day cruise from Newport, Rhode Island to Bermuda. The voyage was plotted with the advice of Yoko's "directional" guru, Yoshikawa.

On June 4th the fledgling sailor embarked with a seasoned crew on board the 43-foot sloop *Megan Jayne*. The trip did the former Beatle a world of good. Upon his return he looked confident and radiant. Apparently Lennon experienced an epiphany of sorts while navigating a violent storm. His ability to handle the crisis buoyed his spirits. He compared the experience to his halcyon days as a rising star in Hamburg, perhaps the happiest days of his life, and the lone period when John felt truly in charge of his own fate.

Fred Seaman observed a man who had rediscovered the vibrant passion of his youth, "a man in the full flush of his power, eager for life, not cowed by it." Water, from which Lennon had always drawn strength, now renewed his spirit.

The journey also served as a catalyst for his final musical resurrection. As John departed on the extended vacation to Bermuda, songs that had only begun to trickle from his pen in the past year now literally poured forth. His creativity was sparked in part by other artists. Lennon was listening to a great deal of Bob Marley, as well as ska and new wave music.

John was enjoying the exhilaration of his latest burst of creativity, only to have Yoko undermine his enthusiasm. Ono was unmoved by his excitement, and her response muted: she seemed distant and preoccupied. For the past month, according to insiders, she'd been carrying on a conspicuous romance with Sam Green. Uda San confided that, while John was at sea, her boss was flaunting the liaison, outfitting herself in provocative lingerie, and giggling like a blushing ingenue. One of the other employees overheard Yoko whispering pillow talk over the phone to Green about the romantic candles she'd lit in her bedroom. While John was off in the Caribbean, the lovers were staying together at the art dealer's hideaway on Fire Island.

Even when she finally flew down to Bermuda on June 27th, where a rejuvenated John unveiled his new repertoire, Yoko remained sullen, distracted, and distant. When she informed him bluntly that she was returning to New York the next day to deal with business, a devastated John blew up. Falling back on a proven gambit, Yoko placated her husband by telling him that she would look into purchasing a place for him in Bermuda after he had made the record. And with that, she was gone.

Over the next few days Lennon turned himself inside out—phoning her, playing her his songs, trying desperately to win a positive reaction. When his attempts fell on deaf ears, John poured his wounded fury into the anguished "Losing You," the lone honest expression of marital discord on the ironically titled *Double Fantasy*. While the Roy Orbison–inspired "Starting Over" was the album's showcase, "Losing You" more accurately depicted Lennon's troubled mind and the crumbling state of his marriage.

On July 4th, while Fred Seaman was on an errand for Yoko, he ran into Sam Havadtoy's one-time lover, Luciano Sparacino, who was doing some renovations for the Lennons. Sparacino told Fred that he was about to move all of John's things—including his clothes, video equipment, books, and furnishings—into the next-door Apartment #71. Yoko, he announced without fanfare, was planning to divorce her monumentally "difficult" husband.

Shortly after Lennon's assassination in 1980 Sparacino, who later died from the complications of AIDS, told his side of the story. He said he had spent a great deal of time with Yoko during John's creative sabbatical in Bermuda, and that she had spoken frankly with him: "She told me, 'I'm bored with John, tired of the Lennon name, and tired of living in his shadow. As soon as the album is off the ground the marriage is over. I'm planning to leave him.' After all the years she and John were together, the spark had gone. There was nothing left. She was also fed up with John just laying about not wanting to work."

Another source who knows Ono well confirmed the story, saying, "She made no bones about it. She was going to leave Lennon. I heard her say, 'I'm very bored with John.'"

However, Ono's indifference to the project changed once she realized that Lennon was going full speed ahead. She decided not only to participate, but that she would cut half the album herself. When she told John, he was stunned. He'd expected she would contribute to the work. But now she was demanding a 50 percent share, and further declared that she was unwilling to confine her material to only one side, insisting they alternate songs as a way of asserting her equality with John. Yoko called John from Fire Island, beginning what soon became a scathing musical dialogue. In "Give Me Something," she

WFIL

HELPING HAND
MARATHON

FEATURING
SPECIAL
GUEST STAR

JOHN
LENNON
(In Person)

Plus Many Other Recording Stars
LIVE - From WFIL/WPVI Parking Area
MEET WFIL AND WPVI PERSONALITIES
★ FREE ENTERTAINMENT ★ FREE REFRESHMENTS
Starting 6 P.M. Friday May 16
and continuing until midnight
Sunday May 18, 1975 and . . . IT'S ALL FREE
WFIL CITY LINE AVENUE & MONUMENT ROAD
PHILADELPHIA

A rare 1975 handbill advertising an even rarer public appearance by Lennon. This
rned out to be a weekend of almost nonstop partying for the former Beatle. (42)

◀ The Lennons leave a Houston court after failing to obtain custody of Yoko's eight-year-old daughter, Kyoko, December 30, 1971. This highly emotional matter vexed John right up until his death. (43)

▶ John and Yoko together in the mid-seventies. The stormy relationship of this charismatic, highly creative couple hid a lot of deeply private pain. (44)

John on the run outside the Dakota, 1975. One can actually *see* the deep paranoia
carried within him during his fragmented final years. (45)

▲ Lennon outside the Federal Courthouse in Manhattan after finally winning his Green Card in 1976, an event that would ultimately prove a hollow victory for the almost perpetually miserable Beatle. (46)

◄ A stressed-out and haggard-looking John. (47)

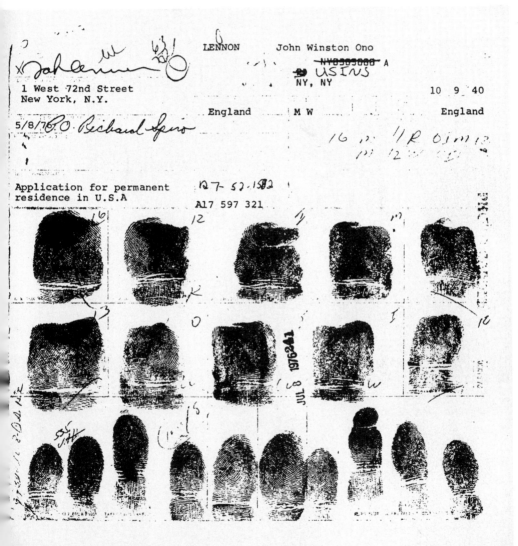

A copy of Lennon's fingerprints taken only days after he was granted permanent residence the United States. (48)

▲ Signing an autograph
outside the posh Dakota,
1976. Frankly, fans were
generally a bother for the
self-involved and often
paranoid musician. (49)

▶Jacqui Dykins, John's troubled maternal half-sister, who
endured a long, sad history of
heroin addiction, Chester,
1978. Today she works as a
shopgirl in a suburban
London green grocer's. Now
long clean and sober, Jacqui
has a son named John. (50)

► On the streets of New York, John's eternal loneliness and indecision was etched on his sad face. (51)

▲ The imposing Dakota complex as seen from Central Park. It was here that Lennon's final psychosis really manifested in a storm of drugs, dreams, magic spells, and emotional isolation. (52)

◀ A busy day at the Record Plant during Lennon's last summer. (53)

▼ An example of one of John's many eccentric notes to former Beatles' roadie Mal Evans. (54)

LUKE WARM!
carry on fucking!
love
John et yoko "

▲ Arriving at the Hit Factory to begin work on John's first record in seven years, *Double Fantasy*, August 12, 1980. Had John lived, he and Yoko were making plans to tour the album worldwide. (55)

▲ A favorite Lennon pastime toward the end of his life, dining out at a posh Manhattan eatery. (56)

▶ As troubled as their relationship was, the Lennons shared a special closeness virtually unfathomable to outsiders. (57)

▼ Satisfying the fans, August 27, 1980. (58)

▲ December 1980, only weeks before his tragic death. (59)

love ,
        your nephew in america.

P.S. one cannot have ones BACK TEETH CAPPED !!!

▲ One of Lennon's final letters to Mimi. (60)

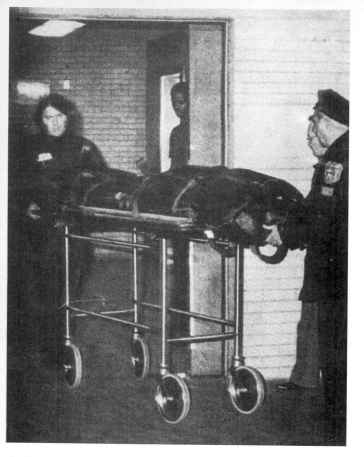

▲ Lennon's body on the way to the Ferncliff Mortuary in Hartsdale for cremation. Yoko is said to keep John's ashes underneath their old bed. (61)

▲ Remembering a genuine cultural hero. (62)

► Julia Baird, Lennon's savvy half-sister, who successfully promoted her brief adult acquaintance with John in her book *John Lennon: My Brother*. Paul McCartney wrote a microscopic introduction that caused the book to sell well. Today, she is a regular at Beatle conventions around the world. (63)

▲ Geoffrey Giuliano with Sean Ono Taro Lennon inside the Dakota during an intensive four-hour interview with the reclusive Mrs. Lennon in 1983. In late 1998, Sean charged that his father was actually murdered at the behest of the U.S. government. (64)

▲ With Harry Nilsson in New York in 1983. It was during this festive night out on the town that Nilsson first approached Giuliano about writing a book utilizing Lennon's lost diaries as source material. (65)

With Julia Baird. Together the pair wrote the authorized biography of Lennon's early life with his Liverpool family, *John Lennon: My Brother*, 1990. Paul McCartney wrote the introduction. (66)

◀ With May Pang, Toronto, 1995. (67)

▲ Sean, Yoko, and Giuliano inside the Lennons' plush apartment, 1983. (68)

wrote, "Your eyes are cold/Your voice is hard." In "Losing You," John fired back, "You say you're not getting enough/But I remind you of all that bad, bad, bad stuff." Yoko replied, "I'm moving on/You're getting phony." Hardly the picture of marital bliss put forth during the album's double-barreled promotion.

Double Fantasy, named for the beautiful but fragile orchid that the lonely composer spotted in the Bermuda botanical garden, suddenly seemed a mockery of his marriage. Lennon was said to be so deflated that he temporarily lost interest in the project. Said Sparacino, "He didn't even want to do *Double Fantasy*, which won a Grammy for them. She pressed him into it."

Suddenly Sam Havadtoy began phoning John in Hamilton, Bermuda, demanding to know what was occurring between Yoko and Sam Green. He pressed John for information about her intimate affairs. Lennon, in a foul mood, hinted that she—like John—needed the occasional fling, but it remains unclear just how much he knew about his wife's indiscretions. He labeled both Sams as sycophants and hustlers trying to fatten their own pockets and reputations.

Lennon returned to Manhattan on July 27th. Eleven days later, on August 7th, he and Yoko hunkered down at the Hit Factory on West 48th Street to record *Double Fantasy* with producer Jack Douglas, who engineered many of Lennon's previous sessions and was well known for his work with Aerosmith and Cheap Trick.

While fans hoped for a passionate, dedicated collaboration between rock's premier couple, the record fell far short of the mark. Tensions were high during the sessions, with the pair often at loggerheads over production issues related to Yoko's songs. Her piercing, off-key vocals—an acquired taste under the best of circumstances—became a profound point of contention during the recording process.

In order to keep focused during the marathon sessions, cocaine was the fuel of choice. One evening Lennon dispatched Fred Seaman in a limousine to fetch several hundred dollars' worth of the drug from one of the studio musicians' regular dealers. Seaman returned with four grams to get them through the all-night session. When Fred wondered how to handle the item on the expense account, Lennon told him, "Write it off as candy."

True to John's rapid-fire recording style, the foundation tracks were laid down in just two weeks. Still without a deal, Ono finally enlisted

David Geffen, who had just formed Geffen Records. Lennon wanted to sign with a larger company and wasn't happy with the development.

In an autumn busy with mixing the album and making the obligatory media rounds, Ono orchestrated yet another publicity stunt. She arranged to shoot a video of the Lennons making love. Yoko sprung this out of the blue one day on John, who had to strip on the spot before the crew and simulate intercourse while Yoko feigned cries of bliss.

Yet, surprisingly, Lennon was taking it all in stride. While in the past such stunts may have driven him into psychological retreat, it was evident that a more mature Lennon had sprouted during the recording experience. The artist told the press this joint project reflected a marriage far from perfect, but one that had endured. He saw it as a kind of family photo album, a documentary of life to be shared with all the couples of his generation who'd traveled so many of the same roads. Despite all the disappointments John's poetic spirit survived, as did his unwavering optimism. "I still believe in love, I still believe in peace," he stated. He added the eerily touching coda, "Where there's life, there's hope."

The highly anticipated release of *Double Fantasy* did not receive the reception the Lennons expected. Reaction to the album was lukewarm from both critics and the public. John's contribution was criticized for the disappointing mediocrity of the music, inspired by retrograde ideas from the fifties and sixties, and venturing nothing bold or new. Yoko, however, fared better. Reviewers found her neo-punk material edgy, though not wildly adventurous. The album simmered disappointingly below the Top Ten. It headed to the top of the charts only after John's assassination. "A very tough way to have a hit," commented Lennon's old friend Vivian Stanshall. While the public once again bought into the romance of the album (subtitled *A Heart Play*), many critics penetrated the smoke screen. Geoffrey Stokes of the *Village Voice* described the work thusly: "vampire woman sucks life out of man who enjoys every minute of his extended destruction." He further observed that it depicted a love "so all-fire powerful it exists without pain, without conflict," and one that doesn't allow "a functioning adult John Lennon."

Then came a couple of odd developments regarding the Lennons' security team. Yoko, in an interview that greatly upset her security chief, described the exact route the couple took from the Dakota to the Hit Factory. In view of their present high-profile itinerary, the security head, an ex-FBI agent turned Lennon bodyguard, Doug MacDougall, had been badgering her for months about increasing their protection. But Ono turned a deaf ear, and MacDougall resigned in protest, returning, as fate and irony would have it, on December 9th. On safety concerns John himself shrugged fatalistically, "If they're gonna get ya, they're gonna get ya. First they kill the fucking bodyguard!"

Looking back on the events of December 8th, fate's hand seemed firmly imprinted on the day's eventual outcome. At 8:00 p.m. that evening Beatles fan Paul Goresh, who'd briefly befriended tourist Mark David Chapman, was unable to convince the waiting assassin to leave the Dakota for the night and return the next morning. Furthermore, Goresh ignored the man's disturbing cryptic remarks: "What if you never see Lennon again? What if something happens to him?"

On the unusually warm evening of December 8th, the first night Jack Douglas had not accompanied his friend John home in weeks, Lennon's worst nightmares converged in the form of troubled nowhere man Mark David Chapman, who fired five shots into Lennon's back, four hitting their target. John managed to stagger away and, in a desperate and vain attempt to escape, made his way up the steps to the Dakota's office, where he pitched forward. As Lennon lay face down, suffering the impact of four hollow-point bullets, his bones were splintered and the life drained out of him. Two items in his possession dropped to the pavement: the blood-spattered glasses Ono would later feature on the cover of her *Season of Glass* album, and a copy of "Walking on Thin Ice," the Yoko dance single John had been producing, and which he accurately predicted would be her most successful work.

Bundled into the back of a patrol car and rushed to nearby Roosevelt Hospital, John was quickly taken into the emergency department headed by Dr. Stephen Lynn. The trauma team had no idea they were working on rock's most celebrated icon. It wasn't until they searched his wallet that they knew who he was. Lynn also later revealed that John had been carrying a "tremendous amount of money."

As Lennon exhibited no vital signs—pulse, blood pressure or respiration—there was only one option: an emergency thoracotomy. John's chest was opened and Dr. Lynn performed a desperate open heart massage in a last-ditch attempt to save his life. But the impact of the three bullets that shattered the left side of his chest destroyed several major heart vessels beyond repair. Lennon was bleeding to death. After feverishly working over his body for nearly half an hour, running transfusions, IV lines, every available surgical procedure, Dr. Lynn pronounced John Lennon dead at 11:15 p.m.

As soon as the news hit the airwaves, the hospital quickly set up an answering service to handle the overload of calls from anxious, devastated fans, many with bizarre questions: Had Lennon's body been frozen? Was his sperm collected? Did the hospital preserve his brain?

Years later, Sean related the strange manner in which Yoko informed him of his father's death. Summoning the boy into her bedroom, she bluntly stated, "'Your dad's dead.' She said it really straight up, like that. 'He's been killed.' I remember wanting to be mature about it for some reason. I said, 'Don't worry, Mom, you're still young. You'll find somebody.' Which is an intense thing to say when I think about it. Then I ran into my bedroom because I didn't want her to see me cry. I didn't want to admit that it was hard. I ran into my room and started crying hysterically."

In the days that followed, while the world mourned a dead hero and showered his grieving widow with sympathy, Ono locked herself behind closed doors and began to bury all that remained of John. The first order of business was the body itself, which doctors found to be in terrible condition due to years of brutal diets, ill-advised fasts, and chronic drug abuse. Although Lennon's often voiced the funeral plans he wanted implemented, Yoko acted not only against his wishes, but against his lifelong objection to cremation, and sent his remains to Ferncliff Mortuary in nearby Hartsdale to be incinerated. John's ashes were later slipped under her bed. Elliot Mintz explained Ono's hasty decision this way: "Yoko wanted John to be thought of not as flesh and bone in varying states of decay, but in the eternal sense in which he lived his life and left this world." Mintz further added that Yoko chose to keep the location of his remains a secret.

In the days following Lennon's murder, Ono pressured his family to stay away, but "allowed" Julian to fly over. It didn't take long for sparks to fly between them. According to Julian, Ono didn't even bother to inform him of his father's death. He had heard about it through the media. Yoko heatedly countered that Cynthia was blocking her calls to Julian, and that it had taken three days to reach him. But the truth is he arrived in New York within 24 hours of his father's death, hustled past the crowds and photographers, and was forced to step over the murder scene and his father's blood. Further, Ono undermined her own version of events by asserting that she asked her stepson if he'd care to see his father before the body was cremated on December 10th. Incidentally, it wasn't Yoko who made the calls to Julian, Mimi, and Paul McCartney, but rather assistant/accountant Rich DePalma who undertook the grim task.

After John's death, Yoko set up the Spirit Foundation, a not-for-profit organization to handle donations from fans, some as much as $10,000. Terming it "John's personal charitable foundation," Ono solicited contributions in a full-page ad in the *New York Times*. The foundation's mission was unclear: "Any money that's sent is directly used for whatever purpose 'we' feel is important."

Ono then made a sweep of her inner circle. Sam Green, Yoko's occasional lover, who had been abruptly demoted to an errand boy during the final sessions for *Double Fantasy*, was ousted. So was Charlie Swan. The tarot reader had become a problem over the past eighteen months, and Yoko felt he disappeared on the family at times of crisis. A particularly thorny issue between them was Swan's resentment when Yoko asked him to tailor readings to her wishes. When Yoko asked him to render readings that would please John, he became angry.

David Geffen, too, was fired. He balked at pushing Ono's *Season of Glass*, an album he found distasteful and substandard. Yoko rushed the record's release, putting it out just six months after John's assassination. Of the Dakota inner circle, only Elliot Mintz remained, the "consummate sycophant," as Seaman dubbed him.

Over the next two years Ono would purge several other "traitors," including bodyguard Doug MacDougall, who bitterly complained of not receiving back pay owed to him. Fred Seaman was also fired. He was later accused of absconding with a mountain of Lennon's personal belongings—including his diaries and several unreleased songs recorded during the *Double Fantasy* sessions—which he later insisted John had designated for Julian. In May of 1983, Seaman pled guilty to second-degree grand larceny in the theft.

Fred, though, wasn't the only Seaman to be dismissed. Ono also fired his Aunt Helen, the once trusted nanny to Sean and wife of longtime confidant Norman. Yoko felt that Helen had taken advantage of her by charging personal expenses to Ono's account. In Yoko's mind, Helen's behavior, however inadvertent, confirmed John's suspicions about the Seamans' dubious integrity. While the release of many Lennon employees may have been justified, there was one brutal, heartless episode that unjustly threatened John's beloved Uncle Norman Birch. Back at the height of Beatlemania, Lennon purchased a modest three-bedroom Liverpool home for his Aunt Harriet and her husband. When Harriet passed away, the deed was never transferred to Norman, even though John intended that he should have the home. Following Lennon's murder, the 78-year-old, nearly penniless Birch received a cruel eviction notice, with the explanation that Ono wanted to sell the place soon. "Yoko sees this as an opportunity to make some extra money," Birch declared to this author, near tears. "Considering her carefully cultivated image as Mrs. Peace and Love, you have to question her sincerity. [John] would probably box her ears and hang her on the line to dry for being so nasty." Yoko's response to the unsavory matter was simply to say that John had never given specific instructions concerning the property. In the end, however, Ono apparently thought better of the greedy move and reluctantly allowed the old man to stay.

Under the new regime Ono opened both her home and her bedroom to Sam Havadtoy. The decorator moved in just days after the shooting, and the couple have been together ever since. There have been reports the pair were secretly married in Budapest in June 1981, a charge Ono vehemently denies. According to insiders, despite her many statements that she was sick of John, Ono has made Havadtoy into a virtual clone of her late husband, dressing him up in Lennon's sweaters, having his hair cut the same way. Yoko also appointed the new man in her life president of the Manhattan Bag One Gallery, specializing in Lennon-related art work. In the fall of 1981, months after Havadtoy was ensconced in the Dakota, she told a writer, "Could I really bring another man into all of this? I don't intend to spend the rest of my life alone, but in this state of mind it would be very unfair to any man who gets involved with me because I'm still very involved."

With John's death, Yoko had an opportunity to heal the rift within the Lennon family, particularly with Julian, who seemed destined to forever be an outsider despite his status as John's firstborn. But no such olive branch was offered. Instead, only a year after John's death, she attacked Julian in a conversation with a colleague of this author. Yoko complained bitterly that she had gone out of her way to make the boy comfortable in the wake of his father's death—providing his favorite libation, beer, offering him a new drum kit, and inviting him to stay as long as he wished. According to Ono, she warmly embraced Julian and assured him that he and Sean now were family. Yoko, however, was quick to point out that Julian's aloof and distant behavior had a disturbing effect on Sean and that furthermore the younger Lennon was jealous of his mom's attention toward his big brother. Ono further complained that she had to contend with the sullen Julian while sacrificing the needs of five-year-old Sean. Her employees, she stated, would confirm her story. But according to many of those people, Ono tapped Havadtoy and Seaman to look after the troubled seventeen-year-old, and even sent the grieving teen off to Canon Hill the day after his arrival in the United States.

The controversy set off a feud between Yoko Ono and Cynthia Lennon. When Ono contacted her following his death, she claims to have graciously offered financial aid. Cynthia counters that Yoko was griping about money, and labeled the widow a mercenary who first stole her husband and was now going after Julian.

Ono lamented that she was in a no-win situation. If she favored Julian, the press would accuse her of trying to wrest him away from his mother. Yet if she compelled him to get permission from his mother to fly to Manhattan she would be depicted as a bad guy.

A year after John's death, journalist Ray Coleman phoned Yoko to read her a December 1981 article in a British tabloid entitled "I'm Penniless, Says Julian. Yoko Only Gives Me Fifty Pounds A Week." In the lengthy notes Coleman took during the call (later given to our researchers by the seasoned journalist), he prepared her by suggesting that the piece insinuated that the boy had an ax to grind. True, Julian was certainly acting like the prodigal son, taking the opportunity to lash out at Yoko. Julian readily admitted he was lazy, didn't want a nine-to-five job, and could be accused of trying to cash in on his father's name.

Upon hearing this, Ono pointed out it was the very reason John could never really draw close to his elder son. She stated that John did not ask Julian to visit often because father and son had little in common and tension ran high between them. Moreover, in an astonishing assertion she declared that her husband secretly accused Julian of being spoiled as a result of being raised by Cynthia. For these reasons, claimed Yoko, John pointedly arranged his will to avoid placing her in the middle of an explosive tug-of-war within the family.

Julian was quoted as saying that when he arrived at the Dakota he didn't even see his stepmother for four days. She hid out in her bedroom, according to him, consulting her legal advisers about the will. Yoko completely ignored Julian, which alienated the grieving teenager even more.

The younger Lennon further charged that Yoko possessed malevolent psychic powers and used intimidation tactics. Julian accused her of using terror to impose her will after he found some of the letters she penned to his father. These notes alleged that Yoko had threatened suicide if John refused to meet with her. "I'm very suspicious of Yoko," said Julian in the piece. "She is very crafty and you have to watch her. She's a very hard lady to get to know, and always kept me at a distance. There always seemed to be great tension in the air when I was with her and with John. . . . *Dad was always totally under her influence.* She is a very strong person and has a lot of power and is a bit scary. She knows I understand what she is about so she is a bit wary of me." He also claimed she offered to put him up in his own New York apartment, but Julian saw that as a trap where Yoko could manipulate his developing musical career.

Ono's reaction to the piece was one of anger, denial, and outrage. For instance, when Julian stated, "The papers say I'm heir to 12 million, but Yoko has total control of everything," Ono exploded that he didn't have a claim to even one penny of his father's estate.

When young Lennon suggested his father's death left his mother "even more upset than Yoko," Ono gasped, "Oh God, how can he say that! Do you believe this?" And when he revealed that during his visits to the Dakota he had to ask permission of the staff to go into his father's bedroom, she retorted, "Not true!"

During the same interview, Julian also aired his fears about becoming a target for a mad gunman or a kidnapping. "I hope that [kidnapping] doesn't ever happen, because Yoko is the only one with any money and she has already told me she will never pay a kidnap ransom for me."

The angry teen also recalled an incident just after his father died, when he offhandedly picked up a recorder John was carrying when he was gunned down. Yoko went ballistic, launching into a hysterical outburst that terrified him. Julian later learned that it was a Japanese custom not to touch any item of someone who had died for a period of forty days. Ono responded that she'd never even heard of such a custom, and insisted she never lost her cool.

Julian's most troubling indictment of his stepmother concerned how she treated his vulnerable half-brother. He alleged Yoko was never a loving parent to Sean and paid little attention to him, leaving his care to nannies. Julian also said his only reason to return to New York would be to see his little brother.

Sean supports that accusation in part. "It was like I didn't know my mom until my dad died. I remember getting dressed in my best clothes to go out for a walk with my mom. Because most of the time I was with nannies, especially when dad died. My mom couldn't deal with me a lot because she was going through a lot of very difficult stuff of her own."

It is important to note that, throughout the interview with Coleman, Yoko's tone changed and she became generously solicitous, allowing young Julian ample slack. After all, she and John had both made mistakes in talking to the press, she pointed out. Here was a young boy with a future ahead of him so she would carefully consider any rebuttal.

The dismaying family animosities underscore John's sad personal legacy, a tale of two sons, one who only knew his father as a legend, the other who knew him only in his troubled final days. Following his own "wild oats" period, Julian set to work honing his musical skills to prove he could make it on his own. His father's influence was stamped upon the sound of his first band, Quasar. Julian's voice bears a remarkable similarity to his father's. Julian has said of his dad, "If he were alive, we would be playing together. We would have made a great team." His 1984 debut album *Valotte*, produced by his father's old colleague Phil Ramone, displayed a promising writing talent, and Julian's plaintive vocals have the unmistakable echoes of his father's voice. It is perhaps that similarity that drove sales for the debut. The public, saddened by Lennon's passing, and hungry for his unique sound, might have turned to the record simply because it reminded them of John. In subsequent releases though, Julian stepped back from re-creating his father's sound, and the records sold poorly. His most recent release was received more warmly by critics than were previous efforts.

In a recent interview he attributed his failures to his sudden, explosive fame complicated by the burden of living up to the impossible expectations of being John Lennon's son. "It was not about me, but about being dad's son," he lamented. When Julian subsequently tumbled into cocaine and alcohol addiction, Cynthia pinned much of the blame on the older, hardened session musicians he worked with. "He was totally lost and screwed up," she conceded. Yet there were signs that a more mature and stronger Julian, now in his thirties, was on the professional rebound with his May 18, 1998 release, *Photograph Smile*. It was dedicated to his stepfather Roberto Bassanini, whom he termed "more a father to (me) than anyone," as much a shot at his biological father as a tribute to his stepfather. Julian went on to accuse his late dad of having fathered a child without bothering to raise it. Julian recently told one interviewer his relationship with his dad was about as cozy as living with a stranger. Although his father proclaimed, "All you need is love" to the masses, he was unable to express his feelings to his own family. "How can you talk about peace and love and have a family in bits and pieces, no communication, adultery, divorce?" cried Julian.

Jumpstarting his flagging career, Julian had to overcome some formidable obstacles. For starters, *Photograph Smile* was released the same day as half-brother Sean's first solo CD, *Into the Sun*. For Julian, this was no mere coincidence; he suggested that someone in the Ono circle was controlling the situation in Sean's favor, no matter what the cost. On the heels of this episode came the inevitable comparisons between the Lennon siblings. Early reviews dismissed Julian's work for following the same tired tracks of his eighties sound while praising Sean for his far more progressive approach. A determined Julian, however, rode out the storm and embarked on a 1999 U.S. tour to promote the February release in the States of *Photograph Smile*. As Lennon played clubs like Los Angeles' legendary House of Blues, American critics took a second, more favorable look at his work, using terms like "glowing" and "masterful." One impressive thumbs-up came from none other than Beatles producer George

Martin: "He's very good by himself. Take away John Lennon and he'd be greater. But you can't do that. He's the son of a famous father."

Financially, too, things were looking up for the musician. After a sixteen-year legal battle over his father's estate, Julian won an undisclosed settlement believed to be worth $10 million plus a share of John's record royalties. The litigation took so long in part because Julian didn't want to appear to be a money grabber.

Furthermore, John's will gave Yoko total control over his son's inheritance and the power to dole out sums as she saw fit. As testament to Ono's "generosity," Julian has framed a royalty check made out to him from his stepmom for a paltry 50 cents!

Although Julian received only a fraction of the several hundred-million-dollar Lennon treasure, Yoko deemed it "more than fair" and curtly labeled her stepson "ungrateful."

Bad blood continues to this day between the estranged pair. Julian has charged, "Yoko tried to negate us from the history books," while blasting Ono for her virtually nonstop, tasteless profiteering from John's doodles and other pseudo artwork. "She has anything and everything of Dad's," he bitterly yet accurately points out, "but the one thing she will never have is the blood and talent of the Lennons."

Sean subsequently hooked up as bass guitarist with the alternative rock band Cibo Matto. In June of 1999 the group released the CD *Stereotype A*, a fusion of R&B, heavy metal, hip-hop, even country waltz. The budding artist promises his next solo effort to be "a kind of gory, horror flick type thing," reflecting his current infatuation with shock rocker Marilyn Manson. This despite Sean's passionate "Mom and me against the world" battle cry over the years.

Sean moved out of the Dakota as soon as he was of age, and has said of Yoko, "She can be very critical sometimes. But I intentionally made a record where I didn't care what she thought." With his bottle-blond hair and tortoiseshell glasses, Sean has been described as very much his father's son: high-strung and given to exuberant hyperbole, once comparing his mother's musical achievements to those of Miles Davis. And like his father, Sean has a refreshing naïveté and generosity of heart.

He also holds John very close in his heart. "People ask me, 'Do you feel he's still around?' And he is, man. He's alive in his music, in my life. Sometimes I walk into a store and 'Instant Karma' is playing and

I feel like that's him talking to me. I wish I could do anything with my dad. Go to a movie. Walk down the street. Watch TV with him, let alone talk about music.

"If there's anything the public doesn't understand, it's that he was a human being. That when he died, he left a real family behind. I miss him every day. I don't miss John Lennon the persona, I miss my fucking dad. I miss the guy who showed me how to clean my penis when I was peeing. Seriously, that's what I miss. I don't at all miss the Beatle."

Of course, there are obvious references to his father in Sean's music, notably the similar nasal vocal style. Even his choice of a companion echoes his father. His lover, keyboard player Yuka Honda, is a Japanese woman some fifteen years his senior, and like his parents, the two write and produce together. Strangely, the younger Lennon is convinced his father's murder was a federal conspiracy. "[He] was a counterrevolutionary and was very dangerous to the government. If he had said 'Bomb the White House tomorrow,' there would have been 10,000 people who would have done it. The pacifist revolutionaries are historically killed by the government, and anybody who thinks Mark Chapman was just some crazy guy who killed my dad for his own personal interest is insane or very naive. It was in the best interest of the United States to have my dad killed. And you know, that worked against them, because once he died, his power grew. So I mean, fuck them! They didn't get what they wanted."

His current opinions are no doubt colored by his childhood experience. "I grew up deathly afraid somebody was going to shoot my mom or me," he confided. This fear is understandable. Ono herself faced numerous death threats in the years following John's assassination. A number of harrowing bomb threats were followed by a threat from a lunatic who, describing himself as a member of the Mark Chapman Fan Club, mailed Yoko a note that read "Death to Ono." The madman was later arrested outside the Dakota, where he had apparently gone with murder on his mind. In the first year after her husband's murder, Ono spent over a million dollars on security. She kept a loaded revolver in her night table, while dour guards armed with submachine guns were posted outside her bedroom and Sean's.

Ono has kept a fairly low profile over the years, holding an art exhibition every now and then, playing occasional club dates, and making sporadic media appearances, once guest-starring as herself on an episode of the NBC sitcom *Mad About You*. A multimillion-dollar book deal with Putnam was in the works in 1982, but when Simon & Schuster (who published *Grapefruit* a decade before) reminded Ono of her contractual option for a second book, the deal soured. At 67 years old she has a small but loyal cult following, but without her late husband she is not nearly as much of a draw as she once was. Her key function is as keeper of the Lennon empire, which today hovers close to an astounding $1 billion, a tribute to her shrewd management of the family fortune.

Yoko Ono will never escape the giant shadow of John Lennon. She was said to be in a "state of shock" following Linda McCartney's death from cancer on April 17, 1998. The tragedy struck her hard, due to her own life-threatening scare with breast cancer, not to mention the striking parallels of their lives: both were divorcées married to Beatles within eight days of each another; both were publicly condemned as unsuitable spouses; both suffered public derision over their musical efforts. Controversy also swirled around the circumstances of McCartney's death. The cover-up of the exact date and place, designed to protect the family's privacy, spurred rumors that the death might have been the result of an assisted suicide.

In the immediate wake of Linda's death, Ono wrote a tribute to her for *Rolling Stone*. Yoko said it was apparent "that our husbands were not all buddy-buddy. John and Paul were both talented but also very strong-willed people. There was some real tension there. Linda and I left them alone. But we didn't go chummy-chummy, wink-wink, 'Aren't they silly boys?' either. We both stood by our men. That was how we were. . . . John would say some nice things. He wouldn't say it to Paul, but when Paul was not around, John would say nice things about him." Ono also revealed that she was invited to the McCartneys' farm after John's death, and noted that Linda showed grace under relentless public criticism. She praised Linda's nobility for putting up with a world that failed to "recognize her for her achievements. Everything that was good," Ono went on, "the good work done, was considered the work of her husband and everything the public did not approve of was considered her doing. . . . Like so many women before her she made a difference in silence."

Curiously, even on the heels of the glowing tribute, Ono was not invited to the June 22nd New York memorial service held for Linda at Riverside Church in Morningside Heights. But Yoko's grief at Linda's passing seemed genuine. "She was so saddened by it," said Ono spokesperson Michael Phillips. As for the snub from McCartney regarding the memorial service, Yoko sent flowers anyway, and said "[Sean and I] were a bit hurt, but I know that Paul's dealing with the tragedy as best as he is allowed."

Perhaps the grieving McCartney had good reason for giving Yoko the cold shoulder. In a BBC radio interview back in December, Ono had callously labeled Paul "Salieri to John's Mozart." It was a remark that Paul, already dealing with a terminally ill spouse, could have done without.

Who among us hasn't wondered now and then about Lennon's role had he lived? He had already booked plane tickets to a December protest rally in San Francisco to support Japanese workers fighting for better wages, which would have been his first such appearance in over eight years. Had he taken the stage at 1985's Live Aid, would his appearance have resulted in the long-anticipated Beatles reunion? What would John have said about Reaganomics, the "Me Generation," the collapse of the Berlin Wall, and the sudden end of communism as a potent world force? Would Lennon's music have provided a saving grace in the nineties atmosphere of disposable, unadventurous, self-serving acts pumped out by the artless, bottom-line industry he had grown to despise? The signs he gave us in late 1980, particularly his plans to do a second and third album, were convincing evidence that he had no intention of once again reverting to his former slump.

Certainly there are those who will take exception to the portrait of John Lennon presented here: the neurotic, often weak, dominated figure given to flare-ups of irrational temper, nearly constant self-pity, and dangerous self-destruction. Others may simply refuse to believe the truth, despite the irrefutable evidence of the man's own words and deeds, preferring instead to bask in the rosy Ono-crafted myth of the past twenty years. Perhaps others will reject this portrayal altogether, unable, or unwilling, to separate John's remarkable artistry from his all-too-human facade. But as Paul McCartney once pointed out, "John was a great guy, but part of his greatness was that he wasn't a saint." Even Lennon at his very worst can't begin to obliterate the finer elements of his incredible legacy:

his cutting wit, mischievous charm, his clarion call to social conscience, his huge heart, and the inimitable echo of that singular Liverpudlian voice. Jack Douglas said of his great friend, "Our generation lost a guide. When things got out of control, there was always John. Without his voice I think we all lost our way." John Lennon created some of the most provocative and stirring music of the twentieth century. His death left a giant void as an artist, icon, and compassionate humanist that no one before or since could possibly even begin to fill. On that at least, everyone must surely agree.

We miss you, John.

Family Tree

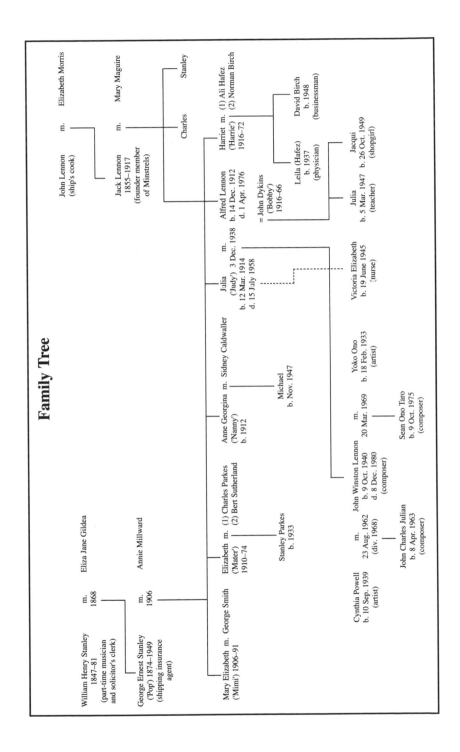

William Henry Stanley
1847–81
(part-time musician
and solicitor's clerk)

m.
1868

Eliza Jane Gildea

George Ernest Stanley
(Pop) 1874–1949
(shipping insurance
agent)

m.
1906

Annie Millward

John Lennon
(ship's cook)

m.

Elizabeth Morris

Jack Lennon
1855–1917
(founder member
of Minstrels)

m.

Mary Maguire

Charles

Stanley

Mary Elizabeth m. George Smith
('Mimi') 1906–91

Elizabeth m. (1) Charles Parkes
('Mater')   (2) Bert Sutherland
1910–74

Anne Georgina m. Sidney Caldwaller
('Nanny')
b. 1912

Julia   m.   Alfred Lennon
('Judy') 3 Dec. 1938   b. 14 Dec. 1912
b. 12 Mar. 1914   d. 1 Apr. 1976
d. 15 July 1958

= John Dykins
('Bobby')
1916–66

Harriet m. (1) Ali Hafez
('Harrie')   (2) Norman Birch
1916–72

Stanley Parkes
b. 1933

Michael
b. Nov. 1947

Leila (Hafez)
b. 1937
(physician)

David Birch
b. 1948
(businessman)

Julia
b. 5 Mar. 1947
(teacher)

Jacqui
b. 26 Oct. 1949
(shopgirl)

Cynthia Powell
b. 10 Sep. 1939
(artist)

m.
23 Aug. 1962
(div. 1968)

John Winston Lennon
b. 9 Oct. 1940
d. 8 Dec. 1980
(composer)

m.
20 Mar. 1969

Yoko Ono
b. 18 Feb. 1933
(artist)

Victoria Elizabeth
b. 19 June 1945
(nurse)

John Charles Julian
b. 8 Apr. 1963
(composer)

Sean Ono Taro
b. 9 Oct. 1975
(composer)

CHRONOLOGY

26 October 1855 John Lennon Senior, John's paternal grandfather (known throughout his life as Jack), is born in Liverpool. He later became a founding member of the famous American traveling musical troupe, the Kentucky Minstrels.

22 August 1874 George Ernest Stanley (Pop), stern patriarch of John's mother's family, is born at 120 Salisbury Street, Everton. He spent many years at sea, later coming ashore to work as an insurance investigator for the Liverpool Salvage Company.

14 December 1912 Alfred (known variously as Alf, Fred, or Freddie) Lennon, John's seafaring father, is born at 27 Copperfield Street, Toxteth Park, Liverpool. His mother, Mary Maguire, had two more sons, Charles and Stanley.

12 March 1914 Julia Stanley (who liked to be called Judy), mother of John Lennon, Victoria Elizabeth Stanley, Julia Dykins, and Jacqui Dykins, is born in Liverpool to Annie Millward and George Stanley.

1916 John Albert Dykins (nicknamed Bobby, Twitchy, or Spiv), Julia's common law husband and the father of their two girls, Julia and Jacqui, is born.

August 1917 John Lennon Senior dies of a liver disease at sixty-one, thus leaving his three sons in the care of Liverpool's Bluecoat Orphanage.

18 February 1933 Yoko Ono is born into the family of a wealthy but aloof Tokyo banker.

3 December 1938 Despite strong objections from the Stanleys, Alfred Lennon marries the free-spirited Julia at the Liverpool Registry Office. Immediately after the austere civil ceremony each returns to their own parents' home. Three days later, Lennon signs on for a three-month tour aboard a cargo ship bound for the West Indies.

10 September 1939 Cynthia Powell, John's first wife, is born in Blackpool.

23 June 1940 Stuart F. Sutcliffe is born in Edinburgh. He will later play bass with the Beatles.

7 July 1940 Richard Starkey (Ringo Starr) is born to Richard and Elsie at 24 Admiral Grove, the Dingle, Liverpool.

9 October 1940   John Winston Lennon enters this world during a German air raid over Liverpool at seven o'clock in the morning. Shortly after his birth he is placed under his mother's sturdy iron bed at the Liverpool Maternity Hospital. He is called John after his grandfather and Winston in honor of Prime Minister Winston Churchill. Once again his father is away at sea.

24 November 1941   Randolph Peter Best, the Beatles' first professional drummer, is born in Madras, India.

18 June 1942   James Paul McCartney is born to Mary Patricia Mohin and James McCartney at home in Liverpool.

1942   Finally giving into family pressure, Julia Lennon reluctantly agrees to temporarily turn over care of her infant son to her sister Mimi and brother-in-law, gentleman dairy farmer, George Smith.

1942   Despairing of her globe-trotting husband ever settling down, Julia finally ends their relationship. She will soon meet and fall in love with a congenial barman, John Albert Dykins. Together they take a small flat in the then tatty Gateacre district of Liverpool.

25 February 1943   George Harold Harrison, the youngest child of Harry and Louise Harrison, is born at 12 Arnold Grove, Wavertree, Liverpool.

19 June 1945   Julia gives birth to her second child, Victoria Elizabeth, at the Salvation Army's Elmswood Infirmary in North Mossley Hill Road, Liverpool. The father is not listed on the birth certificate, but is thought to be an army gunnery officer with the nickname of Taffy. The infant is subsequently adopted and is believed to have been taken by her new parents to Norway. Decades later she goes public with her identity.

September 1945   Young John attends Dovedale Primary just around the corner from Mimi's at 251 Menlove Avenue, Woolton.

July 1946   Fred returns from sea unexpectedly and convinces Mimi to allow John to accompany him on an impromptu holiday to Blackpool, secretly intending to spirit the boy off to New Zealand. Julia locates the two and takes John back to Liverpool.

5 March 1947   Julia Dykins, John Lennon's second sister and the first child of Julia and John Dykins, is born in Liverpool.

26 October 1949   Jacqui Gertrude Dykins is born in Liverpool.

September 1950   Young John is awarded a beginner's swimming certificate by the Liverpool Association of Schoolmasters.

July 1952   John leaves Dovedale Primary.

September 1952   John attends Quarry Bank High School for Boys.

5 June 1955   George Smith dies unexpectedly at home of an undisclosed liver ailment, aged fifty-two. John is heartbroken.

15 June 1956   Paul McCartney meets John for the first time at a Saturday afternoon performance by John's schoolboy skiffle group, the Quarry Men, at St. Paul's Parish Fete in Woolton. Shortly afterward he is invited to join the band by Pete Shotton, a mutual friend of John and Paul (as well as being the Quarry Men's erstwhile washtub player).

September 1957   Cynthia Powell, aged eighteen, enrolls as a lettering student at the Liverpool Junior Art School. She soon transfers to Liverpool Art College where she meets her future husband, fellow student John Lennon.

6 February 1958   Crackerjack guitarist George Harrison joins the Quarry Men. The nucleus of what would later be known as the Beatles is now formed.

Spring 1958   The Maharishi Mahesh Yogi (Mahesh Prasad Varma) arrives in Hawaii to begin propagating his transcendental meditation movement in the West. He will later become John's first guru.

15 July 1958   Julia Lennon is knocked down and killed by a car driven by an off-duty police officer suspected of drinking, just outside Mimi's home on Menlove Avenue. John and his sisters are home with John Dykins, playing outside. Julia's final words to Mimi just before the accident were "Don't worry." Many years later the driver admits that the accident ruined his life.

December 1958   John and Paul perform a few gigs together as the Nurk Twins.

29 August 1959   The Quarry Men are invited to play at the opening night of the Casbah, a teen coffee club run by Mona Best, Pete's fun-loving mother.

5 November 1959   Now renamed Johnny and the Moondogs, the band fails an audition for Carrol Levis at the Manchester Hippodrome.

5 May 1960   The flagging group, renamed once again the Silver Beatles, fail another big audition to back singer Billy Fury. They are, however, chosen to tour with another young crooner, Johnny Gentle, on an upcoming trek through Scotland.

August 1960   Paul McCartney invites Pete Best to join the Beatles as their regular drummer on their first trip to Germany.

Autumn 1960   The Beatles make their first professional recording with members of Rory Storm and the Hurricanes (Ringo is a member), at Akustik Studios, Hamburg. While in Germany they meet Astrid Kirchherr, who takes the first major photos of the Beatles and helps develop the "Mod" look.

5 December 1960   The Beatles' trek to Germany is interrupted after George is found to be underage by German officials and is unceremoniously deported. The other Beatles soon end up back in Liverpool, feeling beaten and dejected. Paul and Pete had to leave for setting fire to the Kaiserkeller. Stuart stays in Germany with Astrid, his new fiancée.

21 March 1961   The Beatles appear at the Cavern for the first time. Over the next two years they will play there some 292 times.

1 October 1961   John and Paul take off on a two-week hitchhiking trip to Paris. While they are there, the famous Beatles haircut is born.

9 November 1961   Wealthy Liverpool record-retailer Brian Epstein unexpectedly drops by the Cavern to hear the Beatles after being deluged with requests for their first official release, "My Bonnie" (a German Polydor import).

3 December 1961   Epstein invites the group to his office to discuss the possibility of taking over as their manager. They readily agree.

1 January 1962   The Beatles travel to London to audition for Decca Records. Despite a rousing performance they are ultimately turned down by Decca executive Rick Rowe who ironically tells Brian that groups with guitars are on the way out.

10 April 1962   Stuart Sutcliffe tragically dies of a brain hemorrhage in Hamburg. He is only twenty-one years old. John is crushed.

9 May 1962   The Beatles are offered a recording contract with Parlophone Records, a tiny offshoot of the vast EMI entertainment empire. Their recording manager is the brilliant and affable George Martin.

16 August 1962   For reasons that remain a mystery to this day, drummer Pete Best is unceremoniously sacked from the group and Ringo Starr is quickly brought in.

23 August 1962   John marries Cynthia Powell in a civil ceremony at the Mount Pleasant Registry Office in Liverpool. Fellow Beatles Harrison and McCartney attend. George Martin is best man.

5 October 1962   The single "Love Me Do" is released.

31 December 1962   The Beatles make their final club appearance in Hamburg.

2 March 1963   "Please Please Me" becomes number one on the *Melody Maker* chart.

8 April 1963   John Charles Julian Lennon is born to John and Cynthia at 6:50 A.M. at Sefton General Hospital, Liverpool.

1 February 1964   "I Want to Hold Your Hand" is the number one record in America.

9 February 1964   The Beatles appear on the *Ed Sullivan Show* in New York. During their performance an estimated seventy-three million television viewers experience John, Paul, George, and Ringo for the first time. Across America not a single crime is committed by a teenager.

23 March 1964   John's first book, *In His Own Write*, is published. Almost overnight it becomes an international bestseller. Thirty years later it will still be in print.

10 July 1964   A civic reception is held in Liverpool to honor its most famous sons; over 100,000 attend. Among them are John's sisters Julia and Jacqui as well as most of his family.

15 February 1965   John finally passes his driving test (after driving illegally for years).

12 June 1965   Buckingham Palace announces that the Beatles will be awarded MBEs later that year.

24 June 1965   John's second book, *A Spaniard in the Works*, is published.

3 August 1965   John buys Mimi a lovely seaside bungalow in Poole, Dorset.

31 December 1965   Alfred Lennon suddenly reappears on the scene, this time to release his one and only record, "That's My Life (My Love and My Home)." Although initially it receives quite a lot of airplay, it is critically panned and sells poorly. John is not amused.

4 March 1966   John makes his infamous remark about the Beatles being more popular than Jesus during an interview with British journalist and Beatle intimate, Maureen Cleave.

31 July 1966   Radio stations across America join together in an ad hoc ban on Beatle music as a result of John's controversial remarks on the decline of Christianity in the West. Over the next few weeks there are reports of record burnings and other protests by groups ranging from the Ku Klux Klan to the Daughters of the American Revolution. In the midst of this furor, John is persuaded by Brian Epstein to publicly to recant his remarks in an effort to calm middle America's shattered faith in the Fabs.

29 August 1966   The Beatles give their final American concert at Candlestick Park, San Francisco. John is thrilled that the Beatles' "performing flea" days are over at last.

9 November 1966   John meets Yoko Ono for the first time at a preview showing of her one-woman conceptual art show, *Unfinished Paintings and Objects*, at the Indica Gallery, London.

26 May 1967   *Sgt. Pepper's Lonely Hearts Club Band* is released just in time to kick off the infamous summer of love.

24 August 1967   The Beatles and an entourage of girlfriends, wives, and hangers-on attend an introductory lecture on transcendental meditation given by the Maharishi at the Hilton Hotel, London. John and George Harrison are particularly impressed.

27 August 1967   While attending a weekend meditation seminar held in Bangor, Wales, the Beatles receive word that Brian Epstein has been found dead in his London townhouse because of an unexplained overdose of drugs. The Maharishi attempts to comfort them.

5 January 1968   Alfred Lennon and his nineteen-year-old fiancée, Pauline Jones, meet John to seek his blessing for their forthcoming marriage. John is not really too happy about this unexpected romance, but reluctantly gives the two of them his support.

16 February 1968   John, Cynthia, George, and his wife, Pattie, join the Maharishi in Rishikesh, India, for an intensive two-month instructor's course in transcendental meditation. The rest of the Beatles entourage arrives four days later.

12 April 1968   The Beatles leave the peaceful mountain ashram two weeks ahead of schedule after a nasty rumor circulates that the giggly Indian fakir attempted to compromise the virtue of fellow mediator Mia Farrow. Mia later confirms the incident in her memoirs.

22 August 1968   Cynthia sues John for divorce, citing adultery with Yoko Ono.

18 October 1968   John and Yoko are busted for possessing one-half ounce of hashish at their flat at 34 Montagu Square, London. A charge of obstructing justice is also brought against the couple who, according to Liverpool chum Pete Shotton, had been warned of the impending bust.

25 October 1968   Word leaks to the press that Yoko is pregnant. John is reportedly the father.

8 November 1968   Cynthia is granted a divorce from John in an uncontested suit brought before magistrates in London.

21 November 1968   Yoko suffers her first painful miscarriage. John remains constantly at her bedside at Queen Charlotte's Hospital, London, where he beds down next to her in a sleeping bag for several days.

While there they record portions of their second avant-garde album, *Life with the Lions.*

28 November 1968   John pleads guilty to unauthorized possession of cannabis at Marylebone Magistrates Court. A fine of £150 is imposed as well as court costs of 20 guineas. The obstruction of justice charges are dropped against both him and Yoko.

29 November 1968   John and Yoko's infamous *Unfinished Music Number One: Two Virgins* is released. The album cover depicts the free-spirited couple nude. There is much media hoopla. Paul McCartney, among others, is none too pleased.

30 January 1969   The Beatles play their last live public performance on the rooftop of the Apple Records building. The impromptu gig is filmed for inclusion in the Beatles' eclectic cinematic swansong *Let It Be.*

2 February 1969   Yoko is granted a divorce from her husband, film-maker Anthony Cox.

20 March 1969   John and Yoko are married in a quiet civil ceremony on the island of Gibraltar.

26 May 1969   The Lennons fly to Montreal to hold an eight-day *Bed-In* for peace at the Queen Elizabeth Hotel. While there they record the now-famous counterculture anthem, "Give Peace a Chance."

1 July 1969   While visiting John's Aunt Mater in Durness, Sutherland, Scotland, the Lennons and their children, Julian and Kyoko, are involved in a car accident in Golspie. Although no one is seriously injured, John requires seventeen stitches on his face and head. Julian is treated for shock.

12 October 1969   Yoko miscarries yet another baby. This time, however, the pregnancy is sufficiently long for the child, a boy, to be given the name John Ono Lennon. He is buried in a tiny white coffin outside London. Only John and Yoko attend the service.

10 April 1970   Paul McCartney publicly quits the Beatles.

31 December 1970   McCartney brings suit against the other Beatles in an effort to legally dissolve the group.

13 January 1971   The Lennons fly to Japan on vacation.

20 January 1971   John meets Yoko's parents in Fujisawa, Japan.

8 March 1971   An exhibit by John and Yoko is included in the Ideal Home Exhibition in Central London.

23 April 1971   The Lennons are held by police in Palma, Majorca, on suspicion of attempting to kidnap Yoko's daughter, Kyoko.

15 May 1971   John and Yoko attend the premiere of their films *Apotheosis* and *Fly* at the Cannes Film Festival.

6 June 1971   The Lennons play the Fillmore in New York with Frank Zappa.

3 September 1971   John and Yoko say good-bye to England forever and fly off to America to make their new home.

9 September 1971   John and Yoko appear on the *Dick Cavett Show* in New York.

9 October 1971   Yoko's *This Is Not Here* art exhibit opens in Syracuse, New York.

28 October 1971   John records "Happy Christmas (War Is Over)" in a New York studio.

10 December 1971   John and Yoko perform at a rally in Ann Arbor, Michigan, in support of jailed left-wing writer/activist John Sinclair.

15 December 1971   John and Yoko are guests at a posh United Nations function.

18 December 1971   John and Yoko fly to Houston, Texas, in search of Kyoko.

22 December 1971   Tony Cox is sentenced to jail for five days for contempt of court after refusing the Lennons permission to see his daughter.

6 January 1972   Joko Films, the Lennons' avant-garde movie company, is formed.

13 January 1972   John and Yoko appear on the *David Frost Show*.

4 February 1972   Right-wing Senator Strom Thurmond advises U.S. Attorney General John Mitchell that it might be better for the current administration if the Lennons were deported from the United States.

5 February 1972   John and Yoko join four hundred demonstrators in an anti-British rally in Manhattan.

14 February 1972   The Lennons begin a five-day stint as co-hosts on the *Mike Douglas Show* in Philadelphia. More than twenty years later it is released on home video.

29 February 1972   John's and Yoko's U.S. visas expire.

6 March 1972   A fifteen-day temporary extension given to the Lennons is canceled by the Deputy Attorney General.

16 March 1972   The Lennons are served with a deportation notice from American immigration officials because of John's 1968 drug conviction in England.

18 April 1972   John and Yoko are present at a deportation hearing in New York.

22 April 1972   The Lennons give a fiery address at the National Peace Rally in Manhattan.

12 May 1972   Yet more immigration hearings on the Lennons' case.

12 June 1972   John's *Some Time in New York City* album is released in America.

29 August 1972   The Lennons head up the *One to One* concert at Madison Square Garden, New York.

6 September 1972   John and company appear on Jerry Lewis's annual *Muscular Dystrophy Telethon*.

18 September 1972   John and Yoko go their separate ways. John moves to Los Angeles while Yoko stays ensconced in their palatial seven-room Manhattan apartment. They have been married four years.

23 December 1972   *Imagine*, the Lennons' film based on the album of the same name, is aired on U.S. television.

22 January 1973   John is sued by Northern Songs Ltd. and Maclen Music Ltd., charging he has assigned certain composing copyrights to Yoko's company, Ono Music Ltd.

23 March 1973   Yoko is allowed to remain in the United States as a permanent resident alien, while John is given sixty days to leave the country.

24 March 1973   John's lawyers appeal the deportation order.

1 April 1973   The Lennons hold a press conference with John Lindsey and Geraldo Rivera to announce the formation of the conceptual country of Nutopia.

29 June 1973   The Lennons attend the Watergate hearings in Washington.

9 September 1973   Tittenhurst Park goes on sale.

18 September 1973   Ringo Starr acquires Tittenhurst.

24 October 1973   John sues the U.S. government over alleged wiretapping improprieties by the FBI.

7 December 1973   John donates £1,000 to a rapidly sinking underground paper, the *International Times* in London.

1 February 1974   John becomes deeply involved in the legal troubles of one Michael X, an alleged murderer who is later hanged for his crimes.

12 March 1974   John is ejected from the Troubador Club in Los Angeles after reportedly heckling the Smothers Brothers during their set.

17 May 1974   John is in Philadelphia assisting radio station WFIL in a fund-raising drive.

17 July 1974   John is again ordered to leave America within two months.

28 September 1974   John gives an interview to WNEW in New York about his music and mounting immigration woes.

16 November 1974   John's "Whatever Gets You Through the Night" hits number one in the *Billboard* charts.

27 December 1974   John holidays at Disneyland in Los Angeles along with his son, Julian, and girlfriend, May Pang.

January 1975   John returns home to New York and is reunited with Yoko. "The separation just didn't work out," he tells the press.

1 March 1975   John attends the Grammy Awards in Los Angeles.

6 March 1975   John officially gets back with Yoko after a separation of eighteen months.

13 June 1975   John appears on a television salute to Sir Lew Grade performing two numbers.

19 June 1975   John files suit against former Attorney General John Mitchell for what his lawyers call "improper selective persecution" relating to the government's deportation proceedings.

23 September 1975   Because Yoko is pregnant once again, immigration officials temporarily halt their deportation proceedings on what they call "humanitarian grounds."

7 October 1975   The U.S. Court of Appeals for the Second Circuit reverses the deportation order against John by a two-to-one vote.

9 October 1975   Yoko gives birth to the Lennons' only child together, a seven-pound boy they name Sean Ono Taro Lennon.

5 January 1976   The Beatles' former road manager and friend, Mal Evans, is shot dead by police in Los Angeles following an incident whereby Evans allegedly pointed a gun at officers responding to a domestic disturbance call. John is said to be deeply disturbed by the tragedy.

1 April 1976   Alfred Lennon dies of cancer at Brighton General Hospital. He was sixty-three.

18 March 1976   Paul McCartney's father, James, dies in Liverpool. John is reportedly very upset.

27 July 1976   John finally receives his Green Card at an immigration hearing in New York. John's only comment to the press: "It's great to be legal again!"

9 October 1976   John begins his self-imposed "retirement" from show business and his so-called househusband period. "From now on," Lennon tells the press, "my only responsibility is to my family."

10 January 1977   The litigation between Allen Klein and the Beatles is finally settled.

20 January 1977   The Lennons attend the inauguration party for Jimmy Carter in Washington.

4 October 1977   John and Yoko meet the press in Japan.

4 February 1978   The Lennons purchase several farms in Delaware County, New York.

3 December 1978   Yoko attends an Apple business meeting in London.

January 1979   The Lennons fly to Geneva and Cairo on a working holiday.

27 May 1979   John and Yoko place a full-page press release in the *New York Times* updating their fans on the particulars of their daily lives.

15 October 1979   The Lennons contribute $1,000 to the New York City Police Department for the purchase of bullet-proof vests for officers.

31 December 1979   Joko Films and Bag Productions Ltd. officially fold.

28 January 1980   The Lennons purchase a sprawling mansion in West Palm Beach, Florida.

23 May 1980   John flies to Cape Town, South Africa, in an effort to gain some independence from the controlling Yoko.

2 July 1980   Yoko sells one of the Lennons' cows for a record $265,000 at the State Fair in Syracuse, New York.

14 July 1980   John and Sean set sail on the 63-foot sloop *Isis*, bound for Bermuda accompanied by a five-man crew. It is during this holiday that John finally begins composing once again.

4 August 1980   John and Yoko begin recording at the Hit Factory in New York for the first time in six years. The music culled from those sessions is later to form the albums *Double Fantasy* and *Milk and Honey*.

9 September 1980   The Lennons are interviewed for *Playboy* magazine.

29 September 1980   *Newsweek* magazine publishes an in-depth interview with John and Yoko.

9 October 1980   John celebrates his fortieth birthday with Sean, who is five on the same day.

15 November 1980   Ringo visits John at the Dakota for the very last time.

17 November 1980   *Double Fantasy* is released worldwide.

21 November 1980   The Lennons pose nude for photographer Allan Tannenbaum.

5 December 1980   John and Yoko are interviewed by *Rolling Stone* in New York.

8 December 1980   In the late afternoon, on his way out of the Dakota John Lennon stops to give an autograph to a young man from Hawaii named Mark David Chapman. The two are photographed together. Chapman inquires from Lennon if there are any jobs available in his office. John tells him to send in a résumé. At 10:49 P.M. Chapman steps out of the shadows and guns down John Winston Ono Lennon as he returns home from a recording session accompanied by Yoko. The world mourns the loss of John.

18 January 1981   Yoko issues a press release thanking people everywhere for their support following John's murder.

15 May 1981   George Harrison releases the poignant single "All Those Years Ago," a loving tribute to John. The McCartneys, Ringo Starr, and Denny Laine also appear on the record.

25 August 1981   Lennon's murderer is sentenced to twenty years to life in Attica Prison, in western New York State.

October 1983   Warner Books publishes May Pang's *Loving John*, a racy memoir of her torrid eighteen-month relationship with the eccentric rock legend.

17 October 1983   Julian Lennon begins recording his debut album, *Valotte*.

29 November 1983   Yoko and Sean visit Great Britain.

20 January 1984   Yoko and Sean visit John's Liverpool family.

27 January 1984   Geffen Records releases John and Yoko's *Milk and Honey*, comprised of unused 1980 *Double Fantasy* tracks.

21 March 1984   Julian joins Sean and Yoko in New York's Central Park for the grim groundbreaking of Strawberry Fields, a memorial garden dedicated to John's memory.

15 October 1984   Julian Lennon debuts his highly successful *Valotte* LP.

25 March 1985   Julian hits the road in support of his new album.

2 November 1985   The musical play *Lennon* opens at London's Astoria Theatre to good reviews.

1986   Julian releases *The Secret Value of Daydreaming*—his follow-up to *Valotte*—to lukewarm reviews and generally poor sales.

27 January 1986   Yoko commences a series of sparsely attended concerts in Cologne, West Germany.

10 February 1986   *John Lennon: Live in New York City*, a recording of his disappointing 1972 *One to One* concert, is released.

12 May 1986   Julian plays the Royal Albert Hall in London.

13 September 1986   Ringo and wife, Barbara Bach, throw a bash at John's former estate, Tittenhurst Park, to celebrate their son Zak Starkey's twenty-first birthday.

8 April 1987   The Beatles and Apple lose a significant portion of their suit against Capitol EMI.

8 December 1990   Fans worldwide mark the tenth anniversary of John's death with radio marathons and teary candlelight vigils.

1993   Yoko contributes three of John's day cassette demos to George, Paul, and Ringo to help resurrect the Beatles on record.

1994   The three surviving Beatles hunker down at Paul's Sussex studio to work on the wistful Lennon ballad "Free as a Bird," originally recorded in 1977 at the Dakota.

December 1994   A two-CD set, *The Beatles Live at the BBC*, is released, a compilation of fifty-six songs from early Beatles radio recordings, March 1962 to June 1965.

20 November 1995   "Free as a Bird" is issued to worldwide hoopla but decidedly mixed reviews.

23 November 1995   The third installment of ABC television's disappointing *The Beatles Anthology* features a second "new" Lennon composition, the heartfelt, but rather mediocre, "Real Love."

26 February 1997   John posthumously picks up three Grammy Awards including one for Best Pop Performance for "Free as a Bird."

17 April 1998   Linda McCartney loses her brave two-year battle with breast cancer. Yoko dedicates a concert to her anonymously. "That's how it was," she later divulged. "We were no-name friends."

18 May 1998   Julian releases his *Photograph Smile* on the same day Sean releases his first CD, *Into the Sun*. Both reportedly sell poorly.

22 June 1998   A high-profile memorial for Linda McCartney is held at New York's Riverside Church. A slighted Yoko, who did not receive an invitation, is said to have been "deeply saddened."

21 October 1998   Yoko flies to South America to open a four-day art exhibit entitled *Wish Trees for Brazil* at Brasilia's National Theater.

3 November 1998   Capitol Records releases *The John Lennon Anthology*, a four-CD box set featuring 100 previously unreleased solo tracks including rare television appearances, outtakes, and home recordings.

25 April 1999   VH1's *Behind the Music* spotlights Julian Lennon. Julian vents his frustrations about Yoko, Sean, and his record company.

30 September 1999   An anonymous bidder purchases John's original lyrics to "I Am the Walrus" for $129,200 at Christie's Pop Auction in London.

1 February 2000   VH1 presents *Two of Us*, a made-for-cable movie about a fictionalized 1976 New York encounter between John Lennon and Paul McCartney. A distorted, inaccurate depiction of events, the film is further marred by its cartoonish characterizations and trite dialogue.

28 March 2000   Capitol Records releases a remastered, remixed version of John's 1971 *Imagine* album. The CD coincides with the British premiere of the hour-long documentary *Gimme Some Truth*, about the making of Lennon's "Imagine" LP.

DISCOGRAPHY

JOHN LENNON AS A BEATLE AND A SOLO ARTIST

Lennon's role on these various recordings may include singer, musician, producer, and/or composer.

Albums

Introducing The Beatles, Vee Jay, United States, 1963
Please Please Me, Parlophone, United Kingdom, March 1963
With The Beatles, Parlophone, United Kingdom, November 1963

Meet The Beatles!, Capitol, United States, January 1964
Twist And Shout, Capitol, Canada, January 1964
The Beatles' Second Album, Capitol, United States, April 1964
A Hard Day's Night, Capitol, United States, June 1964
A Hard Day's Night, Parlophone, United Kingdom, July 1964
Something New, Capitol, United States, July 1964
The Beatles Versus The Four Seasons, Vee Jay, United States, October 1964
Songs, Pictures And Stories Of The Fabulous Beatles, Vee Jay, United States, October 1964 (Double Album Set)
The Beatles' Story, Capitol, United States, November 1964 (Double Record Set)
Beatles For Sale, Parlophone, United Kingdom, December 1964
Beatles '65', Capitol, United States, December 1964

The Early Beatles, Capitol, United States, March 1965
Beatles VI, Capitol, United States, June 1965
'Help!' (Original Soundtrack), Capitol, United States, August 1965
Rubber Soul, Capitol, United States, December 1965
Rubber Soul, Parlophone, United Kingdom, December 1965

Yesterday . . . And Today, Capitol, United States, June 1966
Revolver, Capitol, United States, August 1966
A Collection Of Beatles Oldies, Parlophone, United Kingdom, December 1966

Sgt. Pepper's Lonely Hearts Club Band, Capitol, United States, June 1967
Magical Mystery Tour, Capitol, United States, November 1967

Unfinished Music No.1/Two Virgins, Apple, United States,
   November 1968
The Beatles (White Album), Apple, United States, November 1968

Yellow Submarine, Apple, United States, January 1969
Unfinished Music No. 2/Life With The Lions, Zapple, United States,
   May 1969
Abbey Road, Apple, United States, October 1969
Wedding Album, Apple, United States, October 1969
The Plastic Ono Band/Live Peace In Toronto, Apple, United States,
   December 1969

Let It Be, Apple, United States, May 1970
John Lennon/Plastic Ono Band, Apple, United States, December 1970

Imagine, Apple, United States, September 1971

Some Time In New York City, Apple, United States, June 1972

Mind Games, Apple, United States, November 1973

Walls And Bridges, Apple, United States, September 1974

John Lennon Sings The Great Rock & Roll Hits, Adam VIII Ltd.,
   United States, 1975
Rock 'n' Roll, Apple, United States, February 1975
Shaved Fish, Apple, United States, October 1975

Double Fantasy, Geffen Records, United States, November 1980

Heart Play—Unfinished Dialogue, PolyGram, Canada, 1983

Milk and Honey, Geffen Records, United States, January 1984

Singles

My Bonnie (Lies Over The Ocean)/The Saints (When The Saints Go
   Marching In), Polydor, Germany, June 1961

My Bonnie/Cry For A Shadow, Polydor, United States, April 1962
Love Me Do (Version One)/P.S. I Love You, Parlophone, United
   Kingdom, October 1962

Please Please Me/Ask Me Why, Capitol, United States, January 1963
From Me To You/Thank You Girl, Capitol, United States, April 1963
She Loves You/I'll Get You, Swan, United States, August 1963

I Want To Hold Your Hand/This Boy, Parlophone, United Kingdom,
   November 1963
The Beatles Christmas Record, Fan Club, United States, December 1963

Roll Over Beethoven/Please Mr. Postman, Capitol, Canada, December
1963

I Want To Hold Your Hand/I Saw Her Standing There, Capitol, United
States, January 1964
Please Please Me/From Me To You, Vee Jay, United States, January
1964
Can't Buy Me Love/You Can't Do That, Capitol, United States, March
1964
Do You Want To Know A Secret/Thank You Girl, Vee Jay, United
States, March 1964
Komm, Gib Mir Deine Hande/Sie Liebt Dich, (company not available),
Germany, March 1964
Twist And Shout/There's A Place, Tollie, United States, March 1964
Love Me Do/P.S. I Love You, Capitol, United States, April 1964
Sie Liebt Dich/I'll Get You, Capitol, United States, May 1964
A Hard Day's Night/I Should Have Known Better, Capitol, United
States, July 1964
A Hard Day's Night/Things We Said Today, Capitol, United States, July
1964
And I Love Her/If I Fell, Capitol, United States, July 1964
I'll Cry Instead/I'm Happy Just To Dance With You, Capitol, United
States, July 1964
Do You Want To Know A Secret/Thank You Girl, Capitol, United
States, August 1964
Slow Down/Matchbox, Capitol, United States, August 1964
I Feel Fine/She's A Woman, Capitol, United States, November 1964
Another Beatles Christmas Record, Fan Club, United States,
December 1964

Eight Days A Week/I Don't Want To Spoil The Party, Capitol, United
States, February 1965
Ticket To Ride/Yes It Is, Capitol, United States, April 1965
Help!/I'm Down, Capitol, United States, July 1965
Yesterday/Act Naturally, Capitol, United States, September 1965
Boys/Medley (Kansas City/Hey-Hey-Hey), Capitol, United States,
October 1965
Roll Over Beethoven/Misery, Capitol, United States, October 1965
The Beatles Third Christmas Record, Fan Club, United States,
December 1965
We Can Work It Out/Day Tripper, Capitol, United States, December
1965

Nowhere Man/What Goes On, Capitol, United States, February 1966
Paperback Writer/Rain, Capitol, United States, April 1966

Yellow Submarine/Eleanor Rigby, Capitol, United States, August 1966
The Beatles Fourth Christmas Record, Fan Club, United States,
　　November 1966

Penny Lane/Strawberry Fields Forever, Capitol, United States,
　　February 1967
All You Need Is Love/Baby, You're A Rich Man, Capitol, United States,
　　July 1967
How I Won The War/Aftermath (By Musketeer Gripwood and the
　　Third Troop), (company not available), United Kingdom, October
　　1967
Hello Goodbye/I Am The Walrus, Capitol, United States, November 1967
Christmas Time Is Here Again, Fan Club, United States, December 1967

Lady Madonna/The Inner Light, Capitol, United States, March 1968
Hey Jude/Revolution, Apple, United States, August 1968
1968 Christmas Record, Fan Club, United States, December 1968

Get Back/Don't Let Me Down, Apple, United States, April 1969
The Ballad Of John And Yoko/Old Brown Shoe, Apple, United States,
　　June 1969
Give Peace A Chance/Remember Love, Apple, United States, July 1969
Cold Turkey/Don't Worry Kyoko (Mummy's Only Looking For A Hand
　　In The Snow), Apple, United States, October 1969
Something/Come Together, Apple, United States, October 1969
The Beatles Seventh Christmas Record, Fan Club, United States,
　　December 1969

Hey Jude, Apple, United States, February 1970
Instant Karma (We All Shine On)/Who Has Seen The Wind, Apple,
　　United States, February 1970
Let It Be/You Know My Name (Look Up The Number), United States,
　　March 1970
The Long And Winding Road/For You Blue, Apple, United States, May
　　1970
Mother/Why?, Apple, United States, December 1970

Power To The People/Open Your Box, Apple, United Kingdom, March
　　1971
Power To The People/Touch Me, Apple, United States, March 1971
Imagine/It's So Hard, Apple, United States, October 1971
Happy Christmas (War Is Over)/Listen, The Snow Is Falling, Apple,
　　United States, December 1971

Woman Is The Nigger Of The World/Sisters O Sisters, Apple, United
　　States, April 1973
Mind Games/Meat City, Apple, United States, October 1973

Whatever Gets You Through The Night/Beef Jerky, Apple, United
   States, September 1974
No. 9 Dream/What You Got, Apple, United States, December 1974

Stand By Me/Move Over Ms. L., Apple, United States, March 1975
Imagine/Working Class Hero, Apple, United States, October 1975

(Just Like) Starting Over/Kiss Kiss Kiss, Geffen Records, United States,
   October 1980

Nobody Told Me/O'Sanity, Polydor, United States, January 1984

EPs (Extended Play)

Twist And Shout, Parlophone, United Kingdom, July 1963
Twist And Shout/A Taste Of Honey/Do You Want To Know A
   Secret/There's A Place

The Beatles' Hits, Parlophone, United Kingdom, September 1963
From Me To You/Thank You Girl/Please Please Me/Love Me Do

The Beatles (No. 1), Parlophone, United Kingdom, November 1963
I Saw Her Standing There/Misery/Anna (Go To Him)/Chains

All My Loving, Parlophone, United Kingdom, February 1964
All My Loving/Ask Me Why/Money (That's What I Want)/P.S. I Love You

The Beatles, Capitol, United States, March 1964
Misery/A Taste Of Honey/Ask Me Why/Anna (Go To Him)

Four By The Beatles, Capitol, United States, May 1964
Roll Over Beethoven/All My Loving/This Boy/Please Mr. Postman

Long Tall Sally, Parlophone, United Kingdom, June 1964
Long Tall Sally/I Call Your Name/Slow Down/Matchbox

4 By The Beatles, Capitol, United States, February 1965
Honey Don't/I'm A Loser/Mr. Moonlight/Everybody's Trying To Be My
   Baby

Beatles For Sale (No. 2), Parlophone, United Kingdom, June 1965
I'll Follow The Sun/Baby's In Black/Words Of Love/I Don't Want To
   Spoil The Party

The Beatles' Million Sellers, Parlophone, United Kingdom, December
   1965
She Loves You/I Want To Hold Your Hand/Can't Buy Me Love/I Feel
   Fine

Yesterday, Parlophone, United Kingdom, March 1966
Yesterday/Act Naturally/You Like Me Too Much/It's Only Love

Nowhere Man, Parlophone, United Kingdom, July 1966
Nowhere Man/Drive My Car/Michelle/You Won't See Me

12-Inch Maxi Singles

Give Peace A Chance/Remember Love, Plastic Ono Band, Apple,
   United States, (date not available)

Elton John Band, John Lennon & The Muscle Shoals Horns,
   Metronome Musik GMBH, Germany, (date not available)
Funeral For A Friend/Love Lies Bleeding/Rocket Man/Benny And The
   Jets/Take Me To The Pilot/Whatever Gets You Through The
   Night/Lucy In The Sky With Diamonds/I Saw Her Standing There

Elton John Band, John Lennon & The Muscle Shoals Horns,
   Metronome Musik GMBH, Germany, (date not available)
I Saw Her Standing There/Whatever Gets You Through The
   Night/Lucy In The Sky With Diamonds

John Lennon Imagine, Apple, United States, Plastic Ono Band, (date
   not available)
Imagine/It's So Hard

John Lennon Imagine/Working Class Hero, Apple, United States, (date
   not available)

John Lennon/Yoko Ono, Geffen Records, United States, 1980
(Just Like) Starting Over/Kiss Kiss Kiss

John Lennon Borrowed Time, PolyGram, United States, 1982 (Limited
   Edition)
You're The One/Never Say Goodbye

John Lennon Borrowed Time, PolyGram, United States, 1984
Your Hands/Never Say Goodbye

John Lennon I'm Stepping Out, PolyGram, United States, 1984
Sleepless Night/Loneliness

LENNON FOR OTHERS

These are works for which Lennon composed, produced, performed, or
in some other way contributed. Dates were not available.

Albums

Approximately Infinite Universe, Yoko Ono & Elephant's Memory,
   Capitol, United States

Elephant's Memory, Elephant's Memory, Apple, United States
Fly, Yoko Ono, Apple, United States
Oh! Calcutta!, Original Cast, Aidart Records, United States
The Pope Smokes Dope, David Peel, Yoko Ono & The East Side
    Friends Chorus, Apple, United States
Yoko Ono/Plastic Ono Band, Yoko Ono, Apple, United States

Singles

Across The Universe, David Bowie, (company unknown), United States
Air Male (Tone Deaf Jam), Yoko Ono & The Joe Jones Tone Deaf
    Music Co., Apple, United States
Air Talk, Yoko Ono, Apple, United States
All By Myself, Harry Nilsson, RCA, United States
AOS, Yoko Ono, Apple, United States
Approximately Infinite Universe, Yoko Ono, Apple, United States

Baddest Of The Mean, Yoko Ono, Apple, United States
The Ballad Of Bob Dylan, David Peel & The Lower East Side Friends
    Chorus, Apple, United States
The Ballad Of New York City, David Peel & The Lower East Side
    Friends Chorus, Apple, United States
The Birth Control Blues, David Peel & The Lower East Side Friends
    Chorus, Apple, United States
Black Sails, Harry Nilsson, RCA, United States
Born In A Prison, Yoko Ono, Apple, United States

Catman, Yoko Ono, Apple, United States
The Chicago Conspiracy, David Peel & The Lower East Side Friends
    Chorus, Apple, United States
Chuck 'N' Bo, Yoko Ono, Apple, United States
Cryin' Blacksheep Blues, Yoko Ono, Apple, United States

Death Of Samantha, Yoko Ono, Apple, United States
Don't Count The Waves, Yoko Ono & The Joe Jones Tone Deaf Music
    Co., Apple, United States
Don't Forget Me, Harry Nilsson, RCA, United States
Don't Worry Kyoko, Yoko Ono, Apple, United States
Don't Worry Kyoko (Live No. 1), Yoko Ono, Apple, United States
Don't Worry Kyoko (Live No. 2), Yoko Ono, Apple, United States

Everybody's Smoking Marijuana, David Peel, Apple, United States

F Is Not A Dirty Word, David Peel, Apple, United States
Fame, David Bowie, Apple, United States
Fly, Yoko Ono, Apple, United States

God Save Us, The Elastic Oz Band, Apple, United States
Goodnight Vienna, Reprise, Ringo Starr, Apple, United States
Greenfield Morning I Pushed An Empty Baby Carriage All Over The
    City, Yoko Ono, Apple, United States
Gypsy Wolf, Yoko Ono, Apple, United States

Have You Seen A Horizon Lately, Yoko Ono, Apple, United States
The Hip Generation, David Peel & The Lower East Side Friends
    Chorus, Apple, United States
The Hippie From New York, David Peel & The Lower East Side
    Friends Chorus, Apple, United States
Hirake, Yoko Ono, Apple, United States (Also called Open Your Box)

I Felt Like Smashing My Face In A Clear Glass Window, Yoko Ono,
    Apple, United States
I Have A Woman Inside My Soul, Yoko Ono, Apple, United States
I Saw Her Standing There, Elton John and The Muscle Shoals Horns,
    Apple, United States
I Want My Love To Rest Tonight, Yoko Ono, Apple, United States
I'm Gonna Start Another Riot, David Peel & The Lower East Side
    Friends Chorus, Apple, United States
I'm Running Away, David Peel & The Lower East Side Friends
    Chorus, Apple, United States
I'm The Greatest, Ringo Starr, Apple, United States
Is Winter Here To Stay, Yoko Ono, Apple, United States
(It's All Da-Da-Down To) Goodnight Vienna, Ringo Starr, Apple,
    United States

John John (Let's Hope For Peace), Yoko Ono, Apple, United States

Kite Song, Yoko Ono, Apple, United States

Liberation Special, Yoko Ono, Apple, United States
Life, Yoko Ono, Apple, United States
Listen, The Snow Is Falling, Yoko Ono, Apple, United States
Local Plastic Ono Band, Yoko Ono, Apple, United States
Looking Over From My Hotel Window, Yoko Ono, Apple, United
    States
Loop De Loop, Harry Nilsson, RCA, United States
Lucy In The Sky With Diamonds, Elton John, (company unknown),
    United States

Madness, Yoko Ono, Apple, United States
Many Rivers To Cross, Harry Nilsson, RCA, United States
McDonald's Farm, David Peel & The Lower East Side Friends
    Chorus, Apple, United States
Men, Men, Men, Yoko Ono, Apple, United States

Midsummer New York, Yoko Ono, Apple, United States
Mind Holes, Yoko Ono, Apple, United States
Mind Train, Yoko Ono, Apple, United States
Move On Fast, Yoko Ono, Apple, United States
Move Over Ms. L., Keith Moon, Apple, United States
Mrs. Lennon, Yoko Ono, Apple, United States
Mucho Mungo/Mt. Elga, Harry Nilsson, RCA, United States

Now Or Never, Yoko Ono, Apple, United States

Old Forgotten Soldier, Harry Nilsson, RCA, United States
One Day At A Time, Elton John, Apple, United States
Only You, Ringo Starr, Apple, United States
Open Your Box, Yoko Ono, Apple, United States
O'Wind, Yoko Ono, Apple, United States

Paper Shoes, Yoko Ono, Apple, United States
Peter The Dealer, Yoko Ono, Apple, United States
The Pope Smokes Dope, David Peel & The Lower East Side Friends
   Chorus, Apple, United States
Power Boogie, David Peel, Apple, United States

Remember Love, Yoko Ono, Apple, United States
Rock And Roll People, Johnny Winter, (company unknown), United
   States
Rock Around The Clock, Harry Nilsson, RCA, United States

Save The Last Dance For Me, Harry Nilsson, Apple, United States
She Hits Back, Yoko Ono, Apple, United States
Shirankatta, Yoko Ono, Apple, United States
Sisters O Sisters, Yoko Ono, Apple, United States
Song For John, Yoko Ono, Apple, United States
Subterranean Homesick Blues, Harry Nilsson, RCA, United States

Telephone Piece, Yoko Ono, Apple, United States
Toilet Piece/Unknown, Yoko Ono, Apple, United States
Touch Me, Yoko Ono, Apple, United States

Waiting For The Sunrise, Yoko Ono, Apple, United States
We Love You, The Rolling Stones, Condor, United States
We're All Water, Yoko Ono, Apple, United States
What A Bastard The World Is, Yoko Ono, Apple, United States
What A Mess, Yoko Ono, Apple, United States
What Did I Do, Yoko Ono, Apple, United States
Who Has Seen The Wind, Yoko Ono, Apple, United States
Why, Yoko Ono, Apple, United States
Why Not, Yoko Ono, Apple, United States

Wind Ridge, Yoko Ono, Apple, United States
Winter Song, Yoko Ono, Apple, United States
Woman Power, Yoko Ono, Apple, United States

Yang Yang, Yoko Ono, Apple, United States
You, Yoko Ono & The Joe Jones Tone Deaf Music Co., Apple, United
   States
You've Got To Hide Your Love Away, The Silkie Fontana, United States

A NOTE ON SOURCES/CREDITS

Throughout the sixteen years of research for this book and my many other Beatles-related projects, I have been enormously grateful to the many individuals who have given their time and insight into John Lennon and the Beatles' remarkable life and times. Several Lennon insiders quoted in this book have asked not to be identified and I respectfully honored their request without exception. Most sources, however, enthusiastically lent their experiences and observations to help uncover this complex and wholly human figure who has been too often cloaked in myth and hero worship.

I express my sincere thanks to Peter Brown, Jesse Ed Davis, Clive Epstein, George Harrison, Olivia Harrison, Denny Laine, Jo Jo Laine, Tony Manaro, Angela and Ruth McCartney, Linda McCartney, Mike McCartney, Paul McCartney, Harry Nilsson, May Pang, Mike Pinder, Frederic Seaman, Pete Shotton, Luciano Sparacino, George Speerin, Francie Swartz, Alistair Taylor, Derek Taylor, Pete Townshend, Allan Williams, and Bob Wooler. Special thanks must also go to members of the Lennon family: Julia Baird, Harriet and Norman Birch, Jacqui Dykins, Leila Harvey, Cynthia Lennon, Julian Lennon, Sean Lennon, Yoko Ono, Mimi Smith, and Pauline Smith.

My extended research work was most capably assisted by Deborah Lynn Black, co-author of several popular books. She writes for dozens of magazines around the world, and has worked with me on many past projects, including the CD biographies *That Fateful Night: True Stories of Titanic Survivors* and *Frank Sinatra: A Tribute*.

BIBLIOGRAPHY

Baird, Julia, with Geoffrey Giuliano. *John Lennon: My Brother*. New York: Holt, 1988.

Bego, Mark. *Julian Lennon!* New York: St. Martin's Press, 1986.

Brown, Peter, and Steven Gaines. *The Love You Make*. London: Macmillan, 1983.

Butler, Dougal. *Two Sides of the Moon*. London: Star, 1981.

Carr, Roy, and Tony Tyler. *Beatles: An Illustrated Record*. London: New English Library, 1975.

Colacello, Bob. *Andy Warhol Close Up*. New York: HarperCollins, 1990.

Coleman, Ray. *Lennon*. New York: McGraw-Hill, 1984.

Cott, Jonathan, and Christian Doudna. *The Ballad of John and Yoko*. New York: Rolling Stone Press, 1982.

Gay Liberation Book (no data).

Giuliano, Geoffrey, and Brenda Giuliano. *The Lost Beatles Interviews*. New York: Dutton, 1996.

Giuliano, Geoffrey, and Brenda Giuliano. *The Lost Lennon Interviews*. New York: Adams Media, 1996.

Giuliano, Geoffrey, and Vrnda Devi. *Glass Onion: The Beatles in Their Own Words*. New York: Da Capo Press, 1999.

Giuliano, Geoffrey, and Vrnda Devi. *Things We Said Today: Conversations with the Beatles*. New York: Adams Media, 1998.

Goldman, Albert. *The Lives of John Lennon*. New York: Morrow, 1988.

Green, John. *Dakota Days*. New York: St. Martin's Press, 1983.

Gruen, Bob. *Listen to These Pictures*. London: Sidgwick & Jackson, 1985.

Haclett, Pat. *The Andy Warhol Diaries*. New York: Warner Books, 1989.

Hopkins, Jerry. *Yoko Ono*. London: Sidgwick & Jackson, 1987.

Lennon, Cynthia. *A Twist of Lennon*. London: Star, 1978.

Lennon, John. *John Lennon's 1969 London Diary*. London: Apple, 1969.

Lennon, John. *Skywriting by Word of Mouth*. London: Pan, 1986.

Lennon, Pauline. *Daddy Come Home*. London: HarperCollins, 1990.

Miles, Barry. *Paul McCartney: Many Years from Now*. New York: Holt, 1997.

Miles, Barry, ed. *The Beatles: In Their Own Words*. London: Bobcat Books, 1978.

Miles, Barry, ed. *John Lennon: In His Own Words*. New York: Omnibus, 1981.

Pang, May, and Henry Edwards. *Loving John*. New York: Warner, 1983.

Papolos, Demitri, M.D., and Janice Papolos. *Overcoming Depression*. New York: Harper & Row, 1992.

Peebles, Andy. *The Lennon Tapes*. London: BBC, 1981.

Seaman, Frederic. *The Last Days of John Lennon: An Intimate Memoir*. New York: Carol, 1991.

Sheff, David. *The Playboy Interviews with John Lennon and Yoko Ono*. New York: Playboy Press, 1981.

Shevy, Sandra. *The Other Side of Lennon*. London: Sidgwick & Jackson, 1990.

Shotton, Pete, and Nicholas Shaffner. *John Lennon in My Life*. New York: Stein and Day, 1983.

Solt, Andrew, and Sam Egan. *Imagine*. New York: Macmillan, 1988.
[Stafford Pemberton] The Beatles for the Record. Knutsford, Cheshire, 1981.
[Time Life editors] *Dreams and Dreaming*. Alexandria, Va.: Time Life Books, 1985.
Wenner, Jann. *Lennon Remembers*. San Francisco: Straight Arrow Press, 1971.
Wiener, Jon. *Come Together: John Lennon in His Time*. London: Faber & Faber, 1985.
Woofinden, Bob. *The Beatles Apart*. London: Proteus, 1981.

Periodicals

London Daily Mirror
London Observer
London Star 12/8/81
Melody Maker 10/6/71; 11/73
Newsweek 9/29/80
New Yorker 5/5/99
Q Magazine
Radix 1981
Real Video (Internet Publication) 12/99
Rolling Stone 5/6/75; 1/81 (John Lennon Commemorative Issue); 1/22/81; 10/1/81; 2/5/98
Shukan Bunshun 2/16/70
Sunday Mirror of London 1972
Village Voice 11/80

Broadcast Sources

ABC Television: *20/20* 12/30/99
CBC Television: *The Way It Is* (no date)
E Entertainment: *The Murder of John Lennon* 12/99
Entertainment Tonight 12/31/99
RKO Radio 12/12/80
Tomorrow with Tom Snyder 4/28/75

CREDITS

Illustrations are printed with permission of the owners, as follows.

1. Geoffrey Giuliano Collection.
2. Geoffrey Giuliano Collection.
3. Geoffrey Giuliano Collection.
4. Deliberate Alchemy Archives.

5. Deliberate Alchemy Archives.
6. Sesa Giuliano.
7. Deliberate Alchemy Archives.
8. Deliberate Alchemy Archives.
9. Deliberate Alchemy Archives.
10. Deliberate Alchemy Archives.
11. Deliberate Alchemy Archives.
12. Deliberate Alchemy Archives.
13. Deliberate Alchemy Archives.
14. Deliberate Alchemy Archives.
15. Brazen Images.
16. Deliberate Alchemy Archives.
17. Deliberate Alchemy Archives.
18. Deliberate Alchemy Archives.
19. Deliberate Alchemy Archives.
20. Deliberate Alchemy Archives.
21. Deliberate Alchemy Archives.
22. Deliberate Alchemy Archives.
23. Deliberate Alchemy Archives.
24. Deliberate Alchemy Archives.
25. Brazen Images.
26. DMI.
27. Deliberate Alchemy Archives.
28. Deliberate Alchemy Archives.
29. Deliberate Alchemy Archives.
30. Newspics.
31. Geoffrey Giuliano Collection.
32. Deliberate Alchemy Archives.
33. Deliberate Alchemy Archives.
34. Deliberate Alchemy Archives.
35. Deliberate Alchemy Archives.
36. Deliberate Alchemy Archives.
37. Deliberate Alchemy Archives.
38. Deliberate Alchemy Archives.
39. Brazen Images.
40. Geoffrey Giuliano Collection.
41. Deliberate Alchemy Archives.
42. Geoffrey Giuliano Collection.
43. Deliberate Alchemy Archives.
44. Deliberate Alchemy Archives.
45. Deliberate Alchemy Archives.
46. Deliberate Alchemy Archives.
47. Deliberate Alchemy Archives.
48. Geoffrey Giuliano Collection.
49. Deliberate Alchemy Archives.
50. Brazen Images.
51. Deliberate Alchemy Archives.
52. Sesa Giuliano.
53. DMI.
54. Geoffrey Giuliano Collection.
55. Deliberate Alchemy Archives.
56. Deliberate Alchemy Archives.
57. DMI.
58. DMI.
59. Deliberate Alchemy Archives.
60. Geoffrey Giuliano Collection.
61. Deliberate Alchemy Archives.
62. Geoffrey Giuliano Collection.
63. Sesa Giuliano.
64. Geoffrey Giuliano Collection.
65. Sesa Giuliano.
66. Geoffrey Giuliano Collection.
67. Sesa Giuliano.
68. Geoffrey Giuliano Collection.

INDEX

THE AUTHOR

Geoffrey Giuliano, a top international celebrity biographer, record producer, actor, and popular culture authority, has written more than twenty books, including *The Beatles: A Celebration*; *John Lennon: My Brother* (written with Lennon's sister, Julia Baird); *Dark Horse: The Life and Art of George Harrison*; *Blackbird: The Life and Times of Paul McCartney*; *The Beatles Album: Thirty Years of Music and Memorabilia*; *Rod Stewart: Vagabond Heart*; *The Rolling Stones Album: Thirty Years of Music and Memorabilia*; *The Illustrated Series*; *Paint It Black: The Murder of Brian Jones*; *The Lost Beatles Interviews*; *The Lost Lennon Interviews*; *Behind Blue Eyes: A Life of Pete Townshend*; *Things We Said Today: Conversations with the Beatles*; *Glass Onion: The Beatles in Their Own Words*; and *Two of Us: John Lennon and Paul McCartney, Behind the Myth*.

In addition, Giuliano, who can be heard on the Westwood One Radio Network, has created a best-selling line of audio rocumentaries for Durkin Hayes Publishing, KRB Music, and Jerden Records as well as a series of biographical CD box sets and video documentaries on various popular musicians for Delta Entertainment. Giuliano is also a thirty-year student of Vedic culture and philosophy, dedicated animal rights activist, teacher of Bhakti (Devotional) yoga, and occasional lecturer at Northwestern University, Department of Music. He and his wife, author Vrnda Devi, have four children.